The Book of Revelation

SCM CORE TEXT

The Book of Revelation

Simon Patrick Woodman

scm press

British Library Cataloguing in Publication data

A catalogue record for this book is available
from the British Library

978 0 334 04104 7

First published in 2008 by SCM Press
13–17 Long Lane,
London EC1A 9PN

www.scm-canterburypress.co.uk

SCM Press is a division of
SCM-Canterbury Press Ltd

Typeset by Regent Typesetting, London
Printed in the UK by
CPI William Clowes, Beccles, NR34 7TL

Contents

To Liz,
who has had to cope with my obsession with Revelation
for as long as she has known me.

Preface

If 'a text without a context is a con', there is good reason to suppose that the letter we call 'Revelation' is the source of more interpretative con-tricks than any piece of literature in the history of writing. For some it is an explosively subversive text; for others, a source of fascinating infor-mation about how the world will end. For some it radically challenges the political structures of our own day (because it exposes the dubious mechanics of human power games). For others it underwrites the same political structures (because 'the end of the world is nigh', there is little point challenging its injustices). The author of Revelation has employed such varied and multivalent imagery that any attempt to interpret its contents is prone to suspicion.

Much recent scholarship, however, has sought to locate the message of the book firmly in its historical, literary and biblical context. Simon Woodman's reading of Revelation offers a clear and lively exposition of this quest, while at the same time adding further credibility and momen-tum to it. He achieves this at three levels.

First, this study provides the student with an accessible introduction to the historical realities faced by the letter's initial recipients. The fact that it is addressed to small Christian congregations living in the shadow of the Roman Empire already offers a clue to its interpretation. The military and ideological power exerted by the Empire are symbolized respectively by the images of the beast and the whore: seemingly uncon-querable foes. But the importance of maintaining a faithful witness to Jesus, a description of what this means for Christians, and a prophetic insight into the effects of this action upon the empire, are all emphasized with stunning clarity.

Second, for anyone writing about the universal Lordship of Christ in a world where Caesar is Lord, a particular style of writing is called for: apocalyptic. Simon Woodman introduces this literary genre, and uses it to provide consistent interpretation of the kaleidoscopic array of John's literary pictures. The explication of individual images is based not on some ad hoc 'this is that' hermeneutics, but upon a clear appreciation of how this literary genre functions in this particular historical setting.

Third, this historical setting is one deeply immersed in Hebrew scriptures. Like many others, the present book helpfully reveals the biblical roots of the episodes, dramas and portraits of Revelation. But the greatest scholarly contribution of the present book is to provide a reading of the letter that situates it in deep continuity with the wider narrative of Scripture as a whole. The question of how God will honour his covenant with Abraham echoes throughout the Jewish and Christian scriptures, and Simon Woodman portrays a John who attends repeatedly, decisively and intriguingly to this primal question.

Its scholarly, analytic and lucid character, the provision of substantial amounts of 'hard-to-find' source material and the accessible nature of its layout, all prove this work to be an ideal guidebook for any student. But its value far exceeds that of a technical introduction. Although the book is the fruit of careful analysis and thought, it arises naturally from an obvious love for the text of Revelation itself. As such it would serve as an interpretative aid to all who are interested in exploring the meaning of the letter and its implications for those living in the modern West.

Ultimately, for anyone concerned with the question of how a God of justice can be trusted in a world plagued by injustice, this book has the capacity to provoke thought, inspire hope and compel the reader to enter into the subversive text of Revelation.

Revd Dr Simon Perry

Bloomsbury Central Baptist Church
Advent 2007

Acknowledgements

Thanks are due to my colleagues at South Wales Baptist College for enabling the research leave needed to complete this project, and to Bristol Baptist College for so warmly offering the use of their library. Special mention must also go to Dr W. John Lyons and the Revd Dr Simon Perry for their friendship, support and critical encouragement, and to Miss Helen Reynolds for her careful reading of the text. Any errors which remain are entirely the responsibility of the author. Final mention must go to SCM Press, for their willingness to allow a young scholar the opportunity of producing a book in their prestigious 'Core Texts' series.

Part 1

Introducing Revelation

1

Introducing the Book of Revelation

A personal story

My own love affair with the book of Revelation began many years ago, when I decided as a teenager to read it through in response to a comment made by one of the youth leaders at the church I was attending. He was taking us through a series looking at 'the end times', and he confidently informed us that we were living in what he called 'the last days'.

The upshot of this was that he told us that Jesus was going to return in person to earth and bring an end to all things sometime within the next five years. As a 13-year-old who was already sensing what I believed to be a call to the Baptist ministry, this caused the bottom to fall out of my world for a few weeks. During this time I struggled with the possibility that God seemed to be calling me into something that I would not be able to fulfil until my mid-twenties at the earliest, while simultaneously revealing through scripture that the world was going to end before I had even left my teens!

My youth leader's conviction that the world was about to come to an end was based on his belief that the book of Revelation was written as predictive prophecy, foretelling in some way the events that would immediately precede the end of the world. In other words, he believed that Revelation was written as a kind of guide book to the last days.

The problem with this way of reading Revelation is that it becomes directly relevant *only* to those people who find themselves living in the days that lead up to the end of the world. So there was my youth leader, firmly convinced that all scripture was of relevance to his life, yet equally firmly convinced that Revelation was only relevant to those living in the last days. It was therefore inevitable that he would try and find correlations between the images of Revelation and the events of his own day. In this quest he would doubtless have found much encouragement from the writings of Hal Lindsey, whose book *The Late, Great Planet Earth*[1] related aspects of John's prophetic writings to, for example, the political events occurring in the European Community of the 1970s. So in this way, my youth leader became convinced that he was living in 'the last days', and that the images of Revelation were finding literal fulfilment before his very eyes.

It was at this point I decided that, rather than listening to what people said *about* Revelation, I was actually going to sit down and read it through for myself, to see what all the fuss was about. I must admit, the first time I read it, much went over my head (and if I am honest – some of it still does!). I was, however (and still am), left with a feeling of breathless wonder that my imagination had been engaged in a new way, and a sense that here was a book that was trying to help me understand my world differently. I also came away with a strong conviction that everything I had read must have been intended to make perfect sense to the people for whom it was first written.

To bring my experience of Revelation up to date: here I still am, many years later, a Baptist minister, a lecturer in biblical studies, and still in love with Revelation! I still get the same feeling of breathless wonder when I read it. I still love having my imagination engaged in new ways. I am still challenged by it to see my world differently. And I still believe it all made perfect sense to those who first read it!

So, I've told you something of my story, and I would encourage you now to take a few moments to ponder your own experience of the book of Revelation up to this point: When did you first come across it? What preconceptions do you have about it? How have you experienced it being portrayed in the media? Can you think of any artwork, songs, or novels that utilize images from Revelation? These things are important, because they define the interpretative lenses through which we read the text. Some of what we bring to the text will be helpful, some less so, and a level of self-awareness is important if we are to grow in our understanding of this complex work.

One of the things I have noticed over the years is that many people are far more comfortable reading books *about* Revelation than they are in reading Revelation itself. So at this point I will make an appeal: please have a copy of Revelation by your side as you work through this book. In my view, Revelation was written to be read out loud in one go, and it works best when it is heard as originally intended – so don't be shy about reading it out loud to yourself. The Bible version I would recommend to use for this purpose is the paraphrase by Eugene Peterson called *The Message*, since it is an accessible and readable version.[2]

What is Revelation trying to achieve?

One of my favourite films is *The Matrix*[3] – a cross between a science-fiction, all-action adventure, and a Japanese martial-arts movie. It is a film to which I have returned on a number of occasions, as it is rich in spiritual imagery. There is a wonderful scene in *The Matrix* where Neo, the hero of the film, has his world shattered. Neo has been under the impression for the whole of his life that he is living in late twentieth-century America; pursuing his job as a humble computer programmer by day, and his hobby as a devious computer hacker by night. But suddenly his world is turned upside down. He finds himself being taken out of the world in which he has been living, on the promise of being shown the truth behind the world as he has always perceived it. He suddenly finds out that the reality of the world he inhabits is entirely different from that which he has always imagined.

This questioning of the nature of reality is not something that is simply the preserve of modern sci-fi classics such as *The Matrix*. In a way, Revelation is a kind of first-century equivalent to such films – with their vivid imagery, its stunning special effects, and its questioning of the nature of reality. And as it proceeds to give its answers, it echoes the invitation made to Neo when he asked about the true reality that lies behind his perception of the world. He was told that there is nothing that can be said that will explain this perception, and that he must rather come and see for himself. So it is with John the author of Revelation. The visionary world he creates invites his audience to realize that their world is not as it appears to be, that there is another way of looking at things. This alternative reality that John presents is not something that can simply be explained – rather it is something that needs to be experienced through imaginative engagement with the visionary world of the Apocalypse.

· The book of Revelation engages the imaginations and feelings of those who suspend their disbelief and enter into its visions, taking them on a journey into what it presents as a deeper spiritual reality. Revelation is primarily a narrative to be experienced, rather than a textbook to be studied. It makes its effect by pounding its audience with image after image, with special effect after special effect. And in so doing, it seeks to transform the way they look at the world in which they live.

When someone starts reading Revelation, they might think of themself as an ordinary person, living an ordinary life. They might look at the world around them, and think they see it for what it is – good and bad, truth and lies, beauty and evil. After all, the human tendency is generally to believe what is seen, and to accept the world at face value. However, by the end of a reading of Revelation, John's intention is that the eyes of his audience will have been transformed, and their imaginations will have been engaged, so that they are equipped to see what he believes to be the true reality that lies behind the everyday perception of the world.

To this end, Revelation seeks to provide the heavenly perspective on the earthly situation. It invites its audience to enter heaven, and see the earth from God's perspective, and in so doing provides an insight into the spiritual reality that, its author believes, underlies the perceived facts of life. As Revelation is read, it tells its audience that what is observed on earth, that which is taken in with the senses, is in fact only a part of the true story. It calls its audience to realize that sometimes their perception of reality is far, far removed from the way God sees things.

In *The Matrix*, Neo is taken into another place, from where he can see the true reality of his world. Similarly in Revelation, John attempts to take his audience into a symbolic world that is at once both frightening and confusing. Yet as the audience enter this world with John, and participate with him in his vision, they can have their perception of the world in which they live transformed for ever. Not everyone who comes to the book of Revelation in the twenty-first century brings with them an innate sympathy for John's text. However, the best way to understand his text may be to enter into his visionary world on its own terms. Those who engage the Apocalypse[4] in this way may find that they come to see the world differently. Instead of being limited to looking at the world through their own eyes and experience, they are instead shown the world as John thinks it appears from the perspective of heaven, and this altered viewpoint can in turn present a relevant challenge to one's own experience.

How does Revelation use imagery?

The images John uses in Revelation are weird and wonderful, but they all serve one purpose: they are there to enable his audience to understand the true nature of their experience. In the following introductory section, a broad-brush picture will be drawn of how Revelation utilizes its imagery. More detailed engagement with the images will occur in subsequent chapters.

Revelation's original audience lived in Asia Minor at the turn of the first century. Graeco-Roman power and civilization was at its height, and they were constantly confronted in their everyday lives with the images of the Roman vision of the world. They saw image after image, through architecture and art, through poetry and prose, all underlining the power of Imperial Rome and its pagan religions. These were the dominant images for John's first audience, those who attended the seven churches of Ephesus, Smyrna, Pergamum, Thyatira, Sardis, Philadelphia and Laodicea.

These early Christians lived in a world dominated by Roman political power, by Greek philosophy and by pagan religion; the images of this social, political and cultural environment were all around them, convincing them of the inevitability and correctness of the Graeco-Roman view of the world.[5] In the book of Revelation John seeks to provide a set of subversive images that will help to purify the imaginations of those who imaginatively enter into his visionary world.[6] After experiencing the images of Revelation, his audience are invited to realize that the images that surround them are in fact satanic[7] distractions from the true spiritual reality to which Revelation points.

The first-century audience of Revelation would have walked into their cities through triumphal arches proclaiming the eternal might of the godlike emperors of Rome. They would have walked past statues and shrines to the many Roman and Greek deities who they believed ruled the world. They were constantly confronted with images of Roman might and power. Their works of art spoke in beautiful and dramatic terms of the beauty and drama of Graeco-Roman civilization and domination, while any who dared to claim otherwise faced persecution and the full might of a Roman sword. If John's original audience believed the imagery of their time, Rome was great, the emperor was a god, and the pagan religions were to be followed. It is to these people that John writes, and as he does so he constructs a series of alternative images that enter the imagination and attempt to convince his audience that Rome is corrupt, that the emperor is evil, and that pagan religions are to be resisted.

The problem that many people have when trying to read Revelation is that they get so caught up in the detail that they miss the big picture. A while ago, I went on a visit to Paris, and was fortunate enough to visit the Musée D'Orsay and to see its exhibition of impressionist paintings. I was struck by their size, but I realized that in order to understand the pictures I needed to take a few steps back and try and appreciate the whole effect. If I stepped up too close to the painting, any sense of meaning was lost, and I was simply confronted with a mass of colours and shades, that I could have stared at all day and still been none the wiser as to what the painting was about. However if I stood back, and took in the whole picture at once, suddenly the picture would make sense. The same is true with Revelation. To spend too long on any one image, without taking a step back and viewing the work as a whole, is a sure way to misunderstand John's intended message. Many weird and unconventional readings of Revelation have emerged because people have begun with a detail, with which they have become obsessed, before they have appreciated the book as a whole.

This is certainly not to say that one should *never* concentrate on the detail, but I very firmly think that one should not get too hung up on specific images, until one has first taken a step back and spent some time studying the big picture of why John was writing, and what he was trying to convey. Once we understand what he is trying to do, we will then be able to begin to understand how he does it.

It is my contention that when reading Revelation, we should always remember that John was not writing to confuse people, neither was he writing in some code that needs to be cracked. Everything John wrote would have made sense to those who received it. The problem we have, as readers coming to his work nearly two thousand years after it was penned, is that we come from a very different culture to that of his first and intended audience. Our reading is informed by the history of interpretation, by those distanced from John's context, that overlays the original text. Therefore much of what John's original audience would have understood easily seems very alien to us, and we have to work harder to discern John's meaning than his original recipients would have done. The key premise for the interpretation offered in this book is that Revelation presents its audience with a vision of God, in order to show them the heavenly perspective on their earthly situation, with the aim of transforming the way in which they live their lives.

The Apocalypse is not some bizarre vision generated by too many local mushrooms (as some have suggested) that enables the reader to escape from reality into some dream world where the lucky few can live happily ever after! John has no time at all for those who would seek to escape from this world, and I think he would be horrified if he thought that there were those who were treating his writings as a kind of escapist literature with no bearing on the present reality.

What about genre and context?

Revelation is an example of the kind of text known as an 'apocalypse'. Just as contemporary readers are familiar with different genres of litera-ture (thrillers, science-fiction, detective novels, poetry, historical writing and so on), John's audience would have known apocalypses (along with letters, biographies, legal documents and so on). The problem we have in the twenty-first century is that we don't read apocalypses very often. The situation is further complicated by the fact that the words 'apocalypse' or 'apocalyptic', when used in our society, mean something different from that which they would have meant in the first century AD. Today, such words are reserved for film titles such as *Apocalypse Now*,[8] or phrases like 'post-apocalyptic'. In this kind of usage, they are often understood as referring to the end of the known world; so a 'post-apocalyptic' film is one that depicts the world after some catastrophic event has occurred. How-ever, in John's time apocalyptic literature had relatively little to do with the end of the world. Rather, an apocalypse was a book that 'revealed' God since the Greek word ἀποκάλυψις ('apocalypse') means 'uncovering' or 'revealing'. In this way, apocalypses were texts that gave a glimpse of heaven, making the secrets of heaven available to mere mortals.

The book of Revelation is often classified, along with a number of other similar texts, as forming part of the genre of 'apocalyptic' literature. This type of literature originated among the Jews in the centuries preceding the time of Christ. An apocalypse is a text where the author receives a revelation of heavenly mysteries, which is then communicated to the readers. An often-cited definition of the apocalyptic genre is that of J. J. Collins:

> 'Apocalypse' is a genre of revelatory literature with a narrative frame-work, in which a revelation is mediated by an otherworldly being to a human recipient, disclosing a transcendent reality which is both temporal, insofar as it envisages eschatological salvation, and spatial, insofar as it involves another, supernatural world.[9]

The discussion over whether and how one can speak of certain pieces of literature as 'apocalyptic' continues.[10] The debate is largely centred around whether or not a document should be called 'apocalyptic' be-cause of its literary form, or because of the meaning it is attempting to convey. As is often the case when a debate becomes polarized, pushing either end of the scale to its extreme merely results in a shift further away from a useful working definition. There is therefore a growing consensus among scholars that attempts to define the 'apocalyptic' genre too tightly may be counter-productive. To this end Barry Matlock critiques the use of all the 'apocalyp-' terms, suggesting that 'we relinquish the idea of having some "second term" ... floating around beyond the literature and seeming to make some historical connection with it'.[11] If his approach is followed, the result is to force the reader back to those texts that are relevant for any particular study, exploring once more those parallels and similarities that shed light on the text being read.[12] For ease of discussion, the term 'apocalyptic' will be used below, but only with due caution as to its usefulness as an overarching and all-embracing definition.

The debate over the definition of 'apocalyptic' has centred around *literaryform* or *content* for a good reason; namely because it is in these two areas that the parallels between these texts are most obvious and fruitful. These two areas provide a useful structure within which to con-sider the wider context of Revelation.

Literary form

D. S. Russell states that the literary form of 'apocalyptic' texts is 'that of poetry of a vivid and highly imaginative kind'.[13] In this he strikes at the heart of the matter, because he does not begin with a list of traits;

rather his starting point is a recognition of the non-literal nature of the writing.[14] This approach frees the reader to understand and interpret the texts using those skills and processes more normally applied to reading poetic and metaphorical material.

First-person narrative

Apocalyptic texts are often written as first-person prose narrative, in which the seer describes the content of the vision that has been revealed to them.[15] This becomes tied in with the practice of pseudonymity in later Israelite and early Christian writings, with the writer not revealing their true name or period, but rather constructing their writing as if it came from the pen of an earlier and recognizably holy person. As Koch says, 'this *pseudonymity* is a much discussed but not convincingly explained phenomenon',[16] and indeed not all apocalypses are pseudonymous. Beale regards pseudonymity as 'the least possible' option for the authorship of Revelation, suggesting: 'If an unknown author were attempting to identify himself with a well-known Christian figure like the apostle John, he would probably call himself not just "John" but "John the apostle". This the author does not do.'[17]

Episodic structure

Another aspect of literary form found among these texts is their episodic structure.[18] This is found in most of the apocalyptic texts, and is a technique that the various authors would have consciously utilized for the presentation of their material. The visions and revelatory messages are 'sandwiched between legends and paraenetic material.'[19] It is the use of such a distinctive literary form that leads C. Rowland to conclude that: 'Although one would not want to speak of the apocalypse as a literary genre which was rigidly adhered to, there does seem to be good evidence that the apocalyptic spirit did tend to manifest itself in a particular form.'[20] Rowland suggests that the adoption of this episodic structure signals that what is being written is revelatory material. The use of this form would also point to the heart of the message; which would be found at the central, or climactic point of the text, with other narrative material serving to frame the main revelation.

Letter form

The book of Revelation has seven letters to seven churches in Asia Minor contained within its opening chapters, and this raises the question of the extent to which the entire work should be understood as a letter, and a comparison with other letter-forms is helpful here. The other letters found within the New Testament were mostly written to be read aloud to a congregation of believers, and the content of these letters indicates that they are predominantly aimed at a church rather than at individuals. It is likely that the prescript (1.4–5) and postscript (22.21) of Revelation owe their structure to a familiarity with the Graeco-Roman tradition of letter-writing which also informed the other New Testament epistles.[21] This epistolary framework serves to ground the text of Revelation within the tradition of public oral reading, and points to the original context being that of the worship services of Christian congregations.

An important factor in interpreting the whole text is an awareness of the context in which it was to be received. As G. R. Beasley-Murray comments:

> Failure to grasp this ... has led innumerable readers to misinterpret the book by identifying the figures and events described in it with persons and events of their own times. Such misunderstanding is corrected by every effort to perceive the situation addressed in the book and its message for those living in it and for all subsequent generations.[22]

Thus understanding Revelation as a letter reinforces the point that the message it contains is geared to the specific needs and situation of the addressees. It also means that the text is to be interpreted primarily in terms of historical context, bearing in mind that everything in it ought to have made sense and had meaning for the original recipients.

Prophecy

If an understanding of Revelation as a *letter* forces the interpreter to consider the context of the intended recipients, an understanding of it as *prophecy* points towards the purpose of the composition. John introduces Revelation as prophecy: 'Blessed is the one who reads aloud the prophecy' (1.3).[23] This indicates that his intention is that the words written will convey an oral message, that in turn will 'transmit a word from God that is constitutive for faith and life'.[24] Thus, John understands his text as the work of the Spirit of God, bearing prophetic witness to 'the word of God and the testimony of Jesus' (1.2).[25]

It has been suggested that the primary prophetic material in Revelation is to be found in the seven letters to the churches in Chapters 2—3.[26] Indeed, in terms of form these letters have much in common with the structures of oral prophecy. However, the question remains as to whether or not John's designation of the work as prophecy is to be understood in terms of the whole book, or just certain parts of it. Furthermore it is also important to consider what John meant when describing his work as 'prophecy'.

There had been a shift by New Testament times in terms of what was meant by 'prophecy', partly motivated by the Jewish belief that prophecy had ceased in the decades following the exile. Hence, when John designates his work as 'prophecy' (1.3; 22.7, 10, 18, 19) it is not necessarily certain that he would have regarded himself as a 'prophet' in the Old Testament sense. A further difficulty here is that whereas Old Testament prophecy is largely a record of oral proclamation, Revelation is clearly a literary work, yet still one that designates itself as prophetic.

Hence the question remains how to understand John's repeated signalling of his work as prophecy. One solution is to divide the text up, treating as prophecy only those areas that fit the generic description.[27] However, this does not do justice to the text, which seems to assert that the whole work is prophetic. A more fruitful process is to understand the prophetic aspect of the text in terms of John's purpose for composition, which is that through this text,

> the Holy Spirit who inspires prophecy enables prophets to bear witness to the revelation that Jesus brought and brings ... Revelation is the work of the Spirit, who from Pentecost on has enabled Christians to bear prophetic witness to 'the word of God and the witness of Jesus.' That witness includes God's word concerning his will for humankind in the present and in the future.[28]

Understanding Revelation as prophetic raises the question of whether it is predictive. In one sense, John seems to nail his colours to the mast in the first verse, when he states that the purpose of the prophecy is 'to show his servants what must soon take place'. However, the issue of how this is to be interpreted has raised much discussion. Some have seen in the work a map of human history that extends into the future up to and beyond the parousia.[29] Others however, would contend that John's

> interest in the prophetic portrayal of eschatological events which are regarded as rapidly approaching is really in their significance for John's own time. He offers no review of past history; he is not concerned with predicting events in the near or distant future, but addresses a church presently involved in a situation of stress and oppression.[30]

This approach seems to make best sense of the book's self description as prophecy.

Content

Russell comments that 'the apocalyptic books claim to be revelations or disclosures of divine secrets'.[31] If it is possible to characterize the content of these texts, Russell here provides the key to it. The method and imagery by which the revelation of heavenly mysteries is mediated varies between the texts, and is influenced by the context of the particular author,[32] but it is this revelatory nature that makes them interesting as far as the exploration of the context of the book of Revelation is concerned.

The belief that undergirds these revelatory visions is that in some way the course of human history, and the secrets of the universe, are laid up in heaven.[33] Through recounting their visionary experiences, the apocalyptic authors are giving their audiences a glimpse into the heavenly realm, in order to convey information that should profoundly affect the way they live.

These apocalyptic visions are typically narrated using language rich in imagery, although as Rowland notes, the book of Revelation is far richer in its imagery than some of its contemporaries.[34] This imagery functions in two ways; it either presents a particular truth about existence in symbolic form, or it describes the contents of the heavenly world.[35] When dealing with the imagery of Revelation, a decision therefore needs to be taken about how a particular image is functioning.

The major source for apocalyptic imagery is the Old Testament,[36] but the writers also draw on observations of the natural world,[37] as well as Graeco-Roman mythology. Much has been written concerning the content of these apocalyptic revelations, and various schemes have been devised to categorize and make sense of this diverse material. Russell concentrates on three areas: cosmology, history, and eschatology.[38]

Cosmology

A concern with the created order, and the way in which the cosmos and humanity interrelate, was particularly prominent in the Judaism which gave rise to many of the texts that parallel Revelation. In contrast to the Greek tradition, Jewish cosmology was concerned less with scientific description and more with poetic portrayal.[39] Thus, there is a complex interrelationship between the descriptions of the created order and the theological perspectives at play in the texts. God was seen as the all-powerful creator of the ordered cosmos, and hence the passing of the seasons, and the movements of the stars in the heavens, were seen as reflecting the mysteries of God.

The visionary revelation of these mysteries therefore involved descriptions of creation. The grand vista of the heavens and the earth can be seen in Revelation as a stage, on which is fought the spiritual battle between Michael and his angels, and the dragon and his angels.[40] The events of history are placed within this overarching vision, which goes beyond the world as it is immediately perceived.

Part of the background to John's text is the tradition of *merkabah* mysticism.[41] These descriptions of the throne or chariot of God make use of language that draws on the creation imagery of Genesis 1.[42] The picture is of the transcendent creator God, the ultimate source of the mysteries that can be found in creation.[43]

Merkabah mysticism finds its roots in passages from the Old Testament that contain accounts of visions of God and his angels in heaven.[44] These passages all contain elements that are picked up by the Jewish *merkabah* tradition. I. Gruenwald lists these elements as follows:

(a) God is sitting on a throne; (b) He has the appearance of a man and particularly that of an old, white-haired man; (c) God is sitting in a palace; (d) Fire occupies an important position in the vision; (e) God is accompanied by angels who minister to him; (f) The angels recite hymns.[45]

Of particular importance for the apocalyptic tradition is the vision of God sitting on a throne or chariot, known as the *Merkabah*, which designates him as the supreme being, the sovereign of the heavens. In the book of Revelation, Christ is pictured as being seated on the throne in heaven,[46] an image which confers on him the authority that is uniquely ascribed to God in the Old Testament. This heavenly vision of the deified Messiah is also present elsewhere in the New Testament, for example 'you will see the Son of man seated at the right hand of the Power' (Mark 14.62).[47] In its description of Jesus as a second divine being, early Christianity reworked Jewish visionary accounts concerning God and the angels, using the language of these accounts to express their beliefs about the divinity of Jesus and his role in the judgement of mankind.[48]

History

In apocalyptic texts, God is seen as being in control of the course of history by his very nature as God. The picture of the cosmos as a stage on which transcendent events are acted out is helpful here. Rowland describes this view of history as: 'a play with many scenes which have been written but not all acted out on stage ... [The] seer, however, is privileged to have a total view of the play, including that which is still to be actualized on the stage of history'.[49] Thus the seer could mediate the message in the context of the total view of history that was granted in the vision. The incomprehensible events of human history, such as the persecution of the righteous, are placed within an understanding of history that finds its completion in the God who will bring all things to their proper conclusion.

Eschatology

The end of history is an important theme in exploring the context of Revelation. Within many of the apocalyptic texts, history was thought to comprise two ages: the present age and the age to come. The notion that the current created order would be transformed, and that a new heaven and a new earth would be established, provides the framework within which the eschatological scheme of Revelation has to be understood. Although the two ages are distinct, it is together that they represent the complete purpose of God in history.[50] The present age is not the end of the story; rather what will follow, already known to the seer, is the re-creation of the cosmos and the inauguration of the age to come. Despite appearances to the contrary, God is in complete control of events. The first two themes, cosmology and history, converge in the eschatological expectation that God will bring them to completion.

The re-creation of all things is tied in with the concept of divine judgement; when God, from his *merkabah* seat, will finally right the wrongs of the current age and vindicate 'the righteous', who are in the main designated by the apocalyptic writers as the nation of Israel. Doubtless this has its origin in the nationalistic nature of some earlier Jewish texts. However, even in the later texts, where the distinction is made on ethical rather than on ethnic grounds, 'the tendency is to identify "the righteous" with Israel and "the wicked" with the Gentiles'.[51] Thus, when Revelation speaks of the establishment of the new age in terms of the new Jerusalem, this need not be understood as an ethnic distinction, but rather as a metaphor for the vindication of the righteous people of God.[52]

What about dating?

The question of the dating of Revelation is one of the enduring puzzles of the book, and has in many ways proved more intractable than some of the more famous interpretative concerns. Two major alternatives have emerged, each of which attracts the approval of notable commentators. The most likely period of composition is either some time between the late 60s and early 70s AD or the early-mid 90s AD. The dominant view among twentieth-century scholars was to locate the book late in the reign of Domitian (AD 81–96),[53] reading the references to martyrdom contained within Revelation as referring to persecution of Christians perpetrated under Domitian's reign. However, recent scholarship has cast doubts on the extent to which the situation under Domitian is actually reflected by this implied context of Revelation.[54] This has led to a resurgence in support for an earlier date, either during or shortly after the reign of Nero (AD 54–68), or during the reign of Vespasian (AD 69–79).

If it is correct that the myth of Nero's return from the grave is reflected in some of John's imagery,[55] then this would imply a time of writing after Nero's death.[56] A further factor that deserves consideration is the destruction of the Jerusalem temple at the hands of the Romans in AD 70; the identification of Rome with Babylon certainly has far stronger resonance once both cities have been responsible for the desecration of the temple.[57] However, the description of John measuring the temple (11.1–2) may indicate that it is still standing at the time of writing.[58]

Some have sought to utilize a correlation between first-century Roman emperors and the seven kings represented by the seven heads of the scarlet beast (17.9) as a way of dating Revelation.[59] The problem with this approach however, is that even if one could be sure that the sixth king was Nero, or Vespasian, or Domitian, this would still provide no guarantee that John is not setting a fictional date for his work that is earlier than the actual date of composition.

The position taken here is that the most likely date for composition is during the early years of the reign of Vespasian,[60] who had played a key role in the Judean Wars of the late 60s, commanding two legions sent to suppress the Jewish uprising. Vespasian went on to serve as Procurator of Judea (AD 67–68), breaking off his plans to take Jerusalem by force upon hearing of the suicide of Nero, and becoming emperor a year later.[61] The honour of taking Jerusalem eventually went to his son, Titus. Given John's concern that those in his churches should endure through 'the great ordeal' (7.14), a context of less than a decade after the Neronian persecutions also seems more plausible than one of a generation later. This suggests that the early years of the reign of Vespasian provide a fitting context for the book, and also raises the intriguing possibility that the book of Revelation may pre-date the Gospel of John by some 15 years.[62]

This chapter has introduced John's use of imagery, highlighting the importance of gaining the 'big picture' as the appropriate context for more detailed study. To this end, the genre of the book of Revelation as an 'apocalypse' has been examined, focusing particularly on the Jewish apocalyptic background and issues of dating.

Draw your own conclusions

- How would you express your understanding of the nature of reality?
- What are the dominant images of your own culture?
- In what ways do the alternative images of Revelation critique these?
- How does an understanding of the original context of Revelation help with its interpretation?
- What do you understand by the term 'prophecy'?
- What do you understand by the term 'apocalyptic'?

Notes

1 Hal Lindsey and C. C. Carlson, 1970, *The Late, Great Planet Earth*, Grand Rapids: Zondervan.

2 There are numerous printed editions of *The Message*, and it is also available to read online at http://www.biblegateway.com/versions/. Quotations from the Bible in this Core Text are all from the New Revised Standard Version (NRSV) unless otherwise indicated.

3 Larry Wachowski and Andy Wachowski, 1999, *The Matrix*, Warner Home Video.

4 The phrase 'the Apocalypse' is used interchangeably with 'the book of Revelation' throughout.

5 For a discussion of the Graeco-Roman and Jewish civic background to John's imagery, see Philip Harland, 2000, 'Honouring the Emperor or Assailing the Beast: Participation in Civic Life among Associations (Jewish, Christian and Other) in Asia Minor and the Apocalypse of John', *Journal for the Study of the New Testament*, vol. 77: 99–121. Cf. also Friedrich Nestor Paulo, 2002, 'Adapt or Resist? A Socio-Political Reading of Revelation 2.18–29', *Journal for the Study of the New Testament*, vol. 25.2: 185–211.

6 Richard Bauckham, 1993, *The Theology of the Book of Revelation*, New Testament Theology, Cambridge: Cambridge University Press, p. 17.

7 The word 'satanic' is used in this book to denote John's perception of a tendency on the part of humans to construct idolatrous alternatives to the worship of God on the heavenly throne. Cf. the discussion of Satan as a character within the text of the Apocalypse on p. 148.

8 Francis Ford Coppola, 1979, *Apocalypse Now*, Pathe Distribution.

9 John J. Collins (ed.), 1979, *Apocalypse: The Morphology of a Genre*, Semeia, vol. 14, Chicago: The Society of Biblical Literature, p. 9. Biblical examples of what are usually termed apocalyptic material, in addition to the book of Revelation, include Daniel, Ezekiel, Mark 13, 1 Cor. 15.35–58, 1 Thess. 4.13–18, and 2 Thess. 2.1–12.

10 As Adams comments: 'There has been and continues to be much debate among scholars about how one defines an "apocalypse" or the "apocalyptic" genre. Yet, there is general agreement about the particular Jewish works that are in view when the category apocalypse/apocalyptic is invoked.' Edward Adams, 2007, *The Stars Will Fall from Heaven: Cosmic Catastrophe in the New Testament and Its World*, Library of New Testament Studies, vol. 347, London: T&T Clark, p. 53. Cf. also Lorenzo DiTommaso, 2007, 'Apocalypses and Apocalypticism in Antiquity (Part I)', Currents in Biblical Research, vol. 5.2: 235–6; Lorenzo DiTommaso, 2007, 'Apocalypses and Apocalypticism in Antiquity: (Part II)', *Currents in Biblical Research*, vol. 5.3: 367–432.

11 R. Barry Matlock, 1996, *Unveiling the Apocalyptic Paul: Paul's Interpreters and the Rhetoric of Criticism*, Journal for the Study of the New Testament Supplement Series, vol. 127, Sheffield: Sheffield Academic Press, p. 291. The importance of this suggestion is highlighted by Bauckham in his work on Jewish and Christian apocalypses. Here, he recognizes the difficulty and confusion which the apocalyp- terms can generate. He is speaking particularly of the term apocalypticism, but his comments are apposite with regard to the other

terms also. He says that they 'may suggest too much uniformity in worldview and eschatology'. Richard Bauckham, 1998, *The Fate of the Dead, Studies on the Jewish and Christian Apocalypses*, Supplements to Novum Testamentum, vol. XCIII, Leiden: E. J. Brill, p. 5. Beale concurs, commenting, 'these studies of the apocalyptic genre have yielded diminishing returns, especially in terms of significant new interpretative insights into the book of Revelation. G. K. Beale, 1999, *The Book of Revelation*, The New International Greek Testament Commentary, Carlisle: The Paternoster Press, p. 41.

12 A parallel situation is to be found with the attempts to create a unifying 'theology of the Old Testament'. If such a thing exists, it can only be by virtue of including within itself the contents of each of the texts which make up the Old Testament. Thus, recent theologies of the Old Testament have taken each book separately, rather than trying to force an overarching scheme on the whole canon. This is not to say that individual texts cannot be interrelated and compared and contrasted, or even that the Old Testament cannot be spoken of as a collection of texts with common themes and concerns, but the starting point must be the text of each document, not some grand unifying theory. Cf. John Rogerson (ed.), 1983, *Beginning Old Testament Study*, London: SPCK, p. 95.

13 D. S. Russell, 1978, *Apocalyptic: Ancient and Modern*, London: SCM Press, p. 1.

14 As Caird comments: 'One of the great advantages of describing the apocalyptic merging of concepts as metaphor is that it brings apocalyptic out of the Jewish backwater, to which so much unimaginative scholarship has consigned it, into the main stream of the world's literature; and this, to judge from its influence on art, music and poetry, is where it belongs.' G. B. Caird, 1980, *The Language and Imagery of the Bible*, London: Duckworth, p. 264.

15 David E. Aune, 1997, *Revelation 1–5*, Word Biblical Commentary, vol. 52A, Dallas: Word Books, p. lxxxii.

16 Klaus Koch, 1972, *The Rediscovery of Apocalyptic*, trans. Margaret Kohl, Studies in Biblical Theology, Second Series, vol. 22, London: SCM Press, p. 26.

17 Beale, *Revelation*, p. 34.

18 Aune, *Revelation 1–5*, p. lxxxii.

19 Christopher Rowland, 1982, *The Open Heaven: A Study of Apocalyptic in Judaism and Early Christianity*, New York: Crossroad, p. 51.

20 Rowland, *Open Heaven*, p. 52.

21 Aune, *Revelation 1–5*, p. lxxiv.

22 G. R. Beasley-Murray, 1997, 'Revelation, Book Of', in Ralph P. Martin and Peter H. Davids (eds), *Dictionary of the Later New Testament & Its Developments*, Leicester: InterVarsity Press, p. 1027.

23 Cf. Rev. 10.11; 22.7, 10, 18, 19. David Hill makes a similar point, but goes on to discuss the relative virtues of categorizing Revelation as prophecy or apocalyptic before concluding that Revelation should primarily be considered as prophecy. His grounds for this are that it lacks 'many of the most characteristic features of [the so-called apocalyptic] genre.' Cf. David Hill, 1979, *New Testament Prophecy*, London: Marshall, Morgan & Scott, pp. 70, 75.

24 Robert W. Wall, 1991, *Revelation*, New International Biblical Commentary, Carlisle: Paternoster Press, p. 22.

25 Beasley-Murray, 'Revelation, Book Of', p. 1026.

26 Aune, *Revelation 1−5*, p. lxxv.

27 See for example the approach of Aune who identifies, in addition to the seven letters to the churches (each beginning with 'thus says'), those areas where God or Christ is quoted in the first person singular (e.g. Rev. 1.7−8, 17−20; 16.15; 21.5−8; 22.7, 12−14, 18−20) and those places where oracular speech is evident (e.g. Rev. 13.9−10; 14.6−11; 18.21−24; 19.9; 21.3−4, 5−8). Cf. K. N. Giles, 1997, 'Prophecy, Prophets, False Prophets', in Ralph P. Martin and Peter H. Davids (eds), *Dictionary of the Later New Testament & Its Developments*, Leicester: InterVarsity Press, p. 974.

28 Beasley-Murray, 'Revelation, Book Of', p. 1026, referencing Rev. 1.2, 9; 20.4.

29 'Parousia' is a technical term for the second coming of Christ, deriving from the Greek word παρουσία meaning 'coming' (cf. Matt. 24.27, 37, 39; 1 Cor. 15.23; 1 Thess. 2.19; 3.13; 5.23; James 5.8; 1 John 2.28).

30 Hill, *New Testament Prophecy*, p. 86.

31 D. S. Russell, 1964, *The Method & Message of Jewish Apocalyptic*, London: SCM Press, p. 107.

32 Rowland, *Open Heaven*, p. 52.

33 Rowland, *Open Heaven*, p. 56.

34 Such as, for example, 4 Ezra and Syriac Baruch, large parts of which are dialogue with God or his angel, rather than description of the heavenly realm. Cf. Rowland, *Open Heaven*, p. 61.

35 Rowland, *Open Heaven*, p. 58.

36 Particularly the visions of Daniel 2 and 7.

37 Rowland, *Open Heaven*, p. 60.

38 D. S. Russell, 1992, *Divine Disclosure*, London: SCM Press, p. 83. These three areas roughly parallel the suggestion of Rowland that the content of the mysteries can be summed up in the following categories: What is above, What is below, What had happened previously, and What is to come. Cf. Rowland, *Open Heaven*, p. vii.

39 J. Painter, 1997, 'Creation, Cosmology', in Ralph P. Martin and Peter H. Davids (eds), *Dictionary of the Later New Testament & Its Developments*, Leicester: InterVarsity Press, p. 250.

40 Painter, 'Creation, Cosmology', p. 254.

41 Cf. Rowland, *Open Heaven*, p. 218; Russell, *Divine Disclosure*, p. 84.

42 For example, the sea of crystal in Rev. 4.6 (with its parallel in Ezek. 1.22) draws on Gen. 1.7, cf. Rowland, *Open Heaven*, p. 220.

43 Russell, *Divine Disclosure*, p. 86.

44 Cf. 1 Kings 22.19; Isa. 6.1; Ezek. 1.26; 8.2; 10.1−17; Dan. 7.9−10.

45 I. Gruenwald, 1980, *Apocalyptic and Merkavah Mysticism*, Leiden: E. J. Brill, p. 31.

46 Cf. Rev. 7.17; 22.1.

47 Cf. John 12.41; Col. 3.1; Rev. 5.6.

48 Cf. Mark 8.38; 13.27.

49 Rowland, *Open Heaven*, pp. 143−4.

50 Russell, *Divine Disclosure*, p. 109.

51 Russell, *Divine Disclosure*, p. 94.

52 Wall, *Revelation*, p. 243.

53 Cf. Beale, *Revelation*, p. 4; M. Eugene Boring, 1989, *Revelation*, Interpretation, Louisville: John Knox Press, p. 10; Martin Kiddle, 1940, *The Revelation of St John*, The Moffatt New Testament Commentary, London: Hodder & Stoughton, p. xliii.

54 Ian Boxall, 2002, *Revelation: Vision and Insight: An Introduction to the Apocalypse*, London: SPCK, pp. 86–9. For a helpful summary of the arguments for a lack of widespread persecution during the reign of Domitian see J. Nelson Kraybill, 1996, *Imperial Cult and Commerce in John's Apocalypse*, Journal for the Study of the New Testament Supplement Series, vol. 132, Sheffield: Sheffield Academic Press, pp. 34–6. Cf. also Leonard L. Thompson, 1990, *The Book of Revelation: Apocalypse and Empire*, Oxford: Oxford University Press, pp. 15–17.

55 See p. 164 for more on the Nero Redivivus idea.

56 Although Aune, in his defence of an early origin for Revelation, suggests a multi-stage editing process whereby the Nero imagery is inserted in the later stages. Aune, *Revelation 1–5*, pp. lxvii–lxx.

57 Although Boxall points out that it is not impossible for the Rome/Babylon identification to pre-date the destruction of the temple, citing 1 Peter 5.13 as evidence of a pre-AD 70 document using Babylon as a code for Rome. Boxall, *Vision and Insight*, pp. 96–7.

58 Equally, it may be a reflection upon the destruction of the temple as John moves towards an understanding of the church as the new temple. Cf. Boxall, *Vision and Insight*, p. 97.

59 See the discussion of the seven kings on p. 166.

60 Cf. Stephen S. Smalley, 1994, *Thunder and Love: John's Revelation and John's Community*, Milton Keynes: Nelson Word Ltd., pp. 49–50; Stephen S. Smalley, 2005, *The Revelation to John: A Commentary on the Greek Text of the Apocalypse*, London: SPCK, pp. 2–3.

61 Barbara Levick, 1999, *Vespasian*, Routledge Imperial Biographies, London: Routledge, p. 38.

62 For a useful chapter on 'The Quest for the Johannine School: The Book of Revelation and the Fourth Gospel' see Elisabeth Schüssler Fiorenza, 1998, *The Book of Revelation: Justice and Judgment*, 2nd edn, Minneapolis: Fortress Press, pp. 85–113. She concludes: 'We no longer need to establish a direct literary interrelationship between both works but can assume a dialectical exchange of theological thought between their respective schools and traditions' (p. 107).

2

Are there Different Ways of Reading Revelation?

Anyone wanting to study the book of Revelation and attempting to read around the various literature that has been produced on its interpretation, whether populist or scholarly, will inevitably find themselves confronted with a confusing array of terminology.[1] This is particularly so regarding the various interpretative strategies that people employ as they seek the appropriate 'key' to unlock the 'true meaning' of the book. It may be of some relief to learn that with the exception of the following few paragraphs, these technical terms are largely avoided throughout this Core Text. This is partly out of a desire to try and engage with the text afresh, without seeking to fit it into a predetermined interpretative framework. But it is also because it is this author's conviction that the reason there has been so much confusion regarding these terms is that they are seeking to ask questions of the Apocalypse that it simply does not set out to answer. Hence, to ask whether the correct interpretation of Revelation is historicist, preterist or futurist, premillennial, postmillennial or amillennial, is to ask questions that will never receive a satisfactory answer because they did not concern John when he originally shaped the text.

Relationship to human history

There are four main approaches to the question of whether, and in what ways, the prophecies of Revelation can be related to the course of human history. The historicist, preterist, futurist and idealist views all provide different answers to the question of how the images contained in Revelation correlate with events that have either occurred through the centuries, or are expected to occur in the near future. The following analyses of these four alternatives begin with a diagrammatic representation of the approach under examination. In these diagrams, the four different approaches to the prophecies of Revelation are demonstrated by plotting the extent to which they are interpreted literally against their application to past, present or future.

Historicist

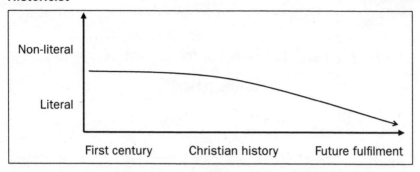

In every age there have been those who have sought to take the symbolism of Revelation and relate it to the course of history that has led to their present circumstances.[2] To this end the historicist approach seeks to identify the content of John's vision with events of human history. The content of the visionary sections of the Apocalypse are seen by historicist interpreters as predictions of events that will happen between the time of the first century and the end of the world. It is typical for interpreters who take this approach to see themselves as living in the days that immediately precede the eschaton,[3] and to take an increasingly literal approach as the 'end times' approach. In this way, the correspondence between Revelation and its original first-century setting is at a largely non-literal level, with the application of the prophecies becoming progressively more literal and specific as the end of the world draws near.

This approach can be seen in numerous interpreters, from the fourth-century commentator Victorinus of Pettau, who saw his generation as living in the time of the sixth seal,[4] to the twelfth-century Calabrian Abbot Joachim of Fiore, who devised a way of reading scripture that allowed him to see patterns in the Bible that were paralleled in the scheme of world history. Joachim thus read the history of humanity back into the Bible, and by following his methodology was able to make detailed predictions about the immediate future.

The difficulty with this approach is that it can reduce Revelation to being of primary relevance only to those who actually inhabit the earth during the last days before the end of the world. Those who have supplied historicist answers in the past are inevitably regarded as having reached incorrect conclusions, in comparison to the current historicist interpreter. This approach also assumes that events of significance in the life of the interpreter have similar significance to God. In other words, events in other parts of the world, unknown to the interpreter, are not covered by the prophecies of Revelation. Given that historicist readings have tended to emerge in Western imperialist contexts, this can create a strongly patriarchal view of the Apocalypse, with the dominant worldview of the historicist interpreter taking precedence over any other.

Preterist

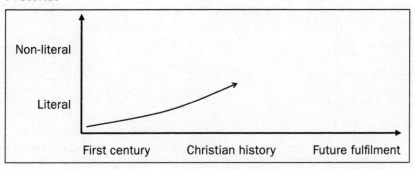

The preterist approach, which takes its name from the grammatical term 'preterite' denoting the past tense, seeks first and foremost to locate the fulfilment of the prophecies of Revelation within the world of the original recipients. In this way, the primary contexts of interpretation are the Roman Empire and Jewish nation of the first century. It is only once correlations to this context have been exhausted that a preterist approach then turns its attention to the course of Christian history, seeing the prophecies concerning the downfall of Babylon as finding their ultimate fulfilment in the fall of the city of Rome in the fifth century. In this way, the approach moves from a literal application of the content of John's visions in the first century, towards a less literal understanding of their application within Christian history. For the preterist interpreter, all the events described in Revelation are understood to be in the past.

This approach came to prominence during the sixteenth-century Reformation, and was promoted by the Roman Catholic Church as an antidote to the historicist approach, some of whose proponents identified the Pope as the Antichrist.[5] This development of a way of reading the text, whereby its fulfilment is located entirely in the past, thus provided a strong refutation of the claims of those who sought to apply the prophecies to their present circumstances.

In many ways the preterist approach prefigures the more recent efforts of historical-critical scholarship, which also locates the text firmly within its original context. However, the difference between the two is that the preterist view still regards the text as predictive prophecy, simply asserting that the fulfilment of the prophecy has now passed. This is in contrast to the historical-critical approach, which seeks to understand the effect John hoped to achieve within the world of his recipients through his construction of the text. In this way, the historical-critical scholar may recognize that John was on occasions encouraging his audience to explore a future eschatological perspective, without seeking to locate that perspective within the early centuries of the Christian Church.

Futurist

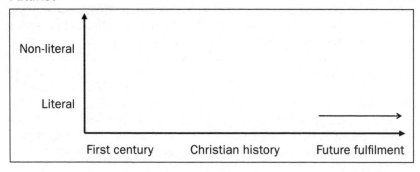

The futurist approach to Revelation locates the fulfilment of the 'prophecies' of Revelation in the future. In this way, the events depicted in the symbols and images are expected to be literally fulfilled on the earth. Those who take a futurist approach usually see themselves as living in the last generation before the time when the prophecies will unfold, and therefore devote much attention to identifying the tell-tale signs that this is the case. In this respect, there is a similarity here to the historicist approach, in that both seek to relate the events of their own day to the prophecies they find in the Apocalypse. The difference, however, lies in the fact that the historicist will see a gradual fulfilment of the prophecies throughout Christian history, whereas the futurist sees a coming fulfilment, beginning with the present and continuing into the future.

The origin of the futurist approach can be found as early as the Church fathers, with Irenaeus and Justin Martyr (second century AD) both of whom take an essentially futurist approach.[6] However, in more recent centuries it has become the dominant approach to Revelation among more conservative (evangelical) traditions. From this group, an influential twentieth-century exponent of the futurist approach is found in Hal Lindsey, who relates the imagery of Revelation to the political events of his own period, continually revising his correlations as alliances and warfare situations change, in order to demonstrate that the events 'predicted' in Revelation are shortly to be fulfilled.[7] In a similar vein American President Ronald Reagan, speaking in 1983, commented:

> You know, I turn back to your ancient prophecies ... and the signs foretelling Armageddon and I find myself wondering if we're the generation that is going to see that come about. I don't know if you've noted any of those prophecies lately, but, believe me, they certainly describe the times we're going through.[8]

The problem with a futurist approach, as with the historicist approach, is that it tends towards a denial of the relevance of the Apocalypse to any except those actually living in the last days. The relevance to the context of the original recipients is diminished, becoming simply a vague hope that one day evil will be judged and the righteous vindicated. The futurist approach also has the effect of freeing the interpreter to utilize ever-more ingenious techniques to try and find correlations between the text and their world, treating the text as a code to be cracked with the application of a suitable key.[9] Another potential drawback with the futurist approach is that it can create a pessimistic view of the immediate earthly future, with war in the Near East, environmental catastrophe, or nuclear holocaust seen as the outworking of God's plan for the earth, and therefore as something to be, if not welcomed, certainly not opposed.[10]

Idealist

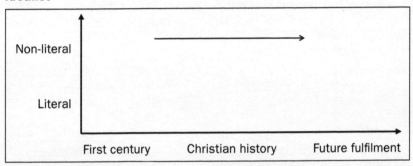

The idealist approach rejects any attempt to find literal correlations between the images of Revelation and any phase of human history, whether this is past, present or future. Instead, the images are seen as allegories for the ongoing cosmic battle between good and evil. Thus attention is paid not to the surface meaning of the words, but to the 'spiritual' meaning behind them.[11] In this way, the images of violence and death that are found in the sequences of seals, trumpets and bowls can be reinterpreted as representations of the ongoing judgement on evil in all times and places, rather than as specific horrors to be enacted on the earth.

This approach has a certain attractiveness in terms of 'sanitizing' the text of those aspects that may otherwise prove problematic or unpalatable. Once again however, a key weakness of this approach, as for the historicist and futurist approaches, is the way in which it distances the images used by John from their specific first-century context, thereby diminishing the pastoral value of the Apocalypse for its original recipients beyond providing an assurance that evil receives judgement. A further problem with this approach is that it is entirely arbitrary, dependent solely on the creativity of the interpreter, which means that any proposed meaning or application is unverifiable. Instead of being a prophetic text speaking words of insight to the Church, the idealist apocalypse faces the danger of becoming what Desrosiers describes as 'a shapeless amalgam of universal truths applied to the believers' life in such an individualistic way as to become completely foreign to the biblical idea of faith and community'.[12]

Summary

The four approaches assessed above all represent attempts to answer the question of how the events of Revelation relate to the course of human history. They also share a concern for locating the contemporary reader within that scheme. As has been demonstrated, they suggest highly divergent answers to the same question, yet each claims to offer an approach that is in accord with the content of the Apocalypse itself.

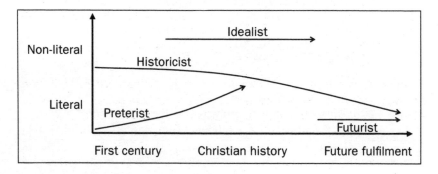

Millennialism

Another interpretative 'key' that is often applied to the Apocalypse is that of how the millennium passage from Rev. 20.1–8 is understood. At its most simple level, this passage is a description of the binding of Satan and the glorious reign of the martyrs. However, the question of exactly *when* this thousand-year reign is expected to take place has occupied far more thought and ink than might be expected for such a short passage. Richard Bauckham comments: 'Millenarianism is the belief that the millennium is a period in the future, and embraces a very wide variety of beliefs about the character of the millennium and how it is to be achieved.'[13] Amillennialism is the belief that there will be no future beginning to the millennium, as it is already occurring in some sense within Christian history. A way of remembering the difference between post- and pre- millennialism is to think of the post- and pre- as referring to the timing of the second coming of Jesus (often called the *parousia*).

Thus, in postmillennialism the parousia comes post- (or *after*) the millennium, whereas in premillennialism it comes pre- (or *before*) the millennium. The following table offers a summary of these three commonly encountered interpretative approaches. Clearly there is a great deal of simplification here, as these positions each in turn contain an enormous variety of nuances.

	Present	*Future*		
Amillennialism	**Millennium**			Return of Jesus
Postmillennialism	Church in history		**Millennium**	Return of Jesus
(Dispensational) Premillennialism	Church in history	Tribulation before Rapture	Return of Jesus	**Millennium**

Amillennialism

Amillennialism arose in an early form during the patristic period, with the attempt to understand scripture in a spiritual rather than literal manner, and can be found in both Origen (AD 185–254) and Jerome (AD 347–420). Another patristic precursor to amillennialism is to be found in the writings of Tyconius (*flor.* AD 370–390),[14] who rejected the notion that the millennium was to be found in the future, and asserted that it had already begun as the period between the first and second comings of Christ.[15] Building on their work, it was Augustine (AD 354–430) who developed what is now termed the amillennial approach. He identified Christ's thousand-year reign on earth as beginning with the binding of Satan at the nativity, and saw it continuing through the Church, with the numerical Christian growth and its increasing influence indicating the ever-expanding nature of the 'kingdom of Christ'.[16] Augustine's approach quickly came to be seen as orthodoxy, although this surely owes as much to political expediency as to the theological reflection on which Augustine based his conclusions. As N. Cohn suggests:

> The Catholic Church was now a powerful and prosperous institution, functioning according to a well-established routine; and the men responsible for governing it had no wish to see Christians clinging to out-dated and inappropriate dreams of a new earthly Paradise.[17]

Largely due to it receiving the endorsement of the Roman Church, Augustine's amillennial viewpoint remained unchallenged for the next thousand years. People accepted that they were living under the millennial reign of Christ, exercised through the Church. According to Augustine's scheme, the millennium was due to end around AD 1000. After a significant enough gap had elapsed since the supposed end of the millennium to allow for errors or disagreements regarding calculations,[18] some started to question what had actually changed. According to a straightforward reading of Rev. 20.7–10, the end of the millennium should have been followed by the release of Satan from his prison, the siege of the Holy City and the banishment of the Devil into the lake of fire and sulphur. So it was that indications were sought in the political and theological context of the eleventh century for signs that the millennium had ended, and that Satan had been released and was rampant upon the earth. Depending of course upon one's political viewpoint, evidence could be found either to support or contradict this expectation. And so from this point, the Augustinian doctrine of amillennialism started to fall out of favour. Those who still wished to preserve a form of amillennialism suggested that it should instead be seen as a symbolic image for the period between the advent of Christ and his second coming, however long that period might be, rather than regarding the millennium as a literal thousand years. In this way, the Roman Church could continue to assert its authority as the agent of the present kingdom of Christ on the earth.[19]

Postmillennialism

The notion that the millennium may lie in the future, at a time preceding the second coming of Christ, is first encountered in the writings of Joachim of Fiore (c. AD 1135–1202). The key to Joachim's interpretation was his understanding that the history of the world from beginning to end was divided into three Trinitarian stages, and that these could be found reflected in the Bible. Each of his three stages represented an *age*, ruled over by the relevant person of the Trinity. Based upon Matthew's genealogy of Jesus (cf. Matt. 1.17), Joachim postulated that each of the ages would last for 42 generations of 30 years, or 1,260 years (cf. Rev. 11.2–3).[20] These ages were consecutive to each other, but each age had a period of incubation during the preceding age before the transition occurred. The following diagram summarizes Joachim's scheme, indicating the period of incubation followed by the age itself.

In this way, Joachim located himself on the cusp of a transition, with the world moving from the *age of the Son* to the *age of the Spirit*. The millennium, for Joachim, was therefore synonymous with the dawning third age, and would continue until the return of Christ and the final judgement.[21]

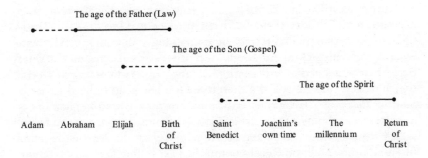

The age of the Father (Law)

The age of the Son (Gospel)

The age of the Spirit

| Adam | Abraham | Elijah | Birth of Christ | Saint Benedict | Joachim's own time | The millennium | Return of Christ |

Joachim's concept of three dispensations, including one still to come, represents a significant move away from the Augustinian amillennial position. It is no coincidence that Joachim was writing just over one thousand years after the point where those who held the amillennial view considered the millennium to have begun. The significance of his radical attempt to re-schematize the history of the world is that it allows the millennium to be placed in the future, rather than within history, thereby removing the problems associated with trying to understand the Church as currently existing in the time after the end of the millennium.

The long-term impact of postmillennialism has been a broadly optimistic approach to human history. If the millennium is seen as something that arises out of the present, then it is incumbent upon the Church to work towards the building of the kingdom of God on earth. Significant postmillennialists include the English Nonconformist Philip Doddridge (1702–51) and the American revivalist preacher Jonathan Edwards (1703–58). Even John Wesley (1703–91), the founder of Methodism, declared a sympathy for postmillennialism.[22] It remains attractive especially to those who understand the progress of the gospel in terms of social justice and improvement.

Premillennialism

The doctrine of premillennialism falls into two main subdivisions. By far the more influential in terms of twentieth-century Western Christianity has been premillennial dispensationalism, a variation on the doctrine of classic premillennialism.

Premillennial dispensationalism

It was Joachim's division of the history of the world into ages past, present and future that paved the way for the development known as dispensationalism.[23] This has its origins proper in the writing and teaching of John Nelson Darby (1800–82), an Anglican priest who went on to become an early leader of the Brethren movement.[24] In the 1830s, Darby became increasingly interested in eschatology, developing a scheme whereby the history of humanity was divided into various dispensations. Darby defined a dispensation as 'any arranged dealing of God in which man ... has failed, and therefore God has been obliged to act by another means'.[25] Darby thus saw human history as a succession of dispensations, each one a fresh act of God in response to the human failure which triggered the end of the previous dispensation. Darby's teaching featured in the notes on Revelation in the best-selling *Scofield Reference Bible* (pub. 1909),[26] and this led to the distinctive theological features developed by Darby coming to exercise enormous influence during the twentieth century on both sides of the Atlantic.

Dispensationalism offers a division of the history of the world into seven ages, paralleling the seven days of creation, with each 'day' approximating to a 'dispensation'. The following chart from 1918 goes a stage further, and lists each dispensation as lasting one thousand years.[27] Assuming a date for the creation of the world of approximately 4000 BC,[28] this would place the expected return of Jesus and inauguration of the millennium at AD 2000.

Those who take a dispensational approach often see themselves as living in the closing decades of the sixth dispensation, on the verge of the millennium. Accordingly, in a similar fashion to Joachim, they seek to comprehend the nascent signs of the coming age. To this end, the letters to the seven churches of Revelation may be utilized to denote seven further subdivisions of the sixth dispensation, with the negative Laodicean letter representing divine judgement on the present state of the Church.[29]

Classic Premillennialism

Through the late nineteenth and twentieth centuries, dispensationalism has tended to go hand-in-hand with the doctrine known as premillennialism. However, the historical precursors to premillennialism can be traced back to the earliest centuries of Christianity, with an imminent parousia expected to inaugurate the thousand-year reign of Christ. This viewpoint was held by Justin Martyr (AD 100–165), Tertullian (AD 155–230), Hippolytus (d. AD 235), and Irenaeus (*flor.* second century AD) among others. However, with the ever-increasing delay in the parousia, the urgency of expectation surrounding the coming millennium receded. Following the rise of amillennialism, the impending return of Christ became less of a theological dogma, and speculation as to the date of an imminent parousia became unnecessary. In this way, early premillennial thought stalled for nearly two millennia in the face of Augustinian

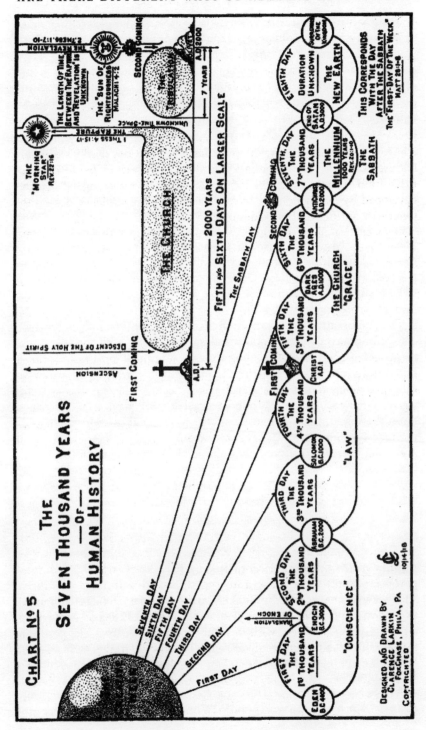

CHART NO 5

THE
SEVEN THOUSAND YEARS
OF
HUMAN HISTORY

THE "MORNING STAR" REV.22:16

THE RAPTURE
1 THESS 4:15-17

DESCENT OF THE HOLY SPIRIT

ASCENSION

FIRST COMING

THE CHURCH

THE LENGTH OF TIME BETWEEN THE RAPTURE AND REVELATION IS UNKNOWN

THE "SUN OF RIGHTEOUSNESS"
MALACHI 4:2

SECOND COMING

THE REVELATION
2 THESS.1:7-10

A.D. 2000

7 YEARS

THE TRIBULATION

UNKNOWN TIME-SPACE

2000 YEARS

FIFTH AND SIXTH DAYS ON LARGER SCALE

THE SABBATH DAY

A.D. 1

EIGHTH DAY

DURATION UNKNOWN

THE NEW EARTH

KINGDOM OF THE KINGDOM

THIS CORRESPONDS WITH THE DAY AFTER THE DAY THE "FIRST-DAY OF THE WEEK"
MATT 28:1-8

END OF SATAN A.D. 3000

SEVENTH DAY
THE 7TH THOUSAND YEARS

THE MILLENNIUM
1000 YEARS
REV.20:1-10

THE SABBATH

ANTICHRIST A.D. 2000

SIXTH DAY
THE 6TH THOUSAND YEARS

SECOND COMING

DARK AGES A.D. 1000

THE CHURCH
"GRACE"

FIFTH DAY
THE 5TH THOUSAND YEARS

CHRIST A.D. 1

FIRST COMING

FOURTH DAY
THE 4TH THOUSAND YEARS

SOLOMON B.C. 1000

"LAW"

THIRD DAY
THE 3RD THOUSAND YEARS

ABRAHAM B.C. 2000

SECOND DAY
THE 2ND THOUSAND YEARS

ENOCH B.C. 3000

TRANSLATION OF ENOCH

"CONSCIENCE"

FIRST DAY
THE 1ST THOUSAND YEARS

EDEN B.C. 4000

SEVENTH DAY
SIXTH DAY
FIFTH DAY
FOURTH DAY
THIRD DAY
SECOND DAY
FIRST DAY

DESIGNED AND DRAWN BY
CLARENCE LARKIN
FOX CHASE, PHILA., PA.
COPYRIGHTED
10/14/18

31

amillennialism. Premillennialism as it is encountered today owes much of its popularity and influence, as with dispensationalism, to the efforts of J. N. Darby and the *Scofield Reference Bible*.

Premillennialism invokes the concept of the 'tribulation',[30] as a time of suffering on the earth. There is however a variance of opinion within premillennialism as to whether the faithful saints will be 'raptured'[31] from the earth before the tribulation (pre-tribulationism), or whether they will have to endure through it (post-tribulationism). Dispensationalists tend to take a pre-tribulationist position, while classic premillennialists tend towards post-tribulationism. In terms of recent popularity, it is dispensational pre-tribulationist premillennialism that has carried the day; for example, this forms the basic premise for the best-selling (fictional) *Left Behind* series of novels by Tim LaHaye and Jerry Jenkins (pub. 1995–). The first book in this series takes the title *Left Behind: A Novel of the Earth's Last Days*, and begins with a description of the rapture of all faithful Christians from the earth, leaving some aeroplanes pilotless and cars driverless. Once the saints have left the earth and gone to be with their Lord in heaven, the sequences of judgement from Revelation are visited upon the earth.[32]

The combination of dispensationalism and premillennialism creates a compelling narrative for understanding the world, with the role of the saints being construed as needing to remain faithful until Jesus returns. Disturbing political events, the threat of nuclear war, or environmental catastrophe do not induce such terror because they are the expected signs of the end times.[33] While such events will have negative effects upon the world, these are not expected to affect those who are part of the true Church, because they will already be safe in heaven while the predicted horrors are visited upon the earth. Whereas postmillennialism has often led to works of social justice, premillennialism tends towards social passivity, with faithful Christian living being interpreted as maintaining moral and ethical purity in the midst of an immoral and impure world.

Asking different questions of the text

In the wake of such a bewildering variety of reading strategies, one could be forgiven for giving up in despair and deciding to read a text that is less complicated. However, this would be to walk away just as things are starting to get interesting, since there have been a number of more recent developments in reading the book of Revelation that shed light on it in new ways.

As has been seen, those who come to the Apocalypse asking questions such as 'When will the world end?' 'When will the millennium be?' and

'When will these things happen?' may find their search for a definitive response frustrated because they are asking the text to yield answers that it has not been constructed to provide. In reaction to these approaches, academic scholarship has for many years focused not so much on the interpretation of the text, as on issues concerning its provenance and textual history.[34] Questions about multiple stages of editing, authorship and possible sources have dominated discussions and there are therefore reams of careful argument devoted to dissecting the text in an attempt to understand it. However, at the end of such analysis, it can prove hard to put the text back together again with a view to appreciating its over-all effect, and one may be left wondering what has been gained in the process.

Feminist readings

The more recent trend towards reader-orientated approaches represents a shift in scholarly engagement with the Apocalypse. Into this category come the approaches of feminist critics such as Elisabeth Schüssler Fiorenza,[35] Catherine Keller[36] and Tina Pippin,[37] who bring to their reading of the text a concern for gender equality.[38] Feminist readings usually articulate a stand against the androcentric ideology they claim is inherent within the text. As Alison Jack comments:

> The dramatically stereotypical female characters who appear in Reve-lation mean that the book is immediately amenable to feminist criti-cism. The prophet Jezebel in chapter 2; the woman clothed with the sun in chapter 12; the whore of Babylon in chapters 17 to 18 and the bride representing the new Jerusalem in chapter 21 are all of great and obvious interest to anyone with an interest in feminism. Little wonder, then, that the tasks of recovering the history of these characters, of reclaiming and translating them, and of reconsidering their subversive role within the deep structures of the text have formed the basis of much writing from a feminist perspective.[39]

Hanna Stenström points to a more positive strand in the feminist ap-proach, describing the feminist exegetical project as 'a quest for a "usable future", that is, visions of a future that inspire work for social change here and now, making our efforts to create a more just world deeply rooted in God's struggle for a world of perfect justice.'[40] Stenström's approach still represents a rejection of the male-dominated ideology of the text, but instead of seeing this as a precursor to necessary rejection of the text itself, she shows how Revelation can provide imagery in sup-port of the liberation of women.

Liberationist readings

Whereas feminist criticism denounces androcentric emphases within the text, liberationist readings look for themes of liberty and the overthrow of oppression, allowing the reader to see the articulation of an agenda for emancipation within the text. To this end, those from third-world contexts who have a concern for issues of liberation are able to bring their contextual circumstances to bear on the reading of the Apocalypse.[41] The basis for a liberationist reading is helpfully summarized by the Chilean commentator P. Richard:

> Revelation arises in a time of persecution – and particularly amid situations of chaos, exclusion, and ongoing oppression. In such situations, Revelation enables the Christian community to rebuild its hope and awareness. Revelation transmits a spirituality of resistance and offers guidance for organizing an alternative world. Revelation is a liberating book, one full of hope; its utopia is political and unfolds in history.[42]

Thus, in a liberationist reading, the Apocalypse becomes a source from which to draw strength, as the reader is enabled to find their own situation of subjugation reflected within the text, and can identify with the author, the recipients, or the characters. Schüssler Fiorenza comments that

> the imagery of chapters 13 and 17—18 as well as chapters 20—21 is very popular with the peasants and poor of Central and South America who are reading the Bible in Christian base-communities. Since Revelation depicts the exploitation of the poor and the concentration of wealth in the hands of the powerful, the injustices perpetrated by the colonialist state, and a society that has grown obscene by perpetrating stark contrasts between rich and poor, they can read it as speaking to their own situation of poverty and oppression.[43]

Postcolonial readings

If liberationist readings have emerged as a conscious effort to read the Apocalypse from the perspective of the oppressed and marginalized, postcolonial readings represent a similarly determined effort to read the text in ways alert to the implications of wealth and privilege. J. P. Ruiz, quoting R. S. Sugirtharajah, defines postcolonial readings:

> Like liberationist criticism, postcolonial criticism emerged in the so-called Third World ... [It] shares the emancipatory commitment

of liberationist criticism inasmuch as it 'offers a space for the once-colonized. It is an interpretive act of the descendants of those once subjugated. In effect, it means a resurrection of the marginal, the indigene and the subaltern ... It is an act of reclamation, redemption and reaffirmation against the past colonial and current neo-colonializing tendencies which continue to exert influence even after territorial and political independence has been accomplished.'[44]

To this end, in postcolonial readings of the Apocalypse, similarities between contemporary Western culture and the first-century Roman Empire are highlighted, and the apocalyptic critique of Rome as Babylon is allowed to speak to the world of the modern Western reader. W. Howard-Brook and A. Gwyther put it thus:

How is the empire of global capital manifested in our world? How is it similar to or different from the Roman Empire of John's day? How might Revelation expect Christians to live in the midst of this powerful imperial reality?[45]

In answer, they observe that:

Behind the veil of divine legitimation, the system of global capital has been and continues to work tirelessly to accomplish the primary mission of empire: ... the transfer of wealth from the poor and middle class to the wealthy.[46]

Just as the Roman Empire looked out at its exploitation of the world of its day and called it good, so do the spokespeople for global capital in our time claim to be serving those whom they systematically impoverish year after year.[47]

Thus, while politicians proclaim the American economy as the best it has been in decades, and empire's preachers brush off world poverty as a temporary effect of 'adjustment' to the emerging global economy, we who call ourselves disciples of Jesus must have the courage and faith to see past this illusion to the apocalyptic truth: as with Rome, so with global capital – empire *is* fallen ... If the Babylon of our time is already, from God's perspective, a smoking ruin, how and where do we find new Jerusalem?[48]

It can be seen from the preceding summaries that feminist, liberationist and postcolonial readings of Revelation all represent attempts to appropriate the text of Revelation according to various worldviews. To put it another way, these approaches self-consciously bring the world of the reader to the text, in order that the text might in turn inform the context of the reader.

Imaginative submission

Another matter that requires consideration is the move that John himself makes in his own readings of and meditations on the Old Testament.[49] The methodology behind his use of texts like Daniel, Ezekiel and Jeremiah may be termed 'imaginative textual submission'. John does not ask of Daniel when the various empires implied in the statue made of different elements will rise and fall (Dan. 2.31–5). He does not ask Ezekiel what is written on the scroll he ingests (Ezek. 3.1–3). Neither does he ask Jeremiah when Babylon will finally be destroyed (Jer. 50.23). Rather, he brings his own first-century world to these ancient texts, and creatively engages with them in order to allow their critique of empire, of power, and of domination to speak to his own context.

Walter Brueggemann offers the following suggestion as to how the book of Jeremiah might function when it is read in contexts later than its original composition: 'When the text is read and heard as a critique of ideology and as a practice of alternative imagination, the text continues to have power and pertinence in many subsequent contexts, including our own.' He further suggests that '[t]he text does not need to be *applied* to our situation. Rather, our situation needs to be *submitted* to the text.'[50] This suggests a process of engagement whereby the situation of later readers is understood in the light of the critique offered by the ancient text. Brueggemann continues:

> If we fail to hear this text, we may succumb to a fraudulent discernment of our situation. Like ancient Jerusalem, we shall imagine that the present is decided by the policies of the empire and not by the pathos of the holy, faithful God ... Everything depends on the text, for without this transformative, critical, liberating, subversive speech, we shall live in a speechless, textless world that is always misunderstood ... It is precisely the text in its odd offer of holiness and pathos, of rending and healing, that dismisses ideology, exposes propaganda, overrides anxiety, and offers forgiveness in the place of brutality.[51]

It was just this kind of meditation on the texts of Jeremiah, Ezekiel and Daniel that led John to write his own text of subversive critique in the face of the idolatrous, coercive and dominating forces of empire. It may be that the most fruitful way of reading John's text today is to do again what he did with his own ancient texts; to submit the world of the reader to the world of the text, so that the text may inform and transform that world.

The preceding chapter has introduced a number of different ways of reading Revelation, ranging from historicist, preterist, futurist and idealist, through varying forms of millennialism, to feminist, liberationist and post-colonial readings. These approaches all represent attempts to ask questions of the text, with the answer received dependent on the question asked. Everybody brings their own set of questions to each text they encounter, and it is therefore important to be aware of these, and of the ways they can affect the answers that we receive.

Draw your own conclusions

- What ways of reading Revelation have you encountered before?
- What concerns or emphases from your own context do you bring to your reading of Revelation?
- Does feminist criticism 'redeem' the text, or 'condemn' it? Why?
- Do you think Revelation has a 'message' for today? If so, what might it be?
- What might the results be of contemporary readers engaging in Brueggemann's process of 'imaginative textual submission'?

Notes

1 For an excellent and useful glossary of apocalyptic terms, see Wes Howard-Brook and Anthony Gwyther, 2001, *Unveiling Empire: Reading Revelation Then and Now*, The Bible and Liberation Series, New York: Orbis Books, pp. 4–5.

2 For example, there were British Baptists during the seventeenth century who identified the Cromwellian protectorate as the millennial reign. Cf. Simon Woodman, forthcoming, 'The Plain and Literal Meaning of the Text: A 17th Century Particular Baptist Perspective on Revelation 20.1–7', in William John Lyons and Jorunn Økland (eds), *The Way the World Ends? The Apocalypse of John in Culture and Ideology*, Sheffield: Sheffield Phoenix Press.

3 The *eschaton* is the final moment of human history.

4 Gilbert Desrosiers, 2000, *An Introduction to Revelation*, T&T Clark Approaches to Biblical Studies, London: Continuum, p. 32.

5 Desrosiers, *Introduction*, p. 31. Charles comments, 'in the thirteenth and fourteenth centuries the Apocalypse was used as the chief weapon of offence against the church of Rome.' R. H. Charles, 1913, *Studies in the Apocalypse*, Edinburgh: T&T Clark, p. 23. It should be noted that the term 'Antichrist' does not appear anywhere in the Apocalypse, despite popular opinion. Rather, it appears in the first and second letters of John (cf. 1 John 2.18, 22; 4.3; 2 John 7), where it denotes what Lieu describes as 'a final manifestation of wickedness

in opposition to God'. Judith Lieu, 1986, *The Second and Third Epistles of John: History and Background*, Studies of the New Testament and Its World, Edinburgh: T&T Clark, p. 79.

6 Desrosiers, *Introduction*, p. 33.

7 Hal Lindsey and C. C. Carlson, 1970, *The Late, Great Planet Earth*, Grand Rapids: Zondervan. This book reportedly sold over forty million copies in the three decades following its publication. Cf. Howard-Brook and Gwyther, *Unveiling Empire*, p. 3.

8 Quoted in Stanley J. Grenz, 1992, *The Millennial Maze: Sorting out Evangelical Options*, Illinois: InterVarsity Press, pp. 19–20. Cf. the chapter 'Apocalyptic Politics in the New Christian Right', in Stephen O'Leary, 1994, *Arguing the Apocalypse: A Theory of Millennial Rhetoric*, Oxford: Oxford University Press, pp. 172–93.

9 Cf. Hal Lindsey, 1997, *Apocalypse Code*, California: Western Front.

10 See the discussion on Revelation and the environment on p. 209.

11 A similar approach is used in the interpretation of the Old Testament, building on the imagery used by John of the Lamb and the bride (19.7–8; 21.2, 9), in the allegorical interpretation of the Song of Songs as depicting the relationship between Christ and his bride the Church. Cf. J. Cheryl Exum, 2005, *Song of Songs*, The Old Testament Library, Louisville, Kentucky: Westminster John Knox Press, pp. 74–6.

12 Desrosiers, *Introduction*, p. 37.

13 Richard Bauckham, 1975, *Tudor Apocalypse*, Oxford: The Sutton Courtenay Press, p. 15.

14 Tyconius was connected with the Donatists, an African Christian movement eventually condemned as heretical.

15 Arthur W. Wainwright, 1993, *Mysterious Apocalypse: Interpreting the Book of Revelation*, Nashville: Abingdon Press, pp. 34–6. Van Oort points to the widespread influence which Tyconius' commentary on the Apocalypse had on Western exegesis, especially on the thinking of Augustine, the classic expositor of the amillennial position. Johannes van Oort, 1991, *Jerusalem and Babylon: A Study into Augustine's City of God and the Sources of His Doctrine of the Two Cities*, Supplements to Vigiliae Christianae, vol. 14, Leiden: E. J. Brill, pp. 259f.

16 Augustine writes: 'Therefore the Church even now is the kingdom of Christ, and the kingdom of heaven. Accordingly, even now His saints reign with Him'. Augustine, *The City of God*, trans. Marcus Dods, The Nicene and Post-Nicene Fathers, First Series, vol. 2, Albany: Sage Digital Library, 20:9, p. 918. For a more detailed analysis of Augustine's interpretation of the millennium see Robert C. Doyle, 1999, *Eschatology and the Shape of Christian Belief*, Carlisle: Paternoster Press, pp. 89–92.

17 Norman Cohn, 1993, *The Pursuit of the Millennium*, London: Pimlico, p. 29.

18 It should be noted that, when the millennium is calculated as 1000(ish) years from the date of the binding of Satan, all that is necessary to push the end of the millennium further into the future is to find a later date for the binding of Satan. Suggested dates ranged from Augustine's original suggestion of the birth of Christ, to the resurrection and even to Constantine's victory over Maxentius

in the fourth century – a dating which would give the end of the millennium as being in 1311. Cf. George Huntston Williams, 1992, *The Radical Reformation*, 3rd edn, Sixteenth Century Essays & Studies, vol. XV, Kirksville, Missouri: Sixteenth Century Journal Publishers, p. 516.

19 Cf. Bauckham, *Tudor Apocalypse*, p. 209.

20 See the discussion of the 1,260 days on p. 103.

21 For a more detailed description of Joachim's scheme see Cohn, *Pursuit of the Millennium*, pp. 108–10; Wainwright, *Mysterious Apocalypse*, pp. 49–53.

22 Wainwright, *Mysterious Apocalypse*, p. 79.

23 Intriguingly, Joachim's scheme can also be found reflected in other, non-Christian, attempts to understand the history of the world as a series of 'ages'. For example, the Rosicrucian Order, a mystery sect with its origins in the seventeenth century, are awaiting the dawning of the 'Aquarian age', which is currently incubating during the present 'Piscean Age', and is expected to come fully in *c.* AD 2600. This coming age of Aquarius is a theme which is also present in much popular New Age philosophy. The 'Third Reich' of Nazi Germany also utilizes Joachimite thinking, presenting itself as the millennial successor to the 'First Reich' of the Holy Roman Empire and the 'Second Reich' of Bismarck's empire.

24 The Brethren emerged during the early decades of the nineteenth century as a conservative evangelical renewal movement, emphasizing a literal approach to the Bible coupled with a separatist approach to the world. It was not until 1948 that a division within the movement led to the split between the Open and the Plymouth Brethren. Cf. Tim Grass, 2006, *Gathering to His Name: The Story of Open Brethren in Britain & Ireland*, Milton Keynes: Paternoster, pp. 9–48, 63.

25 Quoted in Grass, *Gathering to His Name*, p. 104.

26 Howard-Brook and Gwyther comment that, 'the author's ... cross-references and interpretations are included alongside the biblical texts, often confusing readers as to which is which.' Howard-Brook and Gwyther, *Unveiling Empire*, p. 5.

27 This chart was created by Clarence Larkin (1850–1924), an American Baptist pastor. Retrieved from http://www.preservedwords.com/images/history.gif. Accessed 22.10.07. In light of the incredible detail which this chart offers, it is encouraging to discover that some things apparently still eluded Larkin; he comments with modesty: 'The Length Of Time Between The Rapture And "Revelation" Is *Unknown*'.

28 Archbishop James Ussher (1581–1656) famously calculated the date of creation in his work *The Annals of the World*, published in 1650. He suggested that it was the night before 23 October 4004 BC.

29 For an illustration of this scheme see the highly pictorial dispensational chart, originally published in 1893, in Grass, *Gathering to His Name*, p. 173.

30 'Tribulation' is the word used by the King James Version to translate the Greek θλῖψις, meaning pressure. See Rev. 1.9; 2.9, 10, 22; 7.14.

31 The 'rapture' is a doctrine according to which the faithful saints are removed from the earth before the days of tribulation, while the non-Christians are 'left behind'. It is primarily drawn from biblical passages beyond the Apocalypse (Matt. 24.40–42; John 14.2–3; Phil. 3.20–21; 1 Cor. 15.49–55;

1 Thess. 4.15–17; 2 Thess. 2.1–7). For a simplified chart indicating various approaches to understanding the rapture see Mark Wilson, 2007, *Charts on the Book of Revelation: Literary, Historical, and Theological Perspectives*, Kregel Charts of the Bible and Theology, Grand Rapids: Kregel Publications, p. 70. For a fascinating exploration of the relationship between the doctrine of the rapture and contemporary Western society, see 'A Brief History of the Rapture in the United States', in Howard-Brook and Gwyther, *Unveiling Empire*, pp. 3–19.

32 For a critical analysis of these novels see Daniel Hertzler, 2000, 'Assessing the "Left Behind" Phenomenon', in Loren L. Johns (ed.), *Apocalypticism and Millennnialism*, Kitchener: Pandora Press.

33 Cf. 2 Peter 3.10–13.

34 For a useful overview of scholarship on Revelation in the second half of the twentieth century, see the chapter 'Research Perspectives in the Book of Revelation', in Elisabeth Schüssler Fiorenza, 1998, *The Book of Revelation: Justice and Judgment*, 2nd edn, Minneapolis: Fortress Press, pp. 12–32. She concludes: 'When I started my work on Rev. the majority of scholars agreed that the book was an only slightly redacted Jewish apocalypse' p. 25.

35 Schüssler Fiorenza defines her approach as follows: 'First, I translate and read the grammatically masculine language of Revelation as conventional generic language ... Second, I translate and read the sexual language and female images of Revelation first as "conventional" language that must be understood in its traditional and present-meaning contexts. Whoring and fornication as metaphors for idolatry, as well as the symbolic understanding of Israel as bride and wife of Yahweh, are part and parcel of the prophetic-apocalyptic tradition. They must be subjected to a feminist critique, but their gendered meaning cannot be assumed as primary within the narrative contextualisation of Revelation. Finally, I do not read Revelation just in terms of the sex/gender system but with reference to the Western classical patriarchal system and its interlocking structures of racism, classism, colonialism, and sexism.' Elisabeth Schüssler Fiorenza, 1991, *Revelation: Vision of a Just World*, Proclamation Commentaries, Minneapolis: Fortress Press, p. 14. Cf. also Schüssler Fiorenza, *Justice and Judgment*, pp. 211–29.

36 See her important work on feminist approaches to the Apocalypse: Catherine Keller, 1996, *Apocalypse Now and Then: A Feminist Guide to the End of the World*, Boston: Beacon Press. See also Catherine Keller, 2005, 'Territory, Terror and Torture: Dream-Reading the Apocalypse', *Feminist Theology*, vol. 14: 47–67.

37 Pippin outlines her characteristic deconstructive approach as follows: 'I want to focus on the clearly identified women in the text who are destroyed and on the general "apocalypse of women" brought about in the utopian vision of the new Jerusalem ... The text of the Apocalypse, with its female archetypes of good and evil, virgin and whore is an account of a political and religious and also gender crisis of the end of the first century C.E.' Tina Pippin, 1992, *Death and Desire: The Rhetoric of Gender in the Apocalypse of John*, Louisville, Kentucky: Westminster John Knox Press, p. 47. See also Tina Pippin, 1992, 'Eros and the End: Reading for Gender in the Apocalypse of John', *Semeia*, vol. 59: 193–210; Tina Pippin, 1999, *Apocalyptic Bodies: The Biblical End of the World in Text and Image*, London: Routledge.

38 Taking a male perspective, by way of contrast, Stephen Moore provocatively suggests that the cosmic vision of God in the book of Revelation is 'hypermasculine', and that for men reading the text he functions as an object of 'adoration' in a comparable manner to the hypermasculine 'Mr Universe' figures of contemporary body-building magazines. He suggests that 'Revelation's representation of the deity anticipates the publicity poster for the 1984 sword-and-sandal epic, *Conan the Barbarian*, which showed a brooding Arnold Schwarzenegger slumped on a massive throne, his equally massive bulk artfully draped over its contours'. Stephen D. Moore, 1995, 'The Beatific Vision as a Posing Exhibition: Revelation's Hypermasculine Deity', *Journal for the Study of the New Testament*, vol. 60: 27–55, p. 33.

39 Alison Jack, 2001, 'Out of the Wilderness: Feminist Perspectives on the Book of Revelation', in Steve Moyise (ed.), *Studies in the Book of Revelation*, Edinburgh: T&T Clark, p. 149. Cf. also Pamela Thimmes, 2003, 'Women Reading Women in the Apocalypse: Reading Scenario 1, the Letter to Thyatira (Rev. 2.18–29)', *Currents in Biblical Research*, vol. 2.1: 128–144.

40 Hanna Stenström, 'Feminists in Search for a Usable Future: Feminist Reception of the Book of Revelation', in William John Lyons and Jorunn Økland (eds), forthcoming, *The Way the World Ends? The Apocalypse of John in Culture and Ideology*, Sheffield: Sheffield Phoenix Press.

41 The Peruvian theologian Gustavo Gutiérrez (1928–) is often cited as the founder of the liberation theology movement. For an accessible introduction to his writing, see Andrew Bradstock and Christopher Rowland (eds), 2002, *Radical Christian Writings: A Reader*, Oxford: Blackwell, pp. 335–46.

42 Pablo Richard, 1995, *Apocalypse: A People's Commentary on the Book of Revelation*, trans. Phillip Berryman, The Bible & Liberation, New York: Orbis Books, p. 3.

43 Schüssler Fiorenza, *Vision of a Just World*, p. 11. For further reading on liberationist interpretation of the Apocalypse see Jean-Pierre Ruiz, 2003, 'Taking a Stand on the Sand of the Seashore: A Postcolonial Exploration of Revelation 13', in David L. Barr (ed.), *Reading the Book of Revelation: A Resource for Students*, Atlanta: Society of Biblical Literature, pp. 119–35. The South African Allan Boesak suggests: 'The clue to understanding the Apocalypse as protest literature … lies, I think, in Revelation 1:9 … Those who do not know this suffering through oppression, who do not struggle together with God's people for the sake of the gospel, and who do not feel in their own bodies the meaning of oppression and the freedom and joy of fighting against it shall have grave difficulty understanding this letter from Patmos.' Allan A. Boesak, 1987, *Comfort and Protest: The Apocalypse from a South African Perspective*, Philadelphia: Westminster, p. 38.

44 Ruiz, 'Taking a Stand', p. 123, quoting R. S. Sugirtharajah, 2001, *The Bible and the Third World: Precolonial, Colonial, and Postcolonial Encounters*, Cambridge: Cambridge University Press.

45 Howard-Brook and Gwyther, *Unveiling Empire*, p. 237.

46 Howard-Brook and Gwyther, *Unveiling Empire*, p. 242.

47 Howard-Brook and Gwyther, *Unveiling Empire*, p. 245.

48 Howard-Brook and Gwyther, *Unveiling Empire*, p. 260.

49 For a discussion of John's use of the Old Testament, cf. Steve Moyise,

1999, 'The Language of the Old Testament in the Apocalypse', *Journal for the Study of the New Testament*, vol. 76: 97–113.

50 Walter Brueggemann, 1988, *To Pluck up, to Tear Down: A Commentary on the Book of Jeremiah 1—25*, International Theological Commentary, Grand Rapids: Wm. B. Eerdmans, p. 17.

51 Brueggemann, *To Pluck up, to Tear Down*, p. 18.

3

The Book through the Eyes of the Author

One of the problems that many people face when encountering the book of Revelation is that the structure of the book can seem dauntingly complex.[1] In addition to a confusing array of characters, there are repeating cycles of images, which can make it hard to be sure about what is going on at any one time. We will investigate the characters who inhabit this work shortly, but before this it is important to gain an overall appreciation of how the book functions. An effective way to achieve this is to examine how John the author functions as the narrative voice within the text, because an analysis of his presence also provides the key to understanding the overall structure of the book.[2]

An analogy may be helpful at this point. One way of visualizing the structure of Revelation is to think of an old-fashioned collapsible telescope, made up of sections each slightly smaller than the previous one, so that each section can be contained within the one next to it. With its sequences of seals, trumpets, bowls, and visions the central narrative of Revelation has a similar structure: each subsequent section is latent within the previous one, as shown in the diagram.

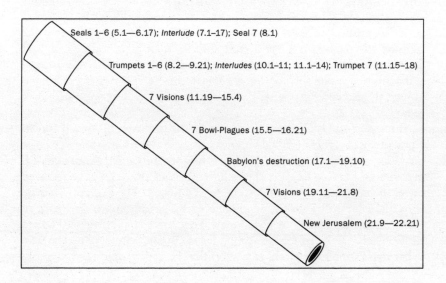

Seals 1–6 (5.1—6.17); *Interlude* (7.1–17); Seal 7 (8.1)

Trumpets 1–6 (8.2—9.21); *Interludes* (10.1–11; 11.1–14); Trumpet 7 (11.15–18)

7 Visions (11.19—15.4)

7 Bowl-Plagues (15.5—16.21)

Babylon's destruction (17.1—19.10)

7 Visions (19.11—21.8)

New Jerusalem (21.9—22.21)

John the narrator

John, the narrator, appears at the beginning of the book and is introduced as a human being who is a servant of Jesus Christ (1.1), and a Christian brother to the recipients of the letter, who shares with them in their experience of persecution and also in their faithful endurance (1.9). The book is cast as a letter from John to seven churches in Asia Minor (1.11), and begins in classic letter-style with a greeting of grace and peace to those in the churches (1.4).[3] Clearly John has a position of pastoral responsibility for these congregations, and this provides a key to understanding all that follows: everything in the book carries pastoral concern and has relevance for the intended recipients. John describes how he received the visions that he records, saying that he was 'in the Spirit on the Lord's day' when he heard a voice like a trumpet instructing him to write down everything he is about to see on a scroll, and to send it to the seven churches (1.10–11).

There is much discussion regarding the precise identity of 'John', particularly with regard to whether he can be correlated with any other character known from the New Testament or the early Church. There are three main suggestions. First, it is claimed that John should be identified with the Apostle John who is known from the Synoptic Gospels.[4] Second, some suggest that he should be identified with John the Elder, the otherwise anonymous author of the letters of 2 and 3 John.[5] The third suggestion is that the work, in common with many other Jewish apocalypses, is *pseudonymous*, written by an anonymous author using the name of John the Apostle to lend credibility and authority to the book. Pseudonymity was the not uncommon Jewish and early-Christian practice of writing a book as if it were written by someone who has already died. However, pseudonymity should not be confused with deception, as the recipients of the text would have known that the claimed author was not the actual author. Such a technique can best be thought of as, 'what X would say to us if s/he were still alive today', and so for example, the book of 2 Peter in the New Testament is almost universally accepted as 'what Peter would say to us if he were still alive today'.[6]

Although John is clearly writing within the tradition of Jewish apocalyptic literature, there is no obvious evidence that he is attempting to cast his vision pseudepigraphically. Rather, he goes into some detail explaining who and where he is, and emphasizing that the visions he received came to him directly from Jesus Christ himself. He explains that he is on the island of Patmos, as a result of his testimony to the word of God and the testimony of Jesus (1.9).[7] He claims that while on Patmos he received a visit from an angel of Jesus Christ, who revealed to him 'what must soon take place' (1.1), and that he has written the book as a record of that revelation (1.2). This experience of a vision through which heavenly mysteries are revealed puts John in the tradition of other Jewish apocalyptic writers, such as the authors of 1 Enoch,[8] 3 Baruch,[9] and the Apocalypse of Adam.[10]

Thus perhaps we should conclude with I. Boxall that: 'A certain agnosticism is perhaps called for as to the precise identity of this early Christian prophet-visionary John of Patmos.'[11] In many ways, the identity of John is not particularly important to the interpretation of the book. Of more significance is the role he plays within his own narrative. As Desrosiers says, 'John ... acts both as a narrator and a character.'[12]

Journeying with John through the Apocalypse

John's opening vision and commission to write to the churches
Revelation 1.1—3.22

Having heard the voice like thunder instructing him to write, John turns to see who has spoken, and sees 'one like a son of man' in the midst of the lampstands (1.12–13). John's use of this phrase draws directly on Dan. 7.13, where the angel of God is spoken of as 'one like a son of man'. However, the language he uses to describe this figure in 1.14 comes from Dan. 7.9, where it is descriptive not of the 'son of man' but of the Ancient One – God himself. The message John is seeking to convey here is clear: the human figure is divine. Accordingly, John falls to the floor in worship and is touched by the 'one like a son of man' and told not to be afraid (1.17). He is then instructed again to write what he sees (1.19), leaving no doubt that John considers his commission to come from none other than Jesus Christ himself. John then receives the first part of the message that he is to write, as he hears the 'one like a son of man' speak a series of seven messages (2.1—3.22) to the seven churches initially mentioned in Rev. 1.11.

John's vision of the throne room
Revelation 4.1–11

After recording seven letters to the seven churches, John sees an open door in heaven, and hears again the voice like a trumpet inviting him to come into heaven to see 'what must take place after this' (4.1). He is then caught up to heaven in the Spirit, and is confronted with the throne of God in heaven (4.2). This ascent into heaven strengthens the identification of John as a visionary in the apocalyptic tradition.[13] There is debate however regarding the meaning of 'what must take place after this' (4.1),[14] with some suggesting that it locates the entire Apocalypse in the future as a kind of guide book to the end times.[15] Others, however, point to the fact that the chronology of the book is far from straightforward, and that John's vision is primarily intended to be significant in the experience of the seven churches. Smalley summarizes as follows: '"What must take place" refers, finally, not so much to *events* as to the coming of Jesus, in time and in eternity, and to the relationships with him and with each other which stem from that advent.'[16]

John's vision of the opening of the first six seals
Revelation 5.1—6.17

Following an extended description of the throne room of heaven, John sees a scroll in the right hand of the one seated on the throne (5.1). The phrase καὶ εἶδον ('and I saw') is spoken by John 33 times in the book.[17] Aune helpfully identifies three ways in which this phrase functions: first, serving to introduce a new vision; second, introducing a scene change (as in 5.1); and third, focusing the audience's attention on a new or significant figure.[18] John weeps bitterly because no one can be found who is worthy to open the scroll (5.4), and he is comforted by one of the elders who tells him that the Lion of Judah is able to do this. However, instead of seeing the Lion he has just heard about, John sees a Lamb with its throat cut, yet somehow still alive and standing between the throne and the four living creatures (5.6). It will turn out that it is the Lamb, rather than the Lion, who will actually open the seals of the scroll. We should note that the difference between what John hears and what he sees is a recurring theme in Revelation, with what is *seen* interpreting what is *heard*.[19] John's view then widens from the narrow focus on the throne and those in its immediate vicinity, and takes in the voices of the innumerable angels surrounding the throne (5.11), and then widens still further as he hears every creature in the whole of creation singing praise to the Lamb (5.13). Although John will go on to describe those who are in opposition to the Lamb, it is significant that here, at the climax of his opening vision, he describes the totality of creation unified in praise of the Lamb. This vision of hope is offered to his fellow Christians in the seven churches, as together they and he struggle to survive in a world where so many forces are experienced as hostile both to them and the one whom they worship.

John then sees the Lamb open the first of the seven seals that are on the scroll (6.1). This initiates a sequence of events linked to the opening of the seven seals. As each seal is opened, John either sees or hears something significant. Following each of the first four seals, he hears the four living creatures in turn call 'come' (6.1, 3, 5, 7), and then sees four riders, each on a different colour horse (6.2, 4, 5, 8). Following the third seal, he also hears a voice in the midst of the living creatures (6.6). The four riders ride forth for battle on the earth, while at the opening of the fifth seal, John turns his attention towards heaven and sees the souls of the martyrs under the altar (6.9), whom he hears crying out for divine justice (6.10). This juxtaposition of the riders on the earth and the martyrs in heaven is a reflection of the pastoral situation of his recipients, who experience Christian existence as a battle, sometimes to the point of death. John hears the martyrs being told to rest a while longer before their vindication, as there are yet more who will join them in martyrdom (6.11). The fact that each seal is seen by John as being opened by the Lamb reassures his recipients that all that happens on earth is ultimately under the control of the one they worship.

At the opening of the sixth seal, John sees a great earthquake, accompanied by images of destructive judgement on a cosmic scale (6.12–17), which serve to remind John's audience that ultimately their Lord will prevail over evil. The events of the sixth seal prefigure the more detailed descriptions of cosmic destruction that are found in the events following the sounding of each of the seven trumpets.

Interlude 1: The naming of the servants of God
Revelation 7.1–17

These events are followed by an interlude, during which John sees the destruction of the earth put on hold while the servants of God are named (7.1–3). He hears the number of the saved as 144,000 (7.4), but sees them as a great multitude that no one can count (7.9). There are extensive debates as to the significance of the 144,000, to which attention will be paid below,[20] yet of interest here is the correlation between the limited number that John hears, and the limitless number that he sees. As noted previously, that which is *seen* interprets that which is *heard*,[21] with the implication being that the total number of those eventually saved will far exceed the number that might initially be expected on careful calculation. In view again here is the universal vision of salvation first encountered at the end of Chapter 5. John is engaged in conversation by one of the twenty-four elders, who asks John if he knows the identity of the 144,000 (7.13). When John replies that he does not, the elder then reveals their identity to be that of those who have come out of the great ordeal (7.14). This conversation serves to reinforce John's role as apocalyptic visionary, underscoring his claim to be reporting heavenly mysteries as they have been revealed to him (cf. 1.2, 11).

47

THE BOOK OF REVELATION

The seventh seal triggering the sounding of the first six trumpets
Revelation 8.1—9.21

After this interlude the seventh seal is opened and John sees the seven
trumpet-bearing angels standing before God (8.1–2). However, before
the trumpets are sounded, and the scenes of judgement restart, John witnesses the prayers of the saints being poured out onto the golden altar
before the throne (8.3–4). For those in John's congregations who must
have wondered if their prayers were futile in the face of massive opposition from the forces of evil, this image of hope must have carried strong
pastoral overtones. It offers assurance that their prayers are indeed heard
before God, and also that divine vindication will follow. John then hears
the first four 'trumpet-angels' sound their instruments, and just as the
prayers of the saints have ascended to heaven, so the judgement of the
wicked descends upon the earth (8.6–12). John then sees an eagle crying
three 'woes' (8.13) which loosely correspond to the events that follow the
final three trumpet blasts.[22] Following the sounding of the fifth trumpet,
John sees 'a star that had fallen from heaven to earth' with the key to
the bottomless pit (9.1). This angelic being unleashes a plague of locusts
upon the earth, and the imagery of judgement and destruction against
the enemies of the people of God intensifies. At the sounding of the sixth
trumpet, John hears a voice from the altar commanding the unleashing
of yet more destruction upon the earth (9.13–19). The significance of the
voice emanating from the altar is that the judgements are seen to be in
response to the prayers of the saints that have already been poured out
upon the altar. However, as with the exodus-plagues (Ex. 7.14—10.29),
the trumpet-plagues fail to bring about a change of heart, and the people
of the earth continue in their idolatry and evil deeds (9.20–21). The dif-
ferentiation that John is making between those who worship and follow
the Lamb, and those who worship and follow the idolatrous gods of
Rome, becomes ever clearer.

Interlude 2: John eats the little scroll
Revelation 10.1–11

Just as there was an interlude before the opening of the seventh seal, so
also there is a delay in the narrative before the end of the second woe
and the sounding of the seventh trumpet. The first part of this interlude
(10.1–11) draws on the Old Testament narrative of Ezekiel's commissioning as a prophet (Ezek. 2.8—3.3), and describes John's own prophetic
commissioning. It seems that John is briefly back on Patmos, as this section of the vision is described from the perspective of earth rather than
heaven. John hears a series of seven thunder-claps, which a reader might

48

expect to function in a similar fashion to the seals, trumpets and bowls. However, John is instructed to refrain from writing their contents down (10.3–4), as there is to be no more delay in revealing the contents of the scroll (10.6c–7; cf. 5.4).[23] The time for warning judgements has passed, and the time for revealing 'what must soon take place' (1.1; 22.6) is now at hand. So John is instructed to take the little scroll from Christ's angel, and to eat it (10.8–9). Although it tastes sweet like honey in his mouth, he finds that it makes his stomach bitter (10.10). John's commissioning as a prophet (10.11) is, it seems, both sweet and bitter: the sweetness of vindication for the righteous and the salvation of the nations is tied to the bitterness of persecution and martyrdom.

Interlude 3: John measures the temple
Revelation 11.1–14

Just as the Church is in view in the interlude before the seventh seal (7.1–9), so also here before the seventh trumpet the followers of the Lamb are depicted as the temple of God, the place of God's dwelling on earth.[24] This interlude begins with John being given a rod with which to measure the temple, the altar and those who worship there (cf. Ezek. 40—42). John's measuring of the temple functions in a similar way to his numbering of the saved in 7.4, marking the elect as distinct from the unrighteous during the time of persecution and trial symbolized by the 42 months of 11.2. John then describes the prophetic ministry of the Church as he narrates the testimony of the two witnesses; with their death, resurrection and ascension paralleling the life, death and resurrection of the faithful saints (11.3–13). It is through this tale of the two witnesses that the content of the scroll begins to be revealed, as John shows his audience that the sweetness of the vindication of the righteous in the sight of their enemies (11.12), and the conversion of the nations through the faithful witness of the Church (11.13), comes only at the bitter cost of persecution and martyrdom (11.7). Only now has the second woe passed (11.14).

The seventh trumpet triggering seven short visions
Revelation 11.15—15.4

Following the seventh trumpet, John hears, not the silence that followed the seventh seal (8.1), but loud voices in heaven proclaiming the coming of the kingdom of God to the earth (11.15). As has already been established, the time for delay in revealing the mystery of the scroll is past and so John finds himself back in heaven, and witnesses the twenty-four

49

elders proclaiming the plagues, which he has so recently witnessed on the earth, as the righteous judgement of God and the vindication of the saints (11.16–18). In the chapters that follow, the contents of the scroll are progressively explicated.

Once again John sees heaven opened to the accompaniment of thunder and lightning (11.19; cf. 4.5; 8.5; 16.18), and receives a series of seven visions.[25] The first vision is of a pregnant woman (the people of God), her child (Jesus Christ), and the satanic dragon (12.1–17), the interpretation of which will be dealt with in greater detail below.[26] However, it is worth noting that the story breaks mid-point (12.10–12), with John hearing a loud voice from heaven which interprets the story for his audience, assuring them that their comrades who have already faced martyrdom have been vindicated, while those who remain on the earth to do battle with the Devil are assured that his time is short. This section closes with the dragon taking his stand on the seashore (12.18), and it is from the sea that John's next visionary encounter arises.

The second of this series of seven visions is that of the beast from the sea, who assumes the power of the dragon (13.2), becomes an object of worship for the people of the earth (12.3–4) and persecutes the people of God for a limited time (12.5–8). The message to John's congregations is clear: Rome may be powerful and evil, but her day will not last for ever. This message is recapitulated in the third vision, that of the beast from the earth (13.11–18), probably best identified as the Roman Emperor Nero,[27] who does the work of the beast from the sea in leading the world astray and persecuting the people of God.

In the fourth of the seven visions in this section of Revelation, John again sees the Lamb first encountered in 5.6 and the 144,000 first encountered in 7.4. The redeemed are now pictured standing with their Lord, participating in the heavenly worship (14.1–3). John's congregations are thereby invited to see their worship in the context of the eternal worship of heaven, rather than as the singing of words of vain hope in small rooms on earth. This message of hope to struggling congregations continues with an interlude to the series of seven visions,[28] in which John sees three angels flying in mid-heaven (14.6–13) who proclaim that first, the people must worship God alone, second, Babylon is doomed, and third, those whose allegiance remains with Babylon are under judgement. This is interpreted by John as a call for the endurance of the saints (14.12), which is confirmed by a heavenly voice proclaiming a blessing on those who 'die in the Lord' (14.13).

The fifth and sixth visions in this series of seven are judgement images of harvesting. The harvesting of the earth by 'one like a son of man' (14.14–16) speaks of the vindication of the 144,000 'first-fruits' (cf. 14.4), while the image of the grape harvest (14.17–20) speaks of judgement on those who remain wedded to Babylon. Then before the final vision in this series begins, John sees seven angels with seven plagues representing God's fury (15.1). However, before the sequence of plagues commences, John catches another glimpse of heavenly worship in the seventh vision of the series (15.2–4). The 144,000, who by this time are in heaven, sing 'the song of Moses, the servant of God' (15.3; cf. Deut. 32.1–43), in which they proclaim: 'All nations will come and worship before you' (15.4). The assurance offered to John's audience is clear: the plagues unleashed by the 'bowl-angels' may well bring suffering and even death, but from a heavenly perspective, the faithful are safe in heaven before the throne of God. Once again, the ultimate vision of salvation is universal in scope (cf. 5.13; 7.9), indicating that the visions of judgement are designed to provoke repentance rather than indicating unambiguous punishment of the wicked.

The seven bowl-plagues
Revelation 15.5—16.21

The seven bowl-angels were first seen by John in the throne room of heaven (15.1). Now however, he sees them coming out from the heavenly sanctuary, and hears a divine voice instruct them to pour out on the earth the seven bowls of God's wrath (16.1). The bowls that John sees are the same bowls he witnessed earlier in his vision, when they contained the prayers of the saints (5.8). Just as the divine judgements initiated by the trumpet-angels originated in the prayers of the faithful (8.3–6), so do the bowls of God's wrath (cf. 14.18–19). The first three bowls are poured out in quick succession (16.2–4), with their judgements reminiscent of the plagues of Egypt (Ex. 7.14–24; 9.8–12). There is then a pause during which John hears the angel of the waters proclaim that the judgements of God are appropriate (16.5–6), and the altar (with the martyrs beneath it) responds that indeed the judgements are just and true (16.7). The violence of the judgement-bowls is, it seems, not inappropriate from the perspective of those facing persecution and martyrdom. The final bowls are then poured out (16.8–21), again recalling the Egyptian plagues,[29] thus emphasizing that the purpose of the judgements is to ensure the vindication of the people of God and their freedom from the slavery and tyranny of a satanic empire.

The destruction of Babylon
Revelation 17.1—19.10

At this point, John is invited by one of the bowl-angels to come and witness the judgement of the great whore (17.1), and thus begins a series of visions focused around Babylon. The judgement of Babylon has already been tantalizingly hinted at earlier in the narrative (14.8; 16.19), but now John describes a series of images for Babylon, culminating in its destruction. John's vision takes him into the wilderness, from where he gets his first glance of a woman seated on a scarlet beast (17.3–6a). After initial amazement and confusion, John has the mystery of the woman on the beast explained to him by the bowl-angel (17.6b–18); she is none other than the great city and ancient enemy of God's people, Babylon itself (17.18). Babylon is seen as a prostitute (17.1), who is drunk with the blood of the Christian martyrs (17.6a).

Similarly the scarlet beast, who originally arose from the sea in 13.1, is also depicted as a cipher for Babylon. This enticing yet corrupt woman riding the powerful and dominating beast forms a damning image for the great city. The manifestation of this 'great city' in John's own day is clearly to be found in the city of Rome, together with the empire that accompanied it. But his failure to name the city indicates that John wants Rome to be understood as simply the most recent expression of the ancient and underlying force of corrupt and corrupting empire, best symbolized as Babylon: the whore and the beast.[30] The horrific vision of the destruction of the whore at the hands of the nations of the world (17.15–17) is therefore an indication to John's audience, struggling to remain pure under the seductive power of Rome, that the seeds of judgement and vindication are already sown.[31] This message is then reinforced as John hears an angel proclaiming the destruction of Babylon as if it were already complete (18.1–3).

From the perspective of John's audience, Babylon was still very much thriving, but from the perspective of heaven, she is seen as already defeated. This then leads into the imperative of 18.4 when John hears a heavenly voice instruct the people of God to 'come out' of Babylon,[32] that is to cease from their participation in the corrupting pleasures of the great prostitute. The voice from heaven continues to proclaim the destruction of Babylon, emphasizing the economic and political strength of the city before its destruction (18.6–20). John then witnesses a prophetic enactment of the destruction and judgement of Babylon, with an angel throwing a millstone into the sea, symbolizing the violence with which Babylon would be destroyed on account of the blood of the innocent saints and prophets (18.21–4).

John then hears a succession of voices; first a large crowd in heaven (19.1–3), then the twenty-four elders and the four living creatures before the throne (19.4), then a single voice from the throne (19.5), and then another large crowd (19.6–8). These voices combine to give heaven's verdict on the judgement of the great whore, emphasizing that the destruction of the great city is both appropriate and just. There is no pity here – evil reaps its own reward, and the suffering righteous are vindicated.

The extravagant attire of the whore is contrasted with the pure and simple clothing worn by the Lamb's bride, symbolic of the righteous behaviour of the Church in contrast to the extravagant evil of Rome (19.7–8). John is then instructed by the bowl-angel to write that those who are invited to the marriage supper of the Lamb are blessed (19.9). If the Church here is the bride and the Lamb the bridegroom, the guests at the wedding may be an indication of the greater number present at the final eschatological banquet (cf. 5.13; 7.9). A liturgical link to the celebration of the Lord's Supper is also to be understood here: in the Eucharist the faithful eat and drink together in a re-enactment of the Passover meal that Jesus shared with his disciples.[33] In this way, the Church participates, through the Eucharist, in John's vision of vindication and unity expressed as the wedding between the Church and its own Passover-Lamb. John then attempts to worship the bowl-angel, but is rebuked and reminded that only God should be worshipped (19.10). This little cameo contributes to the developing Christology of the book, by indicating to John's audience that while it is acceptable to worship both God and the Lamb (5.8–14; 7.10), not all the creatures of heaven are to be worshipped. In fact, John and his fellow disciples are seen as having equal status with the angelic beings of heaven. With this insight, the sequence of the seven bowls is concluded.

Seven short visions
Revelation 19.11—21.8

John then embarks on a final series of seven visions.[34] The sequences of seals, bowls and trumpets have described the judgement of the great city that oppresses the people of God; however the dragon, from which the whore and the beasts took their strength (13.2), has yet to be defeated. The assurance has been given that Rome will experience its judgement in due course, but the underlying force of evil still remains undefeated on the earth.

It is in this context that the rider on the white horse comes back into view in the first of the seven final visions (19.11–16). Having previously been encountered at the opening of the first seal (6.2),[35] where he rode forth to do battle with Babylon, the rider on the white horse makes his reappearance following the sequence of seals, trumpets and bowls, as he once again rides forth – this time to do battle with none other than Satan himself. The army that accompanies him comprises the faithful saints of God, wearing the white robes of their righteous deeds (cf. 19.8). However, the battle itself is fought and won by the rider on the white horse – Christ himself, the crucified and resurrected Messiah.

The second vision in this final sequence begins with John seeing an angel calling the birds of mid-heaven to gather for the great supper of

God (19.17–21). However, this is no wedding banquet for the redeemed with resonances of the Church's practice of Eucharist (cf. 19.9). Rather, it is a horrific image of judgement on the forces of evil in the world. John sees the beast and the false prophet finally thrown into the lake of fire (19.20), while the forces of empire and oppression are destroyed once and for all as they succumb to the sword issuing from mouth of the rider on the white horse. His words of truth are seen to permit no alternative gospel to survive. Their bodies become the food for the birds of mid-heaven, as all evil on the earth is consumed.

The third vision (20.1–3) depicts the binding of Satan, the dragon, for a thousand years. The underlying force of evil in the world is not yet seen by John as destroyed, but merely chained and sealed in the pit from which the plague of locusts emerged in 9.2–3. The final destruction of evil is at hand, and the power of evil in the world bound, but the judgement is not yet complete.

There is then another interlude, in the form of the fourth vision (20.4–6), in which John sees the souls of those who have been martyred for their testimony to Jesus seated on thrones in heaven. The binding of Satan and the heavenly vindication of the martyrs are thus seen to be linked; providing a powerful message of hope for those in John's congregations, who would otherwise have viewed martyrdom as the ultimate victory of the beast over believers. The martyrs, who enter the throne room of God at the point of their martyrdom (the 'first resurrection' 20.5), function as a kind of first-fruit harvest for 'the rest of the dead' (20.5; cf. 14.4, 14–16) who will receive their gift of life at a later time.[36] The martyrs are thus spared participation in the ongoing experience of tribulation, which is the unhappy lot of those who do not receive their vindication until later.

Following this interlude, in the fifth vision of this sequence John returns to the ultimate fate of evil, in the form of Satan, the dragon (20.7–10). The martyrdom of the faithful may have assured the binding of Satan, but from the point of view of John's congregations, Satan is still experienced as being rampant upon the earth (20.7). John thus locates his audience in this in-between time: the martyrs are reigning with Christ, and the power of evil has been broken, but evil is still active on the earth in opposition to the congregations of the faithful, and has yet to go to final judgement (20.8–9a). However, this situation is not allowed to continue for ever, and Satan is cast into the lake of fire, to join the beast and the false prophet (20.9b–10).

The sixth vision continues the theme of judgement on evil (20.11–15). John sees the throne of God in view once again, but in place of the twenty-four elders (4.4), he sees all those who have died now standing before the throne. This vision is the natural counterpart to the vision of the enthroned martyrs (20.4–6). The totality of those before the throne is emphasized in 20.13 where even the sea gives up its dead for judgement. Nearly all humanity is present: only the martyrs are absent, these having already been vindicated through their faithful witness unto death. Thus the scene is set for judgement, and John sees the books which contain the works and deeds of all people opened. Another book is then opened, the Lamb's book of life.[37] On the basis of the content of these books, judgement is passed. Death and Hades are thrown into the lake of fire, together with anyone whose name is not found in the book of life (20.14–15).

The seventh vision changes the tone from judgement and destruction to *re*-creation (21.1–8). The great enemies of God's people – Satan, the beast, the false prophet, Death and Hades – have all been destroyed in the lake of fire, and this paves the way for a recreated heaven and earth. So it is that John reports a vision of a new heaven and a new earth (21.1), with the new Jerusalem as the place where God and his people can live in unity and harmony (21.2–4). It is in this context that John hears a loud voice from the throne proclaiming that the home of God is now among humans. No longer do the people of God live in a world dominated by the powers of evil, but rather in a world focused on the relationship between God and humans. John then hears God speaking directly for the first time since 1.8, and is instructed to write the words just uttered by the voice from the throne as being trustworthy and true (21.5). The vision ends with promise and warning: the blessings just described are promised to those who overcome (21.7), while those who persist in following the ways of the beast are warned that they are in danger of the lake of fire (21.8).

The new Jerusalem
Revelation 21.9—22.21

John then recounts a more detailed vision of the new Jerusalem, as he is carried to the top of a mountain to see the holy city descending from heaven to the earth (21.9–10). He has already described a vision of the destruction of Babylon (17.1—19.10), and both he and his recipients would have been aware of the sacking of the earthly city of Jerusalem at the hands of the Romans in AD 70.[38] In place of these failed cities, John offers his audience a tantalizing alternative: a new Jerusalem, where God lives with his people. After an extended description of the exterior and interior (21.11—22.5),[39] John concludes his vision by reporting an angelic assurance of the trustworthiness of the words of the Apocalypse (22.6), which is coupled with John's testimony of himself as the mediator of the vision. This is only the second time that John names himself (cf. 1.9), and it signals that the visionary material is coming to an end as he returns to the physical reality of Patmos and the seven churches. John's attempt to worship the angel is abortive, as he is once again directed to worship God alone (22.8–9), and his commission to publish the words he has received is shown to be angelic in origin (22.10). In this way the focus moves back from the vision to the world of his recipients: they are to trust the words of the vision as from God, and they are to worship God alone.

John concludes his book with further promises of blessing and warning; offering happiness to those who enter the new Jerusalem, coupled with warnings to those who might seek to exclude themselves (22.12–15). There is then an invitation that emanates from the voice of Jesus and echoes through the Church to the world, for those who hear to answer by 'coming' into the city (22.16–18). There are final warnings against altering the content of the vision (22.18–19),[40] before the concluding verses take a liturgical form with a promise and a prayer: Christ promises he is coming soon and the people respond 'Amen! Come, Lord Jesus' (22.20; cf. 22.7, 12). John completes his work with a traditional grace-blessing in the style of both classical and Pauline epistles,[41] returning thoroughly to the world of his intended recipients as he prepares the letter for distribution.

Draw your own conclusions

- Does it matter to you whether the author of Revelation is positively identified? Why?
- What analogy would you use to summarize the structure of Revelation?
- How does an understanding of the situation of the original recipients affect the way we read the text today?
- Why do you think it is important to John to distinguish between the 'righteous' and the 'unrighteous'?
- What is the significance for John of his visions of the kingdom of God coming to the earth?
- How does John portray the presence of evil in the world?
- How do you respond to John's images of violent judgement?
- Do you think Revelation presents a vision of hope or despair? Why?

Notes

1 Cf. José Adriano Filho, 2002, 'The Apocalypse of John as an Account of a Visionary Experience: Notes on the Book's Structure', *Journal for the Study of the New Testament*, vol. 25.2: 213–34.

2 For a highly detailed analysis of the structure of Revelation, see G. K. Beale, 1999, *The Book of Revelation*, Carlisle: The Paternoster Press, pp. 108–51.

3 For other New Testament examples of a 'grace and peace' greeting see Rom. 1.7; 1 Cor. 1.3; 2 Cor. 1.2; Gal. 1.3; Eph. 1.2; Phil. 1.2; Col. 1.2; 1 Thess. 1.1; 2 Thess. 1.2; 1 Tim. 1.2; 2 Tim. 1.2; Titus 1.4; Phlm 1.3; 1 Peter 1.2; 2 Peter 1.2; 2 John 1.3.

4 References to John the Apostle in the Synoptics are Matt. 4.21; 10.12, 17.1; Mark 1.19, 29; 3.17; 5.37; 9.2, 38; 10.35, 41; 13.3; 14.33; Luke 5.10; 6.14; 8.51; 9.28, 49, 54; 22.8. This character may or may not be synonymous with the Beloved Disciple of John's Gospel. If they are the same person, John the Apostle is to be seen as the author of not only Revelation, but also the Fourth Gospel, as well as the three letters of John.

5 2 John 1.1; 3 John 1.1. It is possible that John the Elder is also the author of the Fourth Gospel. This is not the same as identifying John the Elder as the Apostle John. For example, it is entirely possible that John the Elder wrote the Fourth Gospel based on the testimony of the anonymous Beloved Disciple, and then went on to write the letters and the book of Revelation.

6 Bauckham comments: 'The evidence which really rules out composition *during Peter's lifetime* is that of literary genre and that of date. Either of these might be fatal for any degree of Petrine authorship. Together they must be regarded as entirely conclusive against Petrine authorship.' Richard Bauckham, 1983, *Jude, 2 Peter*, Word Biblical Commentary, vol. 50, Waco, Texas: Word Books, p. 159.

7 Traditionally, John has been thought to have been exiled to Patmos. However, although the island served as a fortress, it is possible that John was there of his own accord.

8 1 Enoch 1.1–2, 'And Enoch ... said, "(This is) a holy vision from the heavens which the angels showed me: and I heard from them everything and I understood."' Translated by E. Isaac in James H. Charlesworth (ed.), 1983, *The Old Testament Pseudepigrapha Volume 1*, The Anchor Bible Reference Library, New York: Doubleday, p. 13. Cf. also George W. E. Nickelsburg and James C. VanderKam, 2005, *1 Enoch: A New Translation*, Minneapolis: Augsburg Fortress.

9 3 Baruch Prologue 1, 'Narration and Apocalypse of Baruch concerning the secret things he saw by the command of God.' Translated by H. E. Gaylord, Jr. in Charlesworth (ed.), *Pseudepigrapha Vol. 1*, p. 663. For a discussion of the nature of the visionary experience in 3 Baruch see Daniel C. Harlow, 1996, *The Greek Apocalypse of Baruch (3 Baruch) in Hellenistic Judaism and Early Christianity*, Studia in Veteris Testamenti Pseudepigrapha, Leiden: E. J. Brill, pp. 16–21.

10 Apocalypse of Adam 1.1, 'The revelation (apocalypse) which Adam taught his son Seth in the seven hundredth year.' Translated by G. MacRae in Charlesworth (ed.), *Pseudepigrapha Vol. 1*, p. 712.

11 Ian Boxall, 2006, *The Revelation of St John*, Black's New Testament Commentaries, London: Continuum, pp. 5–7. Most major commentaries have discussions on the various possibilities for John's identification.

12 Gilbert Desrosiers, 2000, *An Introduction to Revelation*, T&T Clark Approaches to Biblical Studies, London: Continuum, p. 12.

13 Other examples of Jewish apocalyptic material where the seer embarks on a tour of the heavenly realms can be found in 1 Enoch, The Apocalypse of Abraham, and 2 Cor. 12.1–5. 1 Enoch 14.8, 'And behold I saw the clouds: And they were calling me in a vision; and the fogs were calling me; and the course of the stars and the lightnings were rushing me and causing me to desire; and in the vision, the winds were causing me to fly and rushing me high up into heaven.' Translated by E. Isaac in Charlesworth (ed.), *Pseudepigrapha Vol. 1*, p. 20. Apocalypse of Abraham 18.1–3, 'And as I was still reciting the song, the mouth of the fire which was on the firmament was rising up on high ... And as the fire rose up, soaring to the highest point, I saw under the fire a throne of fire'. Translated by R. Rubinkiewicz in Charlesworth (ed.), *Pseudepigrapha Vol. 1*, p. 698.

14 This phrase also occurs in Rev. 1.1; 1.19; 22.6 (cf. Dan. 2.28, 29, 45).

15 For example, Hal Lindsey comments with great detail in his populist and influential book: 'Now we are coming to some of the most important pieces of the prophetic puzzle which are shown in the scriptures. In Revelation 17 the apostle John has a vision which shows the future and precisely what is going to happen on earth the last seven years before Christ returns.' Hal Lindsey and C. C. Carlson, 1970, *The Late, Great Planet Earth*, Grand Rapids: Zondervan, pp. 110–11.

16 Stephen S. Smalley, 2005, *The Revelation to John*, London: SPCK, p. 114. Cf. John Sweet, 1979, *Revelation*, London: SCM Press, p. 115; M. Eugene Boring, 1989, *Revelation*, Louisville: John Knox Press, pp. 100–101; G. K. Beale, 1999, *The Book of Revelation*, Carlisle: The Paternoster Press, p. 318. Victorinus, the third-century theologian who was martyred under Diocletian, understood the content of Revelation as describing what must take place within the context of his own church. Cf. Judith L. Kovacs and Christopher Rowland, 2004, *Revelation*, Blackwell Bible Commentaries, Oxford: Blackwell, p. 42.

17 See p. 99 for an exploration of the difference between what John sees, and what John hears.

18 David E. Aune, 1997, *Revelation 1–5*, Dallas: Word Books, p. 338.

19 See Christopher Rowland, 1998, 'The Book of Revelation', in L. E. Keck (ed.), *New Interpreter's Bible*, Nashville: Abingdon, pp. 622–3.

20 See the discussion of the 144,000 on pp. 96–8.

21 See the discussion of the contrast between what John hears and sees on p. 99.

22 Cf. Rev. 9.12; 11.14.

23 Bauckham argues convincingly that this is the same scroll as was introduced in 5.1. Cf. Richard Bauckham, 1993, *The Climax of Prophecy: Studies on the Book of Revelation*, Edinburgh: T&T Clark, pp. 243–57. See the discussion of the scroll on pp. 186–8 below.

24 For other New Testament imagery of the people of God as the temple see Rom. 12.1; 1 Cor. 3.16–17; 6.19; Eph. 2.21; 1 Peter 2.5

25 Boxall suggests this scheme of seven visions, to parallel the seven seals, trumpets, thunders and bowls. Ian Boxall, 2006, *The Revelation of St John*, London: Continuum, pp. 173–4.

26 See the discussion of the dragon on pp. 150–1.

27 See the discussion of the beast from the earth on pp. 168–71.

28 See Rev. 8.13 for a similar interlude.

29 Cf. Ex. 8.1–15; 10.21–9; 14.21–5.

30 The capitalization of 'Empire' is used to denote the Roman Empire, while the uncapitalized 'empire' indicates the underlying satanic empire which finds expression not just in the Roman Empire, but in all other similar manifestations.

31 For a discussion of the feminist implications of this imagery see p. 162.

32 The command to 'come out' echoes other occasions when the people of God were instructed to leave a corrupt city bound for destruction. Cf. Jer. 51.45; Gen. 19.14.

33 Cf. Luke 22.7–20.

34 This division of the final chapters into seven visions is again suggested by Boxall, *Revelation*, p. 271.

35 For a discussion on whether the rider of 19.11–16 should be identified with that of 6.2 see p. 76.

36 John does not use the phrase 'second resurrection', although it is surely to be found within his scheme at 20.12–13. See the discussion of the 'second resurrection' on pp. 108–9.

37 Cf. Rev. 3.5; 13.8; 17.8; 21.27.

38 See the discussion on dating on pp. 15–16.

39 Cf. David Mathewson, 2003, 'A Note on the Foundation Stones in Revelation 21.14, 19–20', *Journal for the Study of the New Testament*, vol. 25.4: 487–98.

40 Cf. Deut. 4.2.

41 Cf. Rev. 1.4; 1 Cor. 16.23.

Part 2

Meeting the Characters

4

Jesus, God and the Spirit

Whatever else it may be, and it has been described as many things, the book of Revelation is certainly *dramatic* – it is a powerful and complex story, that combines its imagery with an extensive cast of characters. We have already examined the characterization of one of the main players, John himself, as a key to understanding the overall shape of the text. However, one of the potentially confusing features of the text is the way in which different characters appear and reappear at different points in the drama, often having undergone a swift costume-change while in the wings. The purpose of the *dramatis personae* that follows is to help the reader to tease out the different strands of Revelation's characterization, and to allow the characters to emerge as distinct persons who fulfil different roles in the drama.[1]

Jesus

Jesus appears throughout the text of Revelation under a number of different guises. We will initially look at those instances where Jesus is visible as himself, at the Christological titles that are applied to him, and at how these shed light on his portrayal within the text. We will then examine the other Christological images which feature within John's dramatic narrative.

Jesus Christ is named in the first verse of the Apocalypse, appearing before any of the other characters. The reader is told that the revelation that is to follow comes from Jesus, having been given to him by God (1.1a). Jesus has passed this message to John through a divine intermediary, and John is now passing the message to those in the congregations of the churches in Asia Minor (1.1b–2). The centrality of Jesus to the work is thus spelled out at the very beginning, locating the book firmly as a *Christian* apocalypse.

Jesus is mentioned again by John in the opening salutation (1.4–6) where he is listed alongside both the one 'who is and who was and who is to come', and the 'seven spirits who are before his throne'.[2] At this point, Jesus himself is the recipient of a threefold title, and is described as 'the faithful witness, the firstborn of the dead, and the ruler of the kings of the earth' (1.5). This title provides a summary of Jesus' role in terms particularly suited to those among John's recipients who may face martyrdom. First, Jesus is the one who remained faithful in witness even to the point of death, as those in the churches of Asia Minor are called to be.[3] Second, he is the one who has conquered death, and promises a similar victory for those who may experience martyrdom as a result of their faithful witness (2.10). Third, he is the ultimate authority over all earthly powers that may seem to oppose the rule of Christ, which will be shared by those who remain faithful until death (20.4).[4] This is the Messiah who, John says, loves 'us': that is, both him and his recipients. Here, the imprisoned John identifies with his congregations in their suffering, and asserts that Jesus loves them in spite of any perceived evidence to the contrary. Their present difficulties are not to be understood as punishment. Furthermore, Jesus doesn't just love them, but he has also freed them from their sins (1.5). Physical imprisonment may become their experience, but he reminds them that true freedom is theirs through Christ's death, resurrection and ascension to glory.

A major Christological theme is introduced in 1.6, where John asserts that Jesus has made those in his churches into a kingdom of priests serving God. The theme of the divine kingdom forms a significant strand in the Jesus tradition,[5] and it becomes crucial for John in the book of Revelation too. In the Gospels Jesus speaks of the kingdom being 'near',[6] and of his followers already being part of it.[7] However, he also speaks of it as a coming kingdom, the full realization of which lies in the future.[8] John combines these 'now' and 'not-yet' aspects of the kingdom of God, not only speaking of the kingdom as present among the believers of his churches, but also praying for the kingdom to come (cf. 22.20). The hope of the in-breaking kingdom of God entered the early Christian tradition not least through the use of the Lord's Prayer, the opening lines of which resonate strongly with themes that John explores in Revelation: 'Our Father in heaven, hallowed be your name. Your kingdom come. Your will be done, on earth as it is in heaven' (Matt. 6.9–10; cf. Luke 11.2–4). This starting point of God being worshipped in heaven, coupled with prayer for the kingdom of God to come upon the earth, provides a fitting template for understanding much of John's thinking as he seeks to offer an alternative perspective on the earthly kingdoms and powers that currently oppress and seek to control the people of God. Interestingly, John's next phrase in 1.6, 'to him be glory and dominion forever and ever. Amen.' bears a striking resemblance to the traditional (but non-canonical) ending of the Lord's Prayer: 'For yours is the kingdom, the power, and the glory, forever and ever. Amen.'[9] The difference between the two however, is that in the Lord's Prayer 'glory and dominion' are ascribed to God the Father, whereas in Revelation John ascribes these to Jesus. This is a pattern that will be met again throughout the book, with the traditional attributes of God the Father also being applied to Jesus. This 'high' Christology is one of the defining features of John's presentation of Jesus.

The theme of heaven coming to earth continues in 1.7, with the injunction that John's audience should 'look' and see that Jesus is coming to the earth. Thus the fulfilment of the 'Come, Lord Jesus' prayer of 22.20 is already in process here at the beginning of the work, as the kingdom of heaven breaks in upon the earth in the person of Jesus. While at present the coming kingdom may only be visible to those who are already part of it, John holds out the hope that in due course all will see what is at present largely obscured, when all the tribes of the earth cry out at the coming of Jesus. In the meantime however, John and those in his churches share the sufferings of their present situation 'in Jesus' (1.9);[10] not only on account of their faithful witness to Jesus, but also because of their sharing in the faithful witness Jesus gave unto death.[11] The crucifixion of Jesus is referred to specifically in 11.8, where he is spoken of as the crucified Lord of the Church.

The voice of Jesus

There are several instances of an unidentified heavenly voice being heard, where it seems that the exalted Christ is himself speaking directly. In Chapter 10, a voice from heaven instructs John to seal the content of the seven thunders (10.4) and to take the scroll from the angel (10.8). In 14.13, a voice instructs John to write a blessing for the faithful followers who die. There is also a brief interjection in 16.15, where a voice echoes the warning from elsewhere in the New Testament that Jesus will come like a thief in the night,[12] and in 18.4f. a voice from heaven instructs the people of God to cease their compromise with the city of Babylon, since her destruction is assured. Jesus speaks again in 22.7 and his words revisit the theme of the imminent breaking-through of the kingdom of God: 'See, I am coming soon!' (cf. 22.12). This is followed by a blessing on those who keep the words of the Apocalypse, emphasizing that simply hearing is not sufficient, but that response and activity are also expected. The imminent coming of Jesus is linked to his role as judge (22.12), indicating that the final judgement on humanity rests with the one who has defeated the powers of evil and death. Jesus then takes for himself a title which until this point in the text has been applicable only to God: 'I am the Alpha and the Omega' (22.8; cf. 1.8; 21.6). It is this eternal nature of Jesus, the one who is both before and after all things, that qualifies him to be the ultimate judge of humanity.[13]

In 22.16 Jesus speaks again, and confirms the validity of the claim of the book that its message originated with him, albeit mediated by an angel (cf. 1.1). Jesus then takes for himself two Christological titles which have already appeared earlier in the book, describing himself as 'the root and descendant of David' (cf. 5.5 where the title is ascribed to the 'Lion of the tribe of Judah'), and as the 'bright morning star' (cf. 2.28 where the star is promised to those who conquer in the letter to Thyatira). These titles both originate within the Old Testament (cf. Isa. 11.1, 10; Num. 24.17), and the richness and diversity of John's use of this imagery emphasizes the way he creatively reinterprets the prophetic tradition within which he is operating. The final words of Jesus within the Apocalypse are found in 22.20, where once again he utters a promise of his imminent arrival (cf. 22.7, 12).

The 'one like a son of man'

This image for Jesus is presented as a terrifying sight, beginning John's visionary experience in dramatic style. As is the case elsewhere in Revelation, John hears of the vision before he sees it (cf. 7.4, 9), and in this instance, he hears the loud voice like a trumpet (1.10)[14] before he sees the 'one like a son of man' (1.13). The voice commissions John to write down what he sees and send it to the seven churches of Asia Minor. From the point of view of the recipients, this highlights the divine origin of the text they have before them (cf. 22.6). The disembodied voice is then identified as coming from 'one like a son of man' who is seen by John to be standing in the middle of seven golden lampstands. This image recurs in the letter to Ephesus (2.1), while the identity of the lampstands is explained in 1.20 as an image for the seven churches. The reassurance here for John's congregations, that Christ is present with them and among them, is indicative of the ongoing pastoral concerns that drive John's account.

The language that John uses to describe the figure he sees among the lampstands draws on imagery from Daniel and Ezekiel. The phrase 'one like a son of man'[15] (1.13) comes from Dan. 7.13. In its original context in Daniel, the phrase means simply 'a being which looks similar to a human', and as such represents the author's attempt to find words to describe the appearance of the heavenly being encountered in the vision.[16] John's use of this phrase seems chosen to indicate that the being in his vision also has an angelic appearance; certainly this is not initially obviously the ascended Christ. However, that this is no mere repetition of the angelic encounter from Daniel soon becomes clear. The garments worn by the figure are the clothing of a priest (1.13),[17] indicating the high-priestly nature of the figure.[18] In the description of the figure's head (1.14) John returns to Daniel, adapting the description of the Ancient One as having clothing white as snow and hair of pure wool (Dan. 7.9). John overtly applies this description of God to the figure in his vision, further indicating his understanding of the divinity of Jesus. The fiery eyes of John's figure (1.14),[19] and the feet of burnished bronze (1.15) both recur in the letter to Thyatira (2.18, 23).[20] These images come from Dan. 10.6, while the description of the voice like rushing waters comes from Ezek. 1.26; 43.2. These details that John invokes in his description of the 'son of man' figure thus indicate his creative use of the Old Testament as he sought language to describe his visionary experience.

Following the description of the being's location and appearance, John then describes his activity. He is holding seven stars in his right hand (1.16), and these are explained in 1.20 as representing the angels of the seven churches, thus indicating to John's recipients that Christ is not just present with them on earth (as was indicated by the lampstands image), but also that he holds their heavenly existence secure. This image is mentioned again in the letters to Ephesus (2.1) and Sardis (3.1). John then describes a sharp two-edged sword coming from the mouth of the being. Within the New Testament, the only other reference to a two-edged sword is found in Heb. 4.12, where it refers to the word of God, and it seems likely that the same interpretation is to be found here in Revelation. This image draws on Isa. 11.4, recurs in the letter to Pergamum (2.12), and is found again in the vision of the rider on the white horse (19.15), who uses the sword from his mouth to strike down the nations. This image of Christ armed and active in battle is a significant feature of John's Christology, with Christ defeating the forces of evil not through superior military strength, but through the power of the word of God.[21]

The 'one like a son of man' then comforts John, who has understandably fallen prostrate in worship at the sight of this awesome being (1.17),[22] before uttering a largely self-descriptive speech. He describes himself as 'the first and the last', a phrase repeated in the letter to Smyrna (2.8), and that resonates with the 'I am the Alpha and the Omega' statement of 1.8, where it is uttered by God. The adoption of this statement is a further indication of this figure's divinity.[23] The description of the 'one like a son of man' as the living one who was dead but now is alive for ever (1.18) is a clear identification of this figure as the crucified, risen and ascended Christ, and is found again in the letter to Smyrna (2.8). It is the risen Christ who holds the keys of Death and Hades, something that is of great pastoral comfort to those in the churches facing persecution, not least those in Philadelphia whose letter also uses this image (3.7).

The 'one like a son of man' again commissions John to write what he sees (1.19; cf. 1.11) and John does so using a threefold formula referring to what he has seen, what is now, and what is to come.[24] The similarity with the divine designation as the one 'who is, and who was, and who is to come' (1.4, 8; 4.8) should not be lost here. Just as the divine description cannot be broken down into a precise demarcation of the persons of the Trinity,[25] neither should the description of John's vision be seen in terms of precise demarcations either of various parts of the text or indeed of history itself.[26] What is implied here is that John's vision in its entirety is relevant to all periods of human history. It is not to be located entirely in either the past, the present, or the future.

Just in case there remains any lingering doubt as to the Christological identity of the 'one like a son of man', the identification is completed in the introduction to the letter to Thyatira, where the figure is positively identified as 'the son of God' (2.18).[27] In fact this is the only occurrence in Revelation of this designation for Jesus that is so familiar from other parts of the New Testament, and here it serves to demonstrate that the 'son of man' figure is also Jesus Christ the son of God.

The 'one like a son of man' next speaks in 4.1, where he is identified by his voice alone. Within the apocalyptic tradition visionaries such as John would receive angelic revelations of heavenly mysteries,[28] and elsewhere in Revelation this function is fulfilled by a variety of heavenly beings. What is significant about the voice John hears at this point is that, although in the guise of an angelic being, it is actually the voice of the ascended and enthroned Christ himself.[29] The voice invites John to step through the open door into the throne room of heaven, significantly unlike other apocalyptic seers who have to attempt entry through carrying out ascetic practices,[30] or by obtaining the invitation of a lesser angelic intermediary.

The 'one like a son of man' drops out of the narrative of Revelation at this point, with one important exception. In 14.14–16 he comes into view briefly when he is seen by John seated on a white cloud, wearing a golden crown, and carrying a sharp sickle that he uses to reap the whole earth. Although there are strong similarities between this image and the Matthean parable of the wheat and the weeds (Matt. 13.24–43), it must be remembered that there is no evidence that John knew Matthew's work, and so the Gospel's scheme of separating out the wheat and the weeds may not necessarily be what John has in mind here. Certainly however, John does envisage a positive judgement on the earth at the hands of Christ himself, to be contrasted with what follows in the negative judgement enacted by an angel (14.17–20).[31]

The presentation of the 'son of man' figure in Revelation thus locates John's Christology firmly within the apocalyptic messianic interpretations of Ezekiel and Daniel. The image he constructs of Jesus as the glorious son of God reassures his audience that whatever their current earthly context, their future is secure with the mighty one of heaven.

The author of the seven letters

The letters to the seven churches each originate from the lips of Jesus, all beginning with a standard formula: 'These are the words of ...' (2.1, 8, 12, 18; 3.1, 7, 14). This formula is then followed in each case by a different Christological title, each of which links the author to a particular aspect of the vision of the 'one like a son of man' (1.12–18).

In the letter to the church at Ephesus Jesus is described as the one 'who holds the seven stars in his right hand, who walks among the seven golden lampstands' (2.1; cf. 1.13, 16, 20). The pastoral significance of this image for an oppressed and potentially depressed congregation is clear, with its assurance that Jesus is in the midst of his Church, holding their eternal destiny secure. There are also political overtones to this image, as it presents a direct challenge to other powers that might seek to control and influence those in the congregation: it is Jesus who holds the power rather than the Empire.

In the letter to the church at Smyrna Jesus is described as 'the first and the last, who was dead and came to life' (2.8; cf. 1.17–18), reassuring the recipients both of the eternal nature of their Messiah and also of his victory over death. In a context where the power of 'the eternal city'[32] held sway over the life and death of those in John's churches, the title taken by Jesus here serves to relativize the power of Rome.

In the letter to the church at Pergamum Jesus is described as 'him who has the sharp two-edged sword' (2.12; cf. 1.16; 19.15, 21). As has been seen, this weapon is best understood as the word of God (cf. Heb. 4.2), and is likely to have been the only weapon that those in John's congregations would have had available to them as they battled against the dominant ideology of empire. He assures them that the Roman sword may have its own earthly power, but the faithful witness of those in the churches to the word of God will prove more effective in the long term than engaging in guerrilla-style resistance and meeting violence with violence.

In the letter to the church at Thyatira Jesus is described as 'the Son of God, who has eyes like a flame of fire, and whose feet are like burnished bronze' (2.18; cf. 1.14–15). The title 'the Son of God' here recalls Ps. 2.7, where the Israelite king is proclaimed to be a son of God.[33] The inference is that just as the king personified God to the Israelites, so the kingly Jesus personifies God for the Church.

In the letter to the church at Sardis Jesus is described as 'him who has the seven spirits of God and the seven stars' (3.1; cf. 1.4, 16, 20). The seven spirits will be examined in more detail below,[34] but for now it is sufficient to note that they are within the control of Christ. The seven stars are the seven angels of the churches.[35] The spiritual ownership that is being asserted here carries both comfort and warning to the Church.

To the beleaguered congregation, it can be heard as words of consolation. However, to the compromised and complacent church at Sardis, the warning is clear: they ultimately belong not to themselves but to Jesus.

In the letter to the church at Philadelphia Jesus is described as 'the holy one, the true one, who has the key of David, who opens and no one will shut, who shuts and no one opens' (3.7). The titles used here are less obviously derivative of the picture found in Chapter 1. The phrase 'the holy one, the true one' may be an expansion of 'the faithful witness' of 1.5, something that becomes more likely when the ascription 'the faithful and true witness' used in the letter to Laodicea is taken into account (cf. 3.14). The 'key of David' builds thematically on 'the keys of Death and Hades' of 1.18, combining this with Isa. 22.22: 'I will place on his shoulder the key of the house of David; he shall open, and no one shall shut; he shall shut, and no one shall open.' The point here is that Jesus does not simply possess the keys to Death, but that as the Davidic Messiah, he alone has power to open and close the door to the afterlife (cf. 1.8).

In the letter to the church at Laodicea Jesus is described as 'the Amen, the faithful and true witness, the origin of God's creation' (3.14). At issue here is the trustworthiness of the witness provided by Jesus. Isa. 65.16 speaks of invoking a blessing or taking an oath by 'the God of faithfulness', and this clearly lies behind the assertion here that the witness of Jesus is dependable; he is not some created being who needs to take an oath by the faithful God to prove his testimony, rather he is himself the agent of creation, and therefore his witness is inherently both true and faithful.

The Christological titles used in the seven letters, drawing on the vision of the 'one like a son of man', serve to remind John's audience that the great heavenly being they have encountered through his visionary description is also the Lord of their individual congregations. In this way, heaven and earth are joined, and the contents of the vision are rooted in the experiences of those in the seven churches of Asia Minor.

The 'Lion of the tribe of Judah', the 'root of David', the 'bright morning star'

The first two of these messianic titles appear together in 5.5 (cf. 22.16),[36] when John hears one of the elders announce that the 'Lion of the tribe of Judah', also known as the 'root of David', has conquered and is therefore worthy to open the scroll with the seven seals. The image of a conquering Messiah recurs in the vision of the rider on the white horse (6.2),[37] and again in the vision of the 'Lamb that has been slain' (17.14).[38] This theme of conquest is significant for John's audience, as Revelation calls them to imitate their master by themselves becoming conquerors. Thus each of the seven letters concludes with a blessing pronounced on those who conquer (2.7, 11, 17, 26; 3.5, 12, 21), and again towards the end of the work there is a promise that those who conquer will inherit the promised blessings and become children of God (21.7). The victory of the Lion of Judah is stated by one of the elders as his qualification for opening the seals on the scroll, since only the one who has already been victorious in battle is capable of initiating the decisive war against the forces of evil. John's audience are therefore assured that as they engage the battle themselves, they are ultimately guaranteed victory because the one who called them to arms has already proven himself against the enemy.

The image of the Lion of Judah is derived from of Gen. 49.9: 'Judah is a lion's whelp ... He crouches down, he stretches out like a lion, like a lioness – who dares rouse him up?', while the image of the 'root of David' derives from Isa. 11.1, 10: 'A shoot shall come out from the stump of Jesse, and a branch shall grow out of his roots ... On that day the root of Jesse shall stand as a signal to the peoples; the nations shall inquire of him, and his dwelling shall be glorious.' Both passages have a history of Jewish messianic interpretation,[39] and it is within this tradition that John uses them to identify Jesus as a son of the tribe of Judah and as a descendant of King David.[40] The image of Jesus as the 'root of David' recurs in 22.16 where it is paired with the title 'bright morning star', an image that first appears in the letter to Thyatira where it is promised to the one who conquers (2.28). This image should not be confused with the fallen 'day star' of Isa. 14.12, which is part of a passage gloating over the downfall of a feared and hated enemy.[41] Rather, it should be understood in the light of Balaam's prophecy that 'a star shall come out of Jacob' (Num. 24.17),[42] thereby again reinforcing the patriarchal ancestry of Jesus.

The 'Lamb that has been slain'

Following the announcement of the Lion of Judah by one of the elders in 5.5, it is something of a shock when John looks and sees neither a rampant lion, nor the terrifying 'one like a son of man', but instead 'a Lamb standing as if it had been slaughtered' (5.6). The slain Lamb is, for John, a highly significant title for Jesus, occurring 28 times altogether.[43] The dramatic effect of this should not be minimized, and John employs it for great theological effect. Instead of a mighty warrior, setting out to conquer the forces of evil and liberate his followers from oppression, the Messiah is seen as a wounded figure of pathos. It would seem that the one who has just been described as having 'conquered' bears not just the scars of battle, but fatal wounds. Power has been exercised through weakness, and the Lion of Judah has become a sacrificed lamb. The image of Jesus as the 'Lamb of God' occurs outside Revelation only in John's Gospel, where it is twice used by John the Baptist to introduce Jesus (John 1.29, 36). The Old Testament background for this image is less clear, but may draw on several texts, such as Abraham's sacrifice of a ram in place of his son Isaac (Gen. 22.13); the Passover lamb whose blood marked the doors of the Israelite households in Egypt so that the angel of death would pass them by, bringing life and freedom to the exiles (Ex. 12.21; Ezek. 46.13–15); and the suffering servant from Isaiah who goes to the slaughter like a silent lamb (Isa. 53.7).[44] For John in Revelation, the force of this image is that it combines death and resurrection since the Lamb that has been slaughtered is not in fact dead. Rather, he is standing before the throne of God, among the elders and between the four living creatures who surround the throne. Contained in this image are therefore the crucifixion, resurrection and ascension of Jesus.

As John looks more closely, it becomes clear that this is no ordinary-looking lamb, having seven horns and seven eyes.[45] The presence of 'horns' on an animal indicates strength,[46] and the fact that the Lamb has seven horns evokes the Jewish numerological tradition of 'seven' being the perfect number, thereby indicating the completeness of the power that the Lamb wields.[47] Similarly the seven eyes denote the Lamb's complete ability to see all that occurs on the earth. It is this all-powerful, all-seeing, slaughtered, resurrected and ascended Lamb who then takes the scroll directly from God who is seated on the throne (5.7). However, before he starts opening the seals on the scroll, there is a period of worship in the heavenly throne room. The four living creatures and the twenty-four elders begin a hymn of worship to the Lamb, in praise of his worthiness to open the scroll (5.8–14). The hymn-singing then spreads; first to the thousands of angels surrounding the throne, and then to every creature in heaven and earth. No longer is worship limited to the heavenly throne room and directed to God alone (as it was in 4.8–11); now it encompasses all of creation and is directed at the Lamb.[48] Just as the sacrifice of the Passover lamb spared the people of Israel from death in Egypt (Ex. 12.21–23), so the Lamb of God leads all of creation to new life. In a description of worship closely resembling the worship of God in the recently destroyed Jewish temple in Jerusalem, Jesus is proclaimed as God. No longer is God alone on the throne; from here on in Revelation the Lamb is with God at the centre of the throne (7.17; 22.1; cf. 3.21).

The enthronement of the Lamb triggers the opening of the seven seals (6.1, 3, 5, 7, 9, 12; 8.1). The active role of the Lamb in what follows is minimal and is confined to the act of breaking each of the seals in turn. However, this should not obscure the fact that all the judgements that are triggered as the seals are broken have their ultimate origin with the enthroned Messiah in heaven. The Lamb speaks from the throne following the release of the third rider (6.6), proclaiming a judgement on the system that leads to starvation of some while permitting the luxurious lifestyles of others. The deep theological questions that are posed by the violence of such imagery will be addressed in a later chapter,[49] but at this stage it is important to note that the Lamb sets in train all that follows. Hence, it is natural that the kings of the earth should plead to be hidden from the wrath of the Lamb following the opening of the sixth seal (6.16).

The enthroned Lamb comes back into view following the opening of the sixth seal, and is again the object of worship (7.9–17). Once more, those worshipping the Lamb are seen as a great crowd comprising not just heavenly beings, but also an uncountable number of human worshippers clothed in white robes. White functions here as a symbol of purity and of unblemished character, and it becomes clear that these robes are white not because of any great deeds committed on the part of those wearing them, but because they have been washed in the shed blood of the Lamb. The only sacrifice that purifies the human soul is the sacrifice of the Lamb: it is seen that even martyrdom, however much it is to be lauded as an act of faithful witness, is inadequate as a means to vindication. Hence John employs the incongruous image of washing garments in blood and seeing them come out bright white. Only the blood of the Lamb can do this (cf. 3.5, 18). The worshipful interlude then concludes with the Lamb at the centre of the throne (cf. 3.21), and the elder tells John that, in a reversal of the normal course of rural practice, the Lamb will shepherd the people and guide them to springs flowing with the water of life. The resonances with the images of the Good Shepherd and springs of living water in John's Gospel are obvious and highlight the extent to which Johannine Christology holds common themes in both the Gospel and the Apocalypse.[50]

After opening the seventh seal (8.1), the Lamb largely drops from view for some time. He is mentioned in 12.11 when John hears a loud voice in heaven proclaiming that the accuser has been conquered by the faithful through the blood of the Lamb. This provides a further reminder that the true power to defeat evil comes only through the sacrificial death of the Messiah, and not through any other power or action. A concept is introduced in 13.8 that will be crucial in the judgement scenes later in Revelation, that of 'the book of life of the Lamb that was slaughtered' (cf. 17.8; 20.12, 15). The book of life was first encountered in the letter to Sardis, where those who conquer are told that their names will not be blotted from the book (3.5), but it is only in 13.8 and again in 21.27 that the book is linked with the Lamb. The function of the book of life primarily appears to be that of providing assurance to John's audience that their fate is secure for all eternity with the Lamb who holds all power

73

and who sees all deeds, in contrast to a pagan view of life that sees one's fate as being the result of chance or accident of birth. The meaning of the phrase 'from the foundation of the world' (13.8) is greatly contested, and has led to debate around whether the eternal destiny of individuals has been fixed since the beginning of creation. However, Boxall notes the textual difficulty of the Greek at this point, and suggests that it could equally read that it is *the Lamb* who has been *slaughtered* since the foundation of the world, suggesting not a form of predestination, but rather the universal and eternal efficacy of the crucifixion.[51]

The Lamb comes back into view in Chapter 14 where he is pictured, no longer at the centre of the heavenly throne, but standing on Mount Zion, the site of the Jerusalem temple. It should not be thought that John envisages the Lamb as having descended to the earth in an early and partial parousia. Rather, he is employing the image of Zion to communicate the presence of Christ at the centre of his Church. Just as the earthly temple on Zion in Jerusalem was the focal point of the worship of Israel, so the renewed people of God have Christ as the focal point of their worship. The interpretation of the 144,000 is addressed below,[52] but the significant point at hand is that Christ is pictured here as the renewed temple at the centre of his people. In a similar way, the Lamb is also central to the punishment of those who worship the beast (14.10) as they are finally forced to acknowledge that which they have so long denied: the power and divinity of the Lamb.

It has already been noted that the image of the slain Lamb recalls the story of the Passover and exodus. This point is reinforced in 15.3–4, where those who have conquered the beast stand beside the sea of glass and fire, and sing 'the song of Moses, the servant of God, and the song of the Lamb' (15.3). In Exod. 15.1f., the people of God stand beside the sea through which they have just passed on their way out of slavery in Egypt, and Moses leads them in a song of praise to God for the victory over the Egyptians. The point regarding the Lamb here is that as Moses led the people to freedom, so the Lamb is also the agent of freedom and deliverance.

The great final battle between the army of the Lamb and the forces of the beast is introduced in 16.16, where the forces of evil are described as assembling at Harmagedon. In 17.14, John is told that the kings of the earth will make war on the Lamb, and that the Lamb will conquer them and will share his victory with those who have done battle alongside him. The battle itself is described in 19.11–21, where the dominant Christological image changes from the Lamb to the rider on the white horse. But before this, the battle-shout of the faithful is raised, with the great multitude giving praise to God because the time is at hand for the marriage of the Lamb, which encourages the drawing of a comparison between the immorality and unfaithfulness of the forces of the beast and the fidelity of the Lamb towards his Church.[53] The marriage supper of the Lamb and his bride is then prepared, and a blessing pronounced on those who are invited (19.9). The observance of the Lord's Supper in the seven congregations is clearly in view here, as the people of God break bread and drink wine in union with their Lord. This image is in contrast to the horrific 'great supper of God' (19.17–21) where the flesh of the kings of the earth becomes the meal for the birds of mid-heaven.

In the vision of the new Jerusalem, the Lamb has a dual function: he is both temple and light for the city. If the city is understood as the redeemed people of God, then there is no need for any temple or light other than Jesus himself because the marriage of the Lamb has occurred, and the saviour is at one with his people. No longer is there any need for a place to go and meet with God, neither is there any need for a light to show the way to God as both these functions are fulfilled in Jesus the Lamb.[54]

The final image of the Lamb in Revelation is of him enthroned, alongside God, in the new Jerusalem (22.1). The water of life issues from the throne, bringing life and fruitfulness to the city (22.2).[55] In gratitude the servants of the Lamb worship him, see his face, and are marked with his name (22.3–4). Jesus is at one with both God and his Church, and is the perfect intercessor. The people of the Lamb are accorded the privilege denied to Moses, in that they can look upon the face of the divine (Ex. 33.20–23), and as those who have resisted the mark of the beast, they take upon themselves the mark of the Lamb, signifying his absolute and eternal ownership of them.[56]

The Lamb which was slain is thus a key Christological image employed by John. From the initial surprise of seeing the Lamb instead of a lion, through the opening of the seven seals and their consequent effects, to the final battle and the marriage of the Lamb, this deeply subversive image of vulnerability and sacrifice poses a persistent challenge to any who would seek to interpret the defeat of evil as the triumphalistic victory of one segment of humanity over another. The victory of the Lamb is, according to John, won through sacrifice alone.

The 'child who rules the nations with a rod of iron'

This image for Jesus occurs in 12.4–5, where it is stated that the destiny of the child born to the woman crowned with twelve stars will be to rule all the nations with a rod of iron. The origin of the image lies in Ps. 2.9, a coronation psalm that featured heavily in the Jewish messianic tradition.[57] In Revelation, Jesus is cast as the fulfilment of the psalm's prophecy that a Davidic king would arise and exercise authority with an iron rod over the nations of the world.[58] For congregations living under the dominion of Rome, the assurance that ultimate power rests not with the emperor but with Jesus himself provides both reassurance and motivation. Indeed, in 2.27 those in the church at Thyatira are promised that if they conquer they themselves will receive authority over the nations to rule with an iron rod.[59] The Christ-child image of 12.4–5 provides a highly compressed biography of Jesus' life: he is born, threatened by evil, rules the nations, is resurrected and 'taken up' into heaven.[60] The image of Jesus exercising judgement with a rod of iron recurs in 19.15 in the vision of the rider on the white horse, where once again it denotes power and authority over the nations of the earth.

The rider on the white horse

The image of a rider on a white horse occurs at two key points in Revelation – Chapters 6 and 19. The key interpretative question surrounding this image is whether or not these two are to be understood as the same person. The second occurrence is unquestionably Christological, but things are more complex the first time a rider on a white horse is introduced.[61]

As the Lamb opens each of the first four seals (6.1–8), a different rider on a coloured horse is called forth by the four living creatures, with the first described as 'a white horse! Its rider had a bow; a crown was given to him, and he came out conquering and to conquer' (6.2). According to Irenaeus, writing in the second century, this figure is to be identified as Christ.[62] In Revelation there is an obvious attraction to seeing both instances of a rider on a white horse as referring to the same person, particularly given the identical phrase used in both instances, καὶ ἰδοὺ ἵππος λευκός καὶ ὁ καθήμενος ἐπ᾽ αὐτὸν ('and behold, a white horse, and he who sat on it' (6.2; 19.11).[63] By this reading, the bow in the rider's hand functions in a similar fashion to the rod of iron (12.4–5; 19.15) and can be seen as an instrument of judgement, while the crown resonates with that worn by the 'one like a son of man' when he sits enthroned in judgement on the earth (14.14). If this figure is to be understood Christologically, it represents Christ sent forth into the world to make war on the forces of evil which are represented by the next three riders in the series. Clearly the colours of the four horses are important to John, with the white of the first horse recalling the purity and victory symbolized by the colour white elsewhere in the Apocalypse.[64] The image of Christ as a mounted archer recalls the mounted Parthian archers who defeated the Romans in AD 62 at the battle of the Tigris Valley, thereby reinforcing the point that the conquering Messiah will ultimately be victorious over the earthly powers of empire.[65] S. Finamore summarizes: 'The white horse ... symbolizes the primary consequence of the events depicted in Revelation 4 and 5; the witness to the truth in the face of death carried out by those who follow Jesus.'[66]

However compelling this Christological reading of the first rider may be, it needs to be noted that the majority of commentators on Revelation do not view this as the correct reading of this passage.[67] Instead, this figure is more commonly regarded as an integral part of the four horsemen of the first four seals, and is typically seen as a satanic parody of Christ, demonstrating the depths of deception that the forces of evil are capable of achieving in their quest to overcome the world. By this reading the figure represents the myth of salvation through military conquest that was so integral to the Roman doctrine of peace through military might.

If there is confusion surrounding the identity of the rider in 6.2, there are no such problems regarding that found in Chapter 19. John once again sees heaven opened, and finds before him a vision of a rider on a white horse. The rider is then identified through an extended description (19.12–16) which makes it clear beyond all doubt that this is Jesus himself. Both the fiery eyes and the two-edged sword that comes from his mouth have parallels in the description of the 'one like a son of man' (1.14, 16; cf. 2.12, 18). On his head are many diadems indicating his unlimited kingly rule in contrast with the limited number of diadems worn by other lesser characters earlier in the Apocalypse (12.3; 13.1; cf. 6.2), and on his body is a robe dipped in the blood of his crucifixion (cf. 7.14).

To reinforce the identification, the rider is given four names. He is described as: 'Faithful and True', a title used by Jesus of himself in the letter to Laodicea (3.14).[68] He also has a secret name, which John says is inscribed upon his person. Although this name is not revealed, it corresponds to the 'new name' that is given to those who conquer (2.17; 3.12; 14.1; 22.4).[69] In a culture where knowledge of someone's name denoted power over that person,[70] it is not insignificant that the conquering Messiah has a secret name, and that it is this secret name that also marks his followers,[71] preventing anyone from gaining power over either him or them in the final battle. It is debatable as to whether John actually had in mind a name that he intended his recipients to work out; a common suggestion is that he intends the title 'the LORD', the forever unspoken name of God.[72] However, it is more likely that John intends the idea of Jesus having a hidden name to communicate symbolically the unique power of the ascended Messiah. The third designation given to the figure on the horse is 'The Word of God', a phrase that elsewhere in Revelation appears to denote the gospel as distinct from the person of Jesus (1.2; 1.9; 6.9; 20.4). This significantly identifies the messianic figure on the white horse in Chapter 19 as synonymous with the gospel itself. The fourth name is inscribed both on his robe and his thigh: 'King of kings and Lord of lords.' This title derives from Dan. 2.37, 47, and has already been used by John to describe the Lamb in 17.14. In Daniel the title denoted divine power over the earthly rule of Nebuchadnezzar, and similarly in Revelation it signifies the absolute power of Jesus over all earthly authorities.

In addition to being described and named, the rider on the white horse also engages in a number of tasks. He judges in righteousness (19.11),[73] makes war (19.11), and strikes down the nations with the sharp sword coming from his mouth (19.15).[74] These images strike a note of divine vindication, as the powers that oppose the righteous kingdom of the Messiah are engaged by him in battle and defeated. The imagery of ruling the nations with a rod of iron recurs in 19.15,[75] as the supreme authority of Jesus over all earthly powers is underlined once more. The rider is then seen treading the wine press of the fury of the wrath of God (19.15),[76] as the forces of evil are crushed beneath the stamping hooves of the white horse.

The rider on the white horse makes one final appearance in Revelation, at the great battle of Harmagedon (19.19–21; cf. 16.16).[77] The beast and the false prophet gather their forces to wage war on the rider and his army, but they are swiftly captured and consigned to the lake of fire. The now leaderless armies of evil are defeated by the sword that comes from the mouth of the rider, and their bodies are consumed by the birds of mid-heaven (cf. 19.17). It should be noted that the army ranged behind the rider has no part to play in this final battle; it is entirely fought by Christ himself using the sword from his mouth, symbolic of the authority of the gospel message as the forces of evil are consumed by the power of heaven. The image does not necessarily imply the physical death of those who followed the beast, for these same 'kings of the earth' are present in the new Jerusalem (19.19; 21.24).[78] Rather it should primarily be understood as conveying the ultimate defeat of evil by the power of the gospel, as the rider on the white horse conquers those forces that seek to oppress and oppose the coming kingdom of God.

In this way, the image of the victorious warrior trampling his enemies underfoot is subverted to become a symbol for the fragility of the forces of evil when confronted with the truth of the gospel of Christ. It is the gospel of death and resurrection which defeats the armies of the earth, as the cross towers over and relativizes all other powers. For those in John's churches, this would have been received as a message of encouragement, with their participation in the proclamation of the gospel representing their participation in the banishment of evil from the earth.

God

Although in a sense the presence of God permeates the whole of the book of Revelation, nonetheless he also features as a character within the narrative. He appears at the beginning of Chapter 1 as the ultimate source of the revelation, which he gives to Jesus, who in turn makes it known to John through an angel, so that John can then communicate it to his audience (1.1–2). It is significant that God is here presented as the one who lies behind the vision that Jesus communicates to John. In the Fourth Gospel the Father is revealed through the Son (John 1.18; 5.37; 14.9), and it is in this sense that the 'revelation of Jesus Christ' that John receives can be described as 'the word of God' (1.2).[79] The 'word of God' is therefore the testimony borne by Jesus through his life, death, resurrection and ascension, and witnessed to in the images of the Apocalypse. In other words, the 'word of God' in Revelation is to be understood as nothing less than the gospel of Jesus Christ.[80]

The one who is and who was and who is to come

The first of a number of related titles that are applied to God appears in 1.4, where John brings a greeting of grace and peace from 'him who is and who was and who is to come'.[81] This threefold phrase serves to indicate the eternal nature of God, who exists before, after and above all other powers. Similar titles ascribed to God include: 'Alpha and Omega' (1.8; cf. 21.6; 22.13), 'the beginning and the end' (21.6; 22.13), 'the first and the last' (22.13; cf. 1.17), and the one 'who lives forever and ever' (4.9). In all of these titles, it is clear that God is in control of the whole of history, since he both pre- and post-dates the world of John's recipients. For those contemplating the idolatrous claims of Rome, with its deified emperors and 'eternal city',[82] John's assertion that God is both before and after all things provides assurance that however powerful the Empire may appear, its time of dominion is limited in contrast with the eternal kingdom of the one on the heavenly throne.

The voice of God

There are several occasions where an otherwise unidentified heavenly voice should be identified with the voice of God rather than one of the other angelic beings. The loud voice from the temple which orders the pouring out of the bowls upon the earth is the voice of God (16.1), indicating that the sequence of bowl-plagues finds its origin in the activity of God. This same voice is also heard again at the end of the pouring out of the bowls, proclaiming the completion of the divine series of judgements: 'It is done!' (16.17).[83] In a similar manner, the judgement on Babylon finds its source in the anger of God himself: 'God remembered great Babylon and gave her the wine-cup of the fury of his wrath' (Rev.

16.19; cf. 14.10). The judgements on evil are thereby consistently presented as having the righteous anger of God as their trigger. For John's congregations, so often on the receiving end of those forces exercising opposition to the kingdom of God, to know that God's wrath burned against the forces of evil in the world would have been a source of great encouragement as they sought to remain faithful to their calling.

The one seated upon the throne

When John's vision takes him into the throne room of heaven, the first thing he sees is God seated upon his throne (4.1–11). This vision of the enthroned deity draws heavily on the Jewish tradition of *Merkabah* mysticism.[84] The closest parallel in the Jewish non-canonical material is found in 1 Enoch,[85] while within the New Testament Paul describes a visionary experience in terms strongly reminiscent of this tradition (2 Cor. 12.1–4). In the book of Revelation, the image of God enthroned provides a breathtaking introduction to John's ascent into heaven, while firmly establishing within the reader's imagination the supreme power wielded by God. This is to be contrasted with the competing claims for supreme power that John's recipients would have encountered from the forces allied to the Emperor enthroned in Rome. John's point is clear: the Emperor may sit on an earthly throne, but God is on the ultimate throne in heaven. Worship within the throne room is directed at God enthroned, as he is adored by the four living creatures and the twenty-four elders, emphasizing to John's recipients that their earthly worship should mirror the heavenly worship in its focus, despite the many competing idols and ideologies clamouring for adoration.

Continuing the theme of the revelation originating from God himself (1.1), it is significant that the scroll which triggers the sequences of seals and trumpets first comes into view in the right hand of God upon the throne (5.1),[86] before being passed to the Lamb for the seals to be broken. From this point on, the character of God recedes from the forefront of the narrative, and he is not seen again clearly until 20.11. However, the point has already been made: everything that follows originates with the one who is enthroned in heaven.

In 6.15–16 the powerful kings of the earth, together with those under their authority, plead to be hidden from 'the face of the one seated on the throne and from the wrath of the Lamb'. The opposition from the throne of God toward the forces of evil is being played out on the earth, and those who have invested in the corrupt systems of empire are seen to be terrified of the judgement that is being visited upon them. Interestingly the appeal to the one seated on the throne is also cast as an appeal to the Lamb, who will shortly be seen seated on the throne alongside God

(7.17). The frightened cries of those in opposition to the forces of heaven contrast with the security experienced by those who come through the earthly difficulties of the present to enter into a place of sanctuary before the throne of God (7.14–15),[87] where God will wipe away their tears (7.17). God enthroned in heaven comes into view again briefly in 12.5, where the son of the pregnant woman is snatched away from the earth and taken to the throne of God in an image of the birth, resurrection and ascension of Jesus. Once again the point is made: God is no longer alone on his throne in heaven.

The throne of God comes back into sight in Chapter 20, with God seated ready to judge the living and the dead (20.11–15).[88] The separate persons of God and Jesus are here conflated, so that although the figure on the throne is clearly God,[89] nonetheless the presence of Jesus is also implied as the figure prepares to vindicate the righteous and consign Death, Hades and their other forces to destruction in the lake of fire.

In the vision of the new heaven and earth (21.1–8), the one on the throne speaks directly, and proclaims that he is making all things new (21.5).[90] Having definitively dealt with the forces of evil, God is now able to communicate directly with humanity in the transformed creation. The voice from the throne reiterates the command that John should write, together with a renewed assurance that the words he is being given to write are trustworthy and true (21.5; cf. 1.11; 14.13; 19.9). Once again the point is made that John's vision originates from the very throne of God himself. The one on the throne then tells John: 'It is done!' (21.6; cf. 16.17). After all the repetition and delays, the end has finally arrived: the victory won at the crucifixion is at last seen on the earth in all its fullness.[91] Blessings are once again promised to all who overcome (21.6–7), as they are given water from the spring of the water of life.[92] The voice from the throne concludes with a warning against patterns of behaviour that are destined for destruction in the lake of fire (21.8).[93]

The vision of the one seated on the throne is thus a deliberately ambiguous image, evoking both God and the Son as co-occupants of the heavenly seat. This assertion of the supremacy of Christ as having equal status with God serves to locate the worship offered in the seven churches within the heavenly realm, as they worship Jesus as Lord.

The Spirit

One of the accusations that has occasionally been levelled against the book of Revelation is that it has an inadequate pneumatology, with some suggesting that the book treats the Spirit as an aspect of Jesus rather than as a personified character.[94] However, to suggest that the Spirit is not present within the book is to miss a key aspect of John's theological scheme.[95] There are four instances of John describing himself as being 'in the spirit'. The first two of these are associated with his initial entry into his visionary trance (1.10; 4.2). The practice of spirit-possession leading to visionary activity was not unknown within Jewish religious practice, and is found both in the Old Testament,[96] and in Jewish and Christian apocalyptic texts.[97] Similarly, John is carried away 'in the spirit' to witness both the judgement of the great whore (17.3) and the arrival of the bride of the Lamb (21.10). At issue in these passages is whose 'spirit' John is 'in'. It is possible that John is speaking about his own spirit ascending from his body into heaven, in a similar manner to the author of 1 Enoch who claims that: '(Thus) it happened after this that my spirit passed out of sight and ascended into the heavens' (1 Enoch 71.1).[98] However, while this may account for the first two references, it is a less satisfactory explanation of the latter two,[99] for if 'spirit' is understood as the Spirit of God, then John's language becomes a description of the Spirit entering into him in order to facilitate his visionary journey.

Another repeated reference to the Spirit is found in the concluding sections of each of the seven letters, where it is stated: 'Let everyone who has an ear listen to what the Spirit is saying to the churches' (2.7, 11, 17, 29; 3.6, 13, 22). This has the effect of casting the content of each of the letters as being both the words of the Spirit and the words of the Christological 'son of man'.[100] In this way, the Spirit is the one who conveys the message of Jesus to those in the seven churches through John's writings. John is therefore a prophet whose words are Spirit-inspired, so that they effectively communicate the words of Jesus. In a similar manner, the Spirit is heard agreeing with the blessing spoken by the voice from the throne on those who have died in Christ, prophetically confirming to John that the words of Jesus are trustworthy and true (14.3; cf. 21.5; 22.6). This function of the Spirit as conveying the 'testimony of Jesus' is therefore described as being 'the spirit of prophecy' (19.10).[101]

The final direct mention of the Spirit in Revelation is found in the concluding chapter, where the Spirit joins with the bride of the Lamb to issue the summons: 'Come!' (22.17). This passage is discussed below,[102] but for now it is sufficient to note that the function of the Spirit here is to inspire the prayerful response of the Church, just as it has been to inspire the prophetic words of John throughout the Apocalypse.[103]

In terms of indirect references to the Spirit in Revelation, some have suggested that the seven spirits of God should be understood in this way (cf. 1.4; 3.1; 4.5; 5.6). However, the position adopted by this text is that the seven spirits function as a characterization of the omniscient nature of the one seated on the throne.[104] One further possible allusion to the Spirit may be found in the divine seal with which the redeemed are marked (7.2, 3; 9.4).[105]

Thus it can be seen that the Spirit does indeed feature within the

Apocalypse as more than a facet of the presentation of Jesus, and this has implications for those seeking to explore the origins of Trinitarian theology. Although the Spirit in Revelation is not enthroned alongside the Father and the Son, nonetheless there is a definite function which the Spirit fulfils as the presence of Christ among the people of the Lamb.

Draw your own conclusions

• What do you think are the significant features of John's presentation of Jesus?
• Why does John use Old Testament imagery to inform his Christological descriptions?
• Do you agree that the rider on the white horse is Jesus in both Chapters 6 and 19? Why?
• Why is the vision of God on the heavenly throne important for John's audience?
• How might you respond to the claim that the book of Revelation is pneumatologically weak?

Notes

1 For an excellent essay on the plot development and characterization of Revelation, see David L. Barr, 2003, 'The Story John Told: Reading Revelation for Its Plot', in David L. Barr (ed.), *Reading the Book of Revelation*, Atlanta: Society of Biblical Literature, pp. 11–23. Cf. also Gilbert Desrosiers, 2000, *An Introduction to Revelation*, London: Continuum, pp. 10–15.

2 For a more detailed analysis of Trinitarian imagery in Revelation, see Richard Bauckham, 1993, *The Theology of the Book of Revelation*, Cambridge: Cambridge University Press, pp. 23–5. It should be noted however that an advanced Trinitarian understanding should not be forced onto the text at this point, and the 'seven spirits' may not be a direct cipher for the Holy Spirit, rather representing seven angelic mediators (cf. Rev. 8.2). See the discussion on the 'seven spirits' on pp. 119–20.

3 Cf. Rev. 2.7, 11, 17, 26, 28, 3.21.

4 G. K. Beale, *The Book of Revelation*, Carlisle: The Paternoster Press, pp. 190–1.

5 Matthew speaks of the 'kingdom of heaven', while Mark, Luke, John and Paul all use the phrase 'kingdom of God'.

6 Cf. Matt. 3.2; 4.17; 10.7; Mark 1.15; Luke 10.9, 11; 21.31.

7 Cf. Matt. 5.3, 10; 9.35; 11.12; 12.28; 13.11.

8 Cf. Matt. 5.19, 20; 6.33; 7.21; 8.11–12.

9 The earliest known version of the Lord's Prayer containing this closing doxology is found in the Didache, although it should be noted that there are significant discussions concerning the dating of the Didache. For an introduction

to these discussions, and a useful presentation of the text with Matthean parallels indicated, see http://www.didache-garrow.info/

10 Paul uses a similar phrase on a number of occasions, e.g. Rom. 8.1; Gal. 1.22.

11 The phrase 'testimony of Jesus' can support both interpretations, depending whether it is treated as a subjective or objective genitive construction. It is possible that John is being deliberately ambiguous in his use of language here in order to imply both. Cf. Beale, *Revelation*, pp. 183–4. This phrase also occurs in 1.2; 12.17; 19.10; 20.4. The related phrase 'faith of Jesus' occurs in 14.12 and functions in a similar way.

12 Cf. Matt. 24.43; Luke 12.39–40; 1 Thess. 5.2; 2 Peter 3.10.

13 The theme of Jesus sitting in eschatological judgement is found also in Matt. 25.31–3; John 5.22, 27; Acts 10.42; 2 Cor. 5.10; 2 Tim. 4.1.

14 Cf. Rev. 4.1 where the voice is heard again.

15 New American Standard Bible. The NRSV translates this as 'one like *the* Son of Man', inserting the definite article so as to interpretatively identify this character with the 'son of man' self-designation used by Jesus in the Gospels.

16 For a detailed analysis of the Daniel passage, see Ernest Lucas, 2002, *Daniel*, Apollos Old Testament Commentary, vol. 20, Leicester: Apollos, pp. 183–4.

17 The priestly clothing worn by Aaron and his sons is very similar (Ex. 28.39–41; cf. Ex. 28.4; Lev. 16.4). In the Apocalypse, the same garments are worn by the seven angels as they exit the heavenly temple (15.5–6; cf. 19.8, 14).

18 Within John's scheme, both believers and angelic beings serve as priests (1.6; 8.3–5; 15.7–8). The similarity with the imagery of Jesus the High Priest from Hebrews should not be overlooked (e.g. Heb. 4.14–15).

19 Cf. Rev. 19.12 where the rider on the white horse has the same eyes.

20 See the discussion of the letter to Thyatira on p. 69.

21 See the discussion of the white rider on p. 223.

22 Note that there is no rebuke of John's attitude of worship here, as there is later in the book when he attempts to worship angelic intermediaries (19.10; 22.8–9). The point is clear: this is Christ himself, who is worthy of worship.

23 Cf. Rev. 21.6; 22.13.

24 The interpretation of this verse is highly debated. For a thorough discussion see Beale, *Revelation*, pp. 152–70, 216.

25 For example – 'who is' being Christ's present Spirit, 'who was' being the creator Father, 'who is to come' being Christ at the parousia.

26 Some have sought to so divide the text: 1.12–20 'what you have seen' corresponding to the past; Chapters 2—3 'what now is' corresponding to the present age; Chapters 4—22 'what is to take place after this' corresponding to the future. Cf. Ian Boxall, 2006, *The Revelation of St John*, London: Continuum, p. 44.

27 Note the presence of the definite article. John is still drawing on imagery from Daniel; in Dan. 3.25 the mysterious fourth figure in the fiery furnace is described as 'like a son of the gods' (NASB). What is significant is that, unlike his borrowing of the phrase 'one like a son of man' from Dan. 7.13, John does in this instance insert the definite article, thereby ensuring his readers would make the connection to the title used by Christ of himself in the Gospels.

28 For example, Gabriel interprets Daniel's vision for him in Dan. 8.15–17. Also, within the Jewish Enoch tradition, Enoch (cf. Gen. 5.24; Heb. 11.5; Sirach 44.16) is transformed into the archangel Metatron (3 Enoch 9.1–5; 15.1–2) and becomes himself the revealer of heavenly mysteries to others (3 Enoch 13.1–2). Cf. Hugo Odeberg, 1928, *3 Enoch or the Hebrew Book of Enoch*, London: Cambridge University Press.

29 Typically the interpreters for John are either angels or elders.

30 Practices which may be reflected in the self-abasement, worship of angels, and dwelling on visions practised by Paul's opponents in Colossae (cf. Col. 2.18).

31 See the discussion of the two harvest images on pp. 206–7.

32 See the discussion of the 'eternal city' on p. 158.

33 The parallel between the letter to Thyatira and Ps. 2 is reinforced through the similarity of 2.26–27 with Ps. 2.8–9.

34 See the discussion of the seven spirits of God on pp. 119–20.

35 See the discussion of the seven stars on pp. 94–5.

36 The image of a lion also occurs in 4.7 and 10.3, but these are not the same as the Lion of Judah.

37 See the discussion of the rider on the white horse on pp. 76–8.

38 See the discussion of the Lamb which has been slain on pp. 71–5.

39 For example the conquering lion Messiah is found in 4 Esdras: 'And as for the lion whom you saw rousing up out of the forest and roaring and speaking to the eagle and reproving him for his unrighteousness, and as for all his words that you have heard, this is the Messiah whom the Most High has kept until the end of days, who will arise from the offspring of David, and will come and speak with them' (4 Esd. 12.31–32; cf. 11.37), while the 'root of David' appears messianically in the Dead Sea Scrolls: 'He is the branch of David who shall arise with the interpreter of the Law [to rule] in Zion [at the end] of time' (4Q174 I.11–12), and again: '[Interpreted, this concerns the Branch] of David who shall arise at the end [of days] ... God will uphold him with [the spirit of might, and will give him] a throne of glory and a crown of [holiness] and many-coloured garments ... [He will put a sceptre] in his hand and he shall rule over all the [nations]. And Magog ... and his sword shall judge [all] the peoples' (4Q161 Frs 8–10, 15–21). Qumran quotations from Geza Vermes, 2004, *The Complete Dead Sea Scrolls in English*, Revised edn, London: Penguin Books, pp. 526, 498, as identified in Boxall, *Revelation*, p. 97.

40 Other New Testament writers seek to make the same point: cf. Descendant of David (Matt. 1.1; 12.23; 22.42; Mark 10.47; Luke 1.27; 2.4; Rom. 1.3; 2 Tim. 2.8); Descendant of Judah (Heb 7.14).

41 Brevard S. Childs, 2001, *Isaiah*, The Old Testament Library, Louisville, Kentucky: Westminster John Knox Press, pp. 126–7.

42 This passage also appears messianically within the Dead Sea Scrolls: 'A star shall come out of Jacob and a sceptre shall rise out of Israel; he shall crush the temples of Moab and destroy all the children of Sheth.' (4Q175 12–13). Vermes, *Complete Dead Sea Scrolls*, pp. 527–8.

43 As Bauckham notes, 28 significantly equals 7 (the perfect number) x 4. Cf. Bauckham, *Theology*, p. 67. Symbolic numbers in Revelation include: three; four; seven; and twelve; together with various multiples of these numbers. For

a detailed analysis see Richard Bauckham, 1993, *The Climax of Prophecy: Studies in the Book of Revelation*, Edinburgh: T&T Clark, pp. 29–37, and for information on numerology in the Jewish apocalyptic tradition see D. S. Russell, 1964, *The Method & Message of Jewish Apocalyptic*, London: SCM Press, pp. 195–202.

44 Stephen S. Smalley, *Thunder and Love: John's Revelation and John's Community*, Milton Keynes: Nelson Word, pp. 61–2. It is significant that this same imagery may lie behind the Pauline description of the Church as a 'living sacrifice' (Rom. 12:1), with the covenantal mark of the sacrificed lamb becoming a defining feature of the renewed people of Christ.

45 Bauckham sees the seven horns and the seven eyes, along with the seven spirits of God, as representations of the Holy Spirit. Cf. Bauckham, *Climax*, p. 164.

46 See for example Deut. 33.17; 1 Kings 22.11; Ps. 112.9; Dan. 7.21.

47 There are two other characters in Revelation who have multiple horns: The great dragon has seven heads and ten horns (12.3), while the beast from the earth has two horns like a lamb (13.11). The perfect number of seven horns on the Lamb's head is clearly envisaged by John as superior to these alternative claims to power.

48 Cf. L. W. Hurtado, 1985, 'Revelation 4—5 in the Light of Jewish Apocalyptic Analogies', *Journal for the Study of the New Testament*, vol. 25: 105–24; Russell Morton, 2001, 'Glory to God and to the Lamb: John's Use of Jewish and Hellenistic/Roman Themes in Formatting His Theology in Revelation 4—5', *Journal for the Study of the New Testament*, vol. 83: 89–109.

49 See the discussion of the third rider on p. 152.

50 Cf. John 1.29, 36; 4.14; 7.38; 10.1–18.

51 Boxall, *Revelation*, p. 191.

52 See the discussion of the 144,000 on pp. 96–8.

53 The image of marriage between God and the people of Israel is a strong tradition (e.g. Isa. 54.1–8; Ezek. 16.8–14; Hos. 1—3). Cf. Boxall, *Revelation*, p. 269. That the bride of the Lamb is to be identified with the Church becomes clear in 21.9, where she is seen to be synonymous with the new Jerusalem. On this see p. 110.

54 On Jesus as the true light in the Johannine tradition see e.g. John 8.12; 8.5; 1 John 2.8–9; on Jesus as the temple see e.g. John 2.19–21.

55 Cf. Rev. 7.17; John 4.14.

56 Cf. John 6.27. The idea of 'sealing' denoting ownership by God is also found in the Apocalypse of Elijah 1.9–10, 'The Lord said, "I will write my name upon their forehead and I will seal their right hand, and they will not hunger or thirst"'; and 5.4–6, 'Now those upon whose forehead the name of Christ is written and upon whose hand is the seal, both the small and the great, will be taken up upon their wings and lifted up before his wrath. Then Gabriel and Uriel will become a pillar of light leading them into the holy land.' Translated by O. S. Wintermute in James H. Charlesworth (ed.), 1983, *The Old Testament Pseudepigrapha Vol. 1*, New York: Doubleday, pp. 736–7, 750. For further information see the discussion in Stephen S. Smalley, 2005, *The Revelation to John: A Commentary on the Greek Text of the Apocalypse*, London: SPCK, p. 183.

57 Peter C. Craigie, 1983, *Psalms 1—50*, Word Biblical Commentary, vol. 19, Waco, Texas: Word Books, pp. 62–9.

58 Cf. Rev. 1.5; 4.2; 6.17; 11.15–18.

59 Cf. Rev. 5.10; 20.6.

60 Beale identifies a number of other examples within the New Testament of similarly condensed accounts of the life of Jesus: John 3.13; 8.14; 13.3; 16.5, 28; Rom. 1.3–4; Rev. 1.5, 17–18; 2.8. Cf. Beale, *Revelation*, p. 639.

61 For comprehensive discussions of the arguments surrounding the identity of the rider on the white horse in Chapter 6 see Beale, *Revelation*, pp. 375–8, and Smalley, *Revelation*, pp. 148–151.

62 Irenaeus, *Against Heresies*. 4.21.3, 'For to this end was the Lord born, the type of whose birth he set forth beforehand, of whom also John says in the Apocalypse: "He went forth conquering, that He should conquer."' Translated by Philip Schaff. Available from *Christian Classics Ethereal Library* http://www.ccel.org/ccel/schaff/anf01.ix.vi.xxii.html. Victorinus, the third-century AD theologian, makes a similar point when he says: '[T]he white horse is the word of preaching sent to the world with the Holy Spirit' (Ante-Nicene Fathers vii.350). Quoted in Judith L. Kovacs and Christopher Rowland, 2006, *Revelation*, Oxford: Blackwell, p. 79.

63 New American Standard Bible.

64 Cf. Rev. 1.14; 2.17; 3.4–5, 18; 4.4; 6.11; 7.9, 13–14; 19.11, 14; 20.11.

65 Cf. Bauckham, *Theology*, p. 19; Craig R Koester, 2001, *Revelation and the End of All Things*, Grand Rapids: Wm. B. Eerdmans, pp. 82–4.

66 Stephen Finamore, 1997, 'God, Order and Chaos: A History of the Interpretation of Revelation's Plague Sequences and an Assessment of the Value of R. Girard's Thought for the Understanding of These Visions', DPhil Thesis: Oxford University, 1997, p. 261.

67 Some who do identify this rider as Christ are Edmondo F. Lupieri, 2006, *A Commentary on the Apocalypse of John*, trans. Maria Poggi Johnson and Adam Kamesar, Italian Texts and Studies on Religion and Society, Cambridge: Wm. B. Eerdmans, p. 143; Eugene H. Peterson, 1988, *Reversed Thunder: The Revelation of John and the Praying Imagination*, San Francisco: Harper Collins, p. 75; John Sweet, 1979, *Revelation*, London: SCM Press, pp. 137–8. In his forthcoming book, *God, Order and Chaos: René Girard and the Apocalypse* to be published by Paternoster Press, Finamore argues convincingly in favour of this position. Cf. also Finamore, 'God, Order and Chaos', pp. 240–63. These do, however need to be set against the following list of significant commentators who disagree: David E. Aune, 1998, *Revelation 6—16*, Word Biblical Commentary, vol. 52B, Nashville: Thomas Nelson Publishers, p. 393; Richard Bauckham, 1993, *The Climax of Prophecy: Studies on the Book of Revelation*, Edinburgh: T&T Clark, p. 179; Beale, *Revelation*, p. 377; G. R. Beasley-Murray, 1974, *The Book of Revelation*, New Century Bible, London: Oliphants, p. 131; Boxall, *Revelation*, p. 107; G. B. Caird, 1984, *The Revelation of St. John the Divine*, 2nd edn, London: A & C Black, p. 80; Wilfrid J. Harrington, 1993, *Revelation*, Sacra Pagina, vol. 16, Collegeville, Minnesota: The Liturgical Press, p. 91; Howard-Brook and Gwyther, *Unveiling Empire*, p. 141; Grant R. Osborne, 2002, *Revelation*, Baker Exegetical Commentary on the New Testament, Grand Rapids, Michigan: Baker Academic, p. 277; Pablo Richard, 1995, *Apocalypse:*

A People's Commentary on the Book of Revelation, New York: Orbis Books, p. 69; Smalley, *Revelation*, p. 151; Allen Kerkeslager, 1993, 'Apollo, Greco-Roman Prophecy, and the Rider on the White Horse in Rev 6:2', *Journal of Biblical Literature*, vol. 112: 116–21.

68 Cf. 3 Macc. 2.11.

69 Cf. Isa. 62.2–3.

70 From Adam's naming of the created order over which he had dominion (Gen. 3.19–20), to the Jewish tradition of not speaking the divine name aloud, names and power have a long association within Jewish culture.

71 Cf. Isa. 65.15.

72 YHWH; cf. Ex. 3.14. See the detailed discussion in Beale, *Revelation*, pp. 953–7.

73 Cf. Isa. 11.3–4.

74 Cf. Rev. 1.16; 2.12; 19.21; Isa. 11.4; 49.2.

75 Cf. Rev. 12.5; Ps. 2.9.

76 Cf. Rev. 14.19–20; Isa. 63.2–3.

77 The battle of Harmagedon is so named because John describes it as taking occurring at 'the place that in Hebrew is called Harmagedon' (16.16). This is a reference to the hill of Megiddo, the site of two significant battles in antiquity, both against invading Egyptian forces. The first took place in the fifteenth century BC, and the only records of it are found within Egypt itself. The second is recorded in the Old Testament (2 Kings 23.29), and took place in 609 BC, resulting in the death of Josiah. On both occasions, the Egyptian forces prevailed over those of Canaan/Israel. When John symbolically locates the final battle between good and evil, he chooses this historic battle site as his setting.

78 Boxall, *Revelation*, p. 278.

79 Cf. Rev. 1.9; 6.9; 19.13; 20.4.

80 Cf. 1 John 1.1–4.

81 Cf. Rev. 1.8; 4.8; 11.17; 16.15.

82 See the discussion of the 'eternal city' on p. 158.

83 Cf. Rev. 21.6; John 19.30.

84 See the discussion of merkabah mysticism on p. 14.

85 1 Enoch 14.8–22, 'And I kept coming (into heaven) until I approached a wall which was ... surrounded by tongues of fire; and it began to frighten me. And I came into the tongues of the fire and drew near to a great house ... As for its floor, it was of fire and above it was lightning and the path of the stars; and as for the ceiling, it was flaming fire. And I observed and saw inside it a lofty throne – its appearance was like crystal and its wheels like the shining sun; and (I heard?) the voice of the cherubim; and from beneath the throne were issuing streams of flaming fire. It was difficult to look at it. And the Great Glory was sitting upon it – as for his gown, which was shining more brightly than the sun, it was whiter than any snow ... the flaming fire was round about him, and a great fire stood before him. No one could come near unto him from among those that surrounded the tens of millions (that stood) before him.' Translated by E. Isaac in Charlesworth (ed.), *Pseudepigrapha Vol. 1*, pp. 20–1.

86 Cf. Ex. 15.6, 12; Ps. 16.11; 20.6; 44.3; 108.6; Isa. 41.10.

87 Cf. Dan. 12.1.

88 Cf. Matt. 25.31f.

89 This is indicated by the use John makes here of the vision of the enthroned ancient of days from Dan. 7.9.

90 Cf. Isa. 43.19.

91 Cf. John 19.30.

92 Cf. Isa. 55.1.

93 See the discussion of the fate awaiting those whose names are not written in the book of life on pp. 137–9.

94 'Pneumatology' means 'doctrine of the Spirit'. Charles comments: 'There is no definitely conceived doctrine of the Spirit in our author.' R. H. Charles, 1920, *A Critical and Exegetical Commentary on The Revelation of St John*, 2 vols., Edinburgh: T&T Clark, vol. 1, p. cxiv; while Aune ascribes the personified Spirit to a 'Second Edition' of the Apocalypse, commenting that: 'In earlier layers of Revelation, the role and function of the Spirit is primarily associated with an apocalyptic understanding of inspiration.' David Aune, 1997, *Revelation 1–5*, Dallas: Word Books, p. 36.

95 R. Waddell produces an extremely helpful overview of recent attempts to engage with the pneumatology of Revelation, following which he concludes: 'The survey has shown that a consensus has yet to be reached on a definition of the role of the Spirit in Revelation, so that the question, "What is the role of the Spirit in the Apocalypse?" remains open.' Robby Waddell, 2006, *The Spirit of the Book of Revelation*, Journal of Pentecostal Theology Supplement Series, vol. 30, Blandford Forum: Deo Publishing, pp. 36–7. The most comprehensive engagement with this topic before Waddell is in Bauckham, *Climax*, pp. 150–73.

96 Cf. Ezek. 2.2; 3.12.

97 Cf. the second to fourth century AD Christian text The Ascension of Isaiah 6.10–12, 'And while he was speaking with the Holy Spirit in the hearing of them all, he became silent, and his mind was taken up from him, and he did not see the men who were standing before him. His eyes were indeed open, but his mouth was silent, and the mind in his body was taken up from him. But his breath was (still) in him, for he was seeing a vision.' Translated by M. A. Knibb in James H. Charlesworth (ed.), 1985, *The Old Testament Pseudepigrapha Volume 2*, The Anchor Bible Reference Library, New York: Doubleday, p. 165. For Jewish examples of humans being translated into the heavenly realm see Russell, *Method & Message*, pp. 166–9.

98 Translated by E. Isaac in Charlesworth (ed.), *Pseudepigrapha Vol. 1*, p. 49.

99 Cf. Bauckham, *Climax*, p. 151.

100 Cf. Rev. 2.1, 8, 12, 18; 3.1, 7, 14. See also the discussion of the presentation of Jesus as the author of the seven letters on pp. 69–70.

101 This obscure passage can have two possible meanings. Boxall summarizes: '[Either] the witness of Jesus is understood as ... the witness that Jesus himself bore ... [or] it [is] a reference to the Holy Spirit, "the Spirit which inspires prophecy".' Boxall, *Revelation*, p. 270.

102 See the discussion on pp. 113–14.

103 Bauckham observes that, 'traditionally the inspiration of Scripture had as its corollary the inspiration of the reader of Scripture or the reading community. The Spirit who inspired the Scripture also inspires its believing readers to accept

it as God's message and to understand it.' Richard Bauckham, 1998, 'Scripture and Authority', *Transformation*, vol. 15, no. 2: 5–11, p. 6.

104 See the discussion of the seven spirits of God on pp. 119–20. Bauckham treats the seven spirits as a symbol for the Holy Spirit, based on John's use of Zech. 4.1–14. He then goes on to identify the seven spirits with the seven horns and the seven eyes of the Lamb, seeing these functioning together as representing the Spirit of Christ at work in the world. Cf. Bauckham, *Climax*, pp. 162–6. An alternative interpretation is offered by Boxall who suggests that the seven spirits should be understood as the 'angels of the presence' who are before the throne of God in Jewish mythology. Cf. Boxall, *Revelation*, p. 99.

105 Cf. 2 Cor. 1.22; Eph. 1.13; 4.30. See further the discussion of those sealed on pp. 96–8.

5

The People of God

Within the dramatic scheme of Revelation, the people of God assume a surprisingly large number of different guises. The intention of this chapter is to untangle some of this complexity, and to see how John uses the different images to convey his theological understanding of the people of God. In all of these different metaphors for God's people, John has his recipients in mind first and foremost. He is inviting his audience to identify themselves within the text, and to relate to the various situations in which the people of God find themselves in the course of the drama as it unfolds.

The servants of God and of Jesus Christ

The first verse of the Apocalypse introduces the four major characters in the drama: Jesus Christ, God, John, and the servants of God (1.1). These servants are the intended recipients of the revelation, which has passed from God to Jesus to an angel to John before finally being read by those in the seven churches (cf. 22.6). It is unlikely, however, that John is seeking to limit the 'servants' to being just those in the named churches of 1.11; rather, he has in view here all those who comprise the people of God. The defining feature of the faithful in this designation is that they are called *servants* or *slaves* (οἱ δοῦλοι)[1] of *God*; John wants his audience to realize that they exist in a state of perpetual slavery. They may not be the bonded slaves of Roman citizens (although some would have been, as revealed by Paul's instruction to the Ephesian Christian slaves to obey their earthly masters in Eph. 6.5), and some of them may have been slave-owners (cf. Eph. 6.9). However, from John's perspective they are all inevitably subject to a form of ideological slavery to the powerful forces of evil enshrined in the economic, political and social institutions of the Roman Empire. The only freedom he sees from this slavery is to be found in a different form of servitude; namely slavery to God himself (Paul makes a similar point in Rom. 6.16–23). The only way of escaping the dominion of the evil kingdom, manifested in the system represented by the Emperor on the throne in Rome, is to switch allegiance to the one

91

seated on the higher throne in heaven. By John's understanding, people have only two options: they are either enslaved to the beast, or to God, and there is no middle ground.[2] This slavery, unlike physical slavery, is a choice that each person can make; individuals have freedom to decide where their allegiance lies.

The servants of God are presented as those who obey their master's will, through reading, hearing and keeping the words of the prophecy given to them by Jesus, and who are blessed by doing so. They are those who will be the recipients of the seven beatitudes of Revelation as they live out their lives in faithful witness to the gospel of Jesus Christ,[3] and who are encouraged to listen to what the Spirit is saying to the churches through the words of the prophecy.[4] The nature of their obedience to the gospel therefore lies in both hearing and keeping, in listening and obeying.

On three occasions in Revelation, John speaks of God's 'servants' as 'prophets' (10.7, 11.18; 22.9) and in all three instances he clearly has the Church in view. The use of the qualifying phrase 'the prophets' serves to highlight the role that the whole community of believers plays in the prophetic testimony to Jesus (19.10).

In the vision of the new Jerusalem, the servants are seen worshipping both God and the Lamb on the throne (22.3). They are able to surpass Moses' experience as they commune with God face to face (22.4; cf. Exod. 33.20–3), and are marked on the forehead with the name of God and the Lamb (22.4; cf. 7.3; Exod. 28.36–8); the divine mark (contrasting with the mark of the beast in 13.16–17) indicating that their allegiance is now to God as his servants for ever.

The saints

'The saints' is another image John uses for the people of God. As with the image of the 'servants' of God, this is a picture far wider in scope than simply an indication of those who attend the seven churches of Asia Minor. Those saints ransomed by the Lamb are described as coming 'from every tribe and language and people and nation' (5.9). They represent the suffering Church seeking to exist in a world that is hostile to their presence. So it is that within John's vision, Satan and the beast are permitted to make war on the saints (13.7; 20.9). Although these attacks are mitigated by an assurance that the tribulation will not last for ever (13.5; 20.3c), nevertheless the experience of the Church in the world is that blood is still shed in the present (16.6; 17.6; 18.24). The saints are therefore called to remain faithful in their witness even in the face of persecution, as they endure in difficult circumstances (13.9–10), holding fast to the faith of Jesus (14.12), and conquering the forces of evil that would seek to take them captive (2.7, 11, 26, 28; 3.5, 12, 21). Similarly, the people of God are called to come out from the great whore, and to not take part in her sins (18.4). This command to flee should not be understood as a command literally to leave Rome, but rather as a symbolic instruction to disentangle themselves from the corrupt and seductive power structures that are opposed to the coming kingdom of God.[5]

The deeds of endurance and righteousness performed by the saints facing opposition do not pass unobserved, and become in due course the bridal gown of the bride of Christ (19.18).[6] Similarly, the prayers of the suffering, struggling saints are not unheard or unanswered, but rather are seen before the throne of God as the incense in the bowls poured out on the heavenly altar and burned, becoming the fire that is poured back on the earth as the judgements of God (5.8; 8.3–4f.). So it is that the saints are not to be left suffering on the earth for ever; since they have before them a promise that they will be rewarded at the final judgement (11.18), while their present experience of hardship and sorrow should be transformed into rejoicing because God has passed judgement against those who had oppressed them (18.20). Although they are unnamed, it is the saints who are in view in the new Jerusalem as those who no longer experience death, mourning, crying or pain (21.3–4),[7] who receive the promised water of life (21.6),[8] and who have conquered to become the children of God (21.7).[9] In this vision, promises made to the children of Israel are appropriated to whole Church. The divine adoption promise to the Jewish inhabitants of the earthly Jerusalem, 'So shall you be my people, and I will be your God' (Jer. 11.4), is applied to those who dwell in the new Jerusalem as the renewed people of God (21.3). While the Apocalypse opened with an address to the 'servants' of God, the close is addressed to the 'saints'; the conclusion of the words of the prophecy is a blessing on those who overcome and endure to the end (22.21).

The seven golden lampstands

The seven golden lampstands are the first thing John sees in his opening vision in Chapter 1. Having just heard the heavenly voice like a trumpet commanding him to write to the seven churches, he turns to see whose voice has spoken, and sees seven golden lampstands with 'one like a son of man' standing in the middle of them (1.12–13). The mystery of the identity of the lampstands is solved a few verses later, when they are identified as the seven churches (1.20), an image that recurs in the introduction to the Ephesian letter (2.1). The background for the use of golden lampstands lies within the Old Testament, where they feature as part of the furniture both in the tabernacle in the wilderness,[10] and later in the temple in Jerusalem,[11] symbolizing the light of the presence of God. In his vision, the post-exilic prophet Zechariah sees the golden lampstand (*menorah*) with seven lamps on it (Zech. 4.3),[12] symbolizing the all-seeing eyes of the Lord (Zech. 4.10). In John's reworking of this material, the presence of God in the world is now to be found in the midst of the churches, who shine with the divine light of Jesus.[13]

The seven stars, or 'the angels of the churches'

In John's vision of the 'one like a son of man', he sees seven stars held in the figure's right hand (1.16; cf. 2.1). These are identified as being 'the angels of the seven churches' (1.20), and each of the seven letters to the churches is addressed: 'To the angel of the church in …' followed by the name of the relevant city (2.1, 8, 12, 18; 3.1, 7, 14). The initial image of the seven stars is influenced by the description in the book of Daniel of the wise as shining 'like the brightness of the sky', and of those who lead others to righteousness as being 'like the stars for ever and ever' (Dan. 12.3).[14] This representational role of stars as metaphors for groups of the righteous is echoed in John's description of the angels of the churches as stars, shining their light in a world of spiritual darkness.[15] They are held within the right hand of Christ, symbolizing protection and security. The situation facing the seven churches may have been one of darkness and oppression, but when seen from heaven's perspective, their light shines and they are safe within the hand of Christ.

More complex is the relationship between 'the angels of the seven churches', and the seven congregations themselves. Various suggestions have been offered to account for the fact that the letters are addressed to the 'angels' rather than to the congregations directly.[16] Some have pointed to the idea of 'guardian angels', whereby each congregation has a specific angelic being watching over it in the heavenly realm.[17] Others have suggested that the angels should be equated with the pastoral leaders of the individual congregations, or the 'messengers' carrying the text to each congregation. Others point to the Zoroastrian understanding of human communities having heavenly counterparts.[18] One of the more interesting approaches to this text is that offered by W. Wink, who suggests that the angel of each church is a spiritual representation of the totality of that congregation. This is not simply a dramatic personification, but is rather a coalescing of the spiritual identity of the congregation into a single entity: 'Angel and people are the inner and outer aspects of one and the same reality … The one cannot exist without the other.'[19] In this way, when the letters are addressed to the 'angels' they are simultaneously addressed to the congregations. Wink provocatively suggests that all Christian communities exist in this way on both an earthly and spiritual plane, and that it is therefore appropriate to speak of (and to) the 'angel' of any congregation. He says: 'The angel gathers up into a single whole all the aspirations and grudges, hopes and vendettas, fidelity and unfaithfulness of a given community of believers, and lays it all before God for judgement, correction, and healing.'[20]

The twenty-four elders

The twenty-four otherwise unidentified elders have provided fertile ground for the imaginations of interpreters over the centuries. They have been variously identified as, among others, the twenty-four descendents of Levi,[21] the twelve patriarchs of Israel plus the twelve apostles, the twenty-four star gods of the zodiac, and twenty-four martyrs.[22] However, the most satisfying solution is to see them as another heavenly representation of the people of God. It has been seen already that within John's scheme, angelic beings can function as heavenly symbols of the earthly Church (cf. 1.20). In the image of the twenty-four elders therefore, the Church is seen in glory, ranged before the throne of God, offering worship to the one on the throne and encouraging John in his visionary activity.

The word John uses to describe the twenty-four, $\pi\rho\epsilon\sigma\beta\acute{u}\tau\epsilon\rho\sigma\varsigma$, ('elders'), is found elsewhere in the New Testament as a descriptor for individuals who function representatively for the wider body of the Church (cf. Titus 1.5; James 5.14). John sees them seated on twenty-four thrones arranged around the throne of God (4.4), forming part of the heavenly court which passes judgement on evil and vindicates the righteous (cf. 1 Kings 22.19; Rev. 20.4). Their white robes, golden crowns, and harps echo the description of the Church found elsewhere in Revelation (4.4; 5.8),[23] and the Lamb is seen standing among the elders in a similar fashion to the 'son of man' figure standing among the lampstands (5.6).[24] Significantly, the twenty-four elders hold the bowls of incense which are the prayers of the saints (5.8).[25] When the four living creatures sing, the elders fall before the one on the throne in worship, casting their crowns before him in a symbolic gesture of subservience (4.9–10).[26] Their song continues that of the living creatures, affirming God's role as creator of all things, in direct opposition to competing claims that come from the seat of power in Rome (4.11).

In all of the cases cited above, the twenty-four elders function as a unit. However, there is an additional role undertaken by one of the elders, who speaks to John directly. If the elders are thought of as being an angelic representation of the Church, then this puts the elder who addresses John in the role of the interpreting angel.[27] He comforts John when he is in distress because no one can be found to open the scroll, and points to the one who can break the seals (5.4–5). This elder appears on his own again when he asks John to identify the great multitude and, when John declares his ignorance, goes on to supply the answer that they are those who have come out of the great ordeal (7.13–14).

The 144,000 who have the seal of God on their foreheads

There are occasional images in Revelation that have attracted dispro-portionate attention within the interpretative tradition (for example, the number of the beast in 13.17–18, the millennium in 20.1–7), and the image of the 144,000 easily falls into this category.[28] They first come into view in Chapter 7, before the opening of the seventh seal (8.1). The series of judgements that have followed the opening of the first six seals are paused, and an angel proclaims: 'Do not damage the earth or the sea or the trees, until we have marked the servants of our God with a seal on their foreheads' (7.3). It has already been noted that the 'servants of God' are to be equated with the Church, and that the mark they receive on their foreheads from the angel with the seal of God is indicative of their allegiance to God in heaven rather than to the forces of evil in the world.[29] The nature of the 'seal of God' with which the 144,000 are marked is left undefined, although it is described as 'the father's name' (14.1).[30] However, a possible explanation of its nature may be found in the Pauline language of being sealed with the Holy Spirit. In his letter to the church in Ephesus, one of the seven churches of Asia Minor,[31] Paul twice speaks of the Spirit as God's seal on believers (Eph. 1.13; 4.30; cf. 2 Cor. 1.22). This is in contrast with the seal of Judaism, which Paul equates with the practice of circumcision (Rom. 4.11).[32] If this under-standing lies behind John's use of the 'seal of God', then it is the presence of the Spirit in believers that marks them as the people of God.

In the vision of the 144,000 that follows, the Church is seen by John as 12,000 from each of the twelve tribes of Israel (7.4).[33] Throughout Revelation, John appropriates imagery from the Old Testament, par-ticularly in relation to the Israelites as the people of God, and reapplies it to the Christian churches. Here in Chapter 7, the Church is pictured as a large but finite number, contrasting with the small and fragile size of the seven congregations of Asia Minor. The number 144,000 should not be understood literally;[34] in common with other numbers in Revela-tion it carries symbolic significance. The number 12 typically indicates completeness, and in this case (12 × 12,000) it represents the complete number of those who comprise the renewed Israel, the army of the Lamb, who are at war in the world with their master against the forces of evil.

The contrast between those marked with the seal of God on their foreheads and those marked with the seal of the beast becomes appar-ent in 9.4, where the Church is spared from the persecution wrought by the locusts from the bottomless pit. Just as the Israelites were spared the worst excesses of the plagues of Egypt,[35] so the renewed Israel are spared the plague of locusts in Revelation 9. However, it should not be thought that being sealed by God grants the Church immunity from all experiences of tribulation. Contemporary pre-tribulationist interpretations[36] that suggest the Church can expect to be removed from the earth, rather than having to endure and overcome through difficulty,[37] generally fail to take into account the fact that Revelation is written to congregations facing persecution and difficulty. John's intention is to indicate to these churches that their status as those who belong to God means that they will be spared the judgements due upon those systems that continue to oppose the lordship of Jesus.

The 144,000 come into view again in Chapter 14, where they are seen as the army of the Lamb, standing with him on Mount Zion. This image of the Church arrayed behind the Lamb, as a mighty army prepared for battle, is heaven's perspective on the struggling churches addressed by the book of Revelation. They might experience their present circumstances as a time of failure and difficulty, as they seek to remain faithful to their Lord in the face of overwhelming opposition, but in John's vision they are a great force on the brink of victory over the very forces that would seek to crush them (14.1). The sound of heavenly worship is heard echoing over the battlefield (14.2), and the 144,000 are the only people who can learn this new song of heaven (14.3; cf. 5.9–10). The worship offered in the seven churches may not have always have resounded with the echo of divine harpists, but from heaven's perspective the worship of the Church is the dramatic accompaniment to the final victory of good over evil. The content of the new song is hinted at by the fact that the 144,000 are twice described as $\dot{\alpha}\gamma o\rho\dot{\alpha}\zeta\omega$ ('redeemed' 14.3, 4), reminding John's audience that their status as those sealed with the name of God came about at the price of the Lamb's death. The only other occurrence of 'redeemed' in Revelation is found in the 'new song' sung by the four living creatures and the twenty-four elders (5.8–10), where praise is directed to the Lamb who has ransomed the saints for God by his shed blood. Only the Church, it seems, can sing of the victory won through the sacrifice made by Jesus on the cross. The redeemed Church is then described as the 'first fruits' (14.4), recalling the Jewish practice of offering the first fruits of the harvest as a sacrifice to indicate that the greater harvest also belongs to God (Ex. 23.16–19). The Church, namely the symbolic 144,000 who have taken the path of sacrifice and who have endured through tribulation, are therefore to see themselves as the first fruits of a greater harvest which is still to come.

The description of the 144,000 as those 'who have not defiled themselves with women, for they are virgins' (14.4) is another aspect of this ecclesiological image that has attracted an undue level of speculation and interpretative ingenuity,[38] largely due to the image of male virginity being misunderstood as a literal characteristic of the redeemed. John's use of this image is dependent on his understanding of the Church as priests before God (1.6; 5.10; 20.6), since in the Levitical law, the act of sexual intercourse was regarded as making both partners ritually unclean for the next day (Lev. 15.18), thus requiring the Jewish priests to abstain from sexual relations before entering a period of priestly service in the temple. In John's image, the Church is seen as ritually pure – not just through a temporary abstinence from behaviour that would defile, but pure in a virginal sense as befits the bride of the Lamb (19.7; 21.9f.). The Church has been washed pure by the blood of the Lamb, and is now dressed in white robes indicative of this purity (7.14; cf. 3.5, 18). Also possibly in view here is the Jewish practice of soldiers ensuring they were ritually pure before a battle (e.g. 1 Sam. 21.4–5),[39] giving rise to an image of the 144,000 as the army of the Lamb, ritually pure and ready to fight. Their purity is emphasized by the statement that 'in their mouth no lie was found; they are blameless' (14.5), an image dependent on a Christological reading of the suffering servant from Isaiah, who is 'like a lamb that is led to the slaughter' (Isa. 53.7), and who after death is declared innocent with the phrase, 'there was no deceit in his mouth' (Isa. 53.9). The innocence of the Lamb is imputed to those redeemed by his shed blood; the purity of the suffering servant (Isa. 53.11) becomes the purity of 'the servants' who endure through suffering.[40]

John sees the army of the Lamb singing once again in 15.2–4 standing beside the sea of glass and fire, just as the Israelites stood beside the Red Sea having come out of slavery in Egypt (Ex. 15.1f.). The song offered here by the 144,000 is described as the song of Moses and of the Lamb, and this parallel makes it clear that the Church is in the process of a new exodus. They have passed through the waters (of baptism), they are no longer under the tyranny of the beast, and they are embarking on their journey to the new promised land, the new Jerusalem, led on the journey and in song not by Moses, but by the Lamb.

The 144,000 appear again as the army of heaven, assembled behind the rider on the white horse at the final battle of Harmagedon. They are still dressed in white linen but now they are also riding white horses (19.14). The beast and the kings of the earth gather to make war on the rider and his army (19.19), but the army of heaven have no need to participate in this battle: their fight against the forces of evil in the world is already over for the forces of the beast have been defeated by the rider on the white horse. Ultimately the battle against evil is won, not by the efforts of the Lamb's army, but through the truth of the gospel as it comes from the mouth of Christ himself (19.21). Those who have 'conquered' are victorious through their faithful witness to the one who conquers.

The great multitude

In Chapter 7, John *hears* the number of the redeemed as 144,000 (7.4–8), and it has been suggested above that this should be understood as a figurative representation of the whole Church, the army of the Lamb (14.1). This image, while not a literal enumeration of the saints, portrays the Church as a subset, albeit a vast subset, of the totality of humanity. It is therefore significant that within John's scheme, the number he *hears* is contrasted with what he then *sees*: 'After this I looked, and there was a great multitude that no one could count, from every nation, from all tribes and peoples and languages, standing before the throne and before the Lamb, robed in white, with palm branches in their hands' (7.9). John *hears* a vast but finite number from Israel, but *sees* an uncountable number from every nation. The relationship between what John *hears* and what he *sees* here is greatly debated among interpreters. Suggestions include:

1) John *hears* the salvation of all ethnic Israel, but *sees* the salvation of the worldwide Church;
2) John *hears* the salvation of Jewish Christians, but *sees* the salvation of Gentile Christians;
3) John *hears* the salvation of Christian martyrs, but *sees* the salvation of all Christians;
4) John *hears* the salvation of all Christians as the renewed Israel, but *sees* the salvation of all Christians as a multi-ethnic totality;
5) John *hears* the salvation of all Christians as the first-fruits (cf. 14.4), but *sees* the salvation of a much greater number as the full harvest.

If the 144,000 are to be understood as the Church in its totality, then either 4) or 5) become the most likely suggestion. The relationship between what John *hears* and what he *sees* in Revelation is complex,[41] but there is a clear pattern that *vision* frequently clarifies *audition*. The table overleaf illustrates something of the relationship between what John *hears* and what he *sees*.

If item 4) in the above list is correct, then the 144,000 and the great multitude are to be understood as two different images for the same group of people, with the Church being in view in both instances. However, the description of the 144,000 as the 'first-fruits' in 14.4 renders this reading problematic, because the full harvest signified by the first-fruits moves out of sight. A more satisfying solution is to adopt suggestion 5) which sees the 144,000 as the Church, with the great multitude signifying the ultimate presence before the throne of God and the Lamb of a far greater number than those who have enlisted in the army of the Lamb. In this way, the vision of the great multitude (the full harvest) represents the ultimate fulfilment of the task undertaken by the 144,000 (the first-fruits). This reading is strengthened by the imagery John uses

John Hears		John Sees	
1.10, 4.1	A loud voice like a trumpet	1.12	Seven golden lampstands
		1.13	One like the son of man
		4.1	In heaven an open door
5.13	Every creature in heaven and on earth and under the earth and in the sea, and all that is in them, singing	6.1	The Lamb opening the seven seals
6.1, 3, 5, 7	The four living creatures call out 'Come!'	6.2, 4, 5, 8	The four coloured horses with their riders
7.4–8	The number of those who were sealed as 144,000 from Israel	7.9	A great multitude that no one could count, from every nation
9.16	The number of the troops of cavalry as two hundred million	9.17	The horses with riders wearing breastplates the colour of fire
14.2–3	A new song which no one could learn except the 144,000	14.6	An angel with an eternal gospel to proclaim to those who live on the earth – to every nation and tribe and language and people
14.13	A voice from heaven	14.14	One like the son of man
19.9	An angel saying, 'Write this: blessed are those who are invited to the marriage supper of the Lamb'	19.11	Heaven opened and a white horse with a rider called Faithful and True
21.3	A loud voice from the throne saying, 'See, the home of God is among mortals'	21.22	No temple in the city, for its temple is the Lord God the Almighty and the Lamb

of the 'palm branches' in the hands of the great multitude (7.9), recalling the Jewish festival of Booths held at the end of the harvest (Lev. 23.39–43; Neh. 8.15). At this festival the Jews made shelters out of palm branches and lived in them for seven days, as a reminder that they lived in shelters when they fled from slavery in Egypt at the time of the Exodus. John's use of this image signifies that the great harvest is now complete, as the great multitude have made their own new exodus out from slavery. Interestingly, the vision of the great multitude is one in which ethnic and linguistic variety can still be distinguished; this is no monochrome vision of cloned saints in glory, but is rather a representation of the full diversity of humanity before the throne of God.

The victory that the Lamb has won for the multitude is further symbolized by the 'white robes' (7.9, 13–14; cf. 3.5; 19.8) they wear as they cry out in worship to God and the Lamb (7.10, 15). The victory garments of the martyrs (6.11) have become the clothing of the great multitude, as the faithful witness of the first fruits under persecution is seen to have resulted in the ingathering of the great harvest. The robes of the multitude are said to have been washed clean by the blood of the Lamb (7.14); a complex and stark image indicating that forgiveness and purity are available to humanity only through the sacrificial death of Jesus on the cross. This image of the great multitude is located in the future, after the time of tribulation has ended, with John recording the end result of the endurance of the saints in the present. For the great multitude, the time of punishment, suffering and judgement has now passed (7.16), and they are shepherded by the Lamb who leads them to the water of life and removes their tears of pain and loss (7.17).

Having been glimpsed proleptically in Chapter 7 following the sequence of seal-openings, the great multitude are heard singing in heaven following the sounding of the seventh trumpet (11.15), before returning to view towards the end of the Apocalypse in Chapter 19 after the vision of the destruction of Babylon. Here they participate once again in the heavenly worship directed towards the one on the throne (19.1–3, 6–8). God's judgements on the oppressive and evil systems of Babylon are now complete, and the great multitude proclaim that, 'his judgements are true and just; he has judged the great whore who corrupted the earth with her fornication' (19.2). They then continue in praise, as they rejoice at the marriage of the Lamb and his bride, the Church (19.7). The final sight of the great multitude in Revelation is found just a few verses from the end, where the voice of Jesus proclaims a blessing on those who wash their robes, because they have 'the right to the tree of life and may enter the city by the gates' (22.14). The reference to washed robes is a recurrence of the image of robes washed white in the blood of the Lamb (7.14), indicating that those who are the recipients of this blessing can only be so because of the sacrificial death of Jesus. The tree of life stands beside the river of the water of life in the new Jerusalem (22.2), and the great multitude gain entrance to it as promised (7.17). In a reversal of the situation in Eden where access to the tree is ultimately denied to humanity,[42] in the new creation the nations have access to the tree of life through the open gates of the new Jerusalem.[43]

Every creature in heaven and on earth and under the earth and in the sea

The image of universal praise implicit in the image of the great multitude is explicit in the song of praise offered to the Lamb by 'every creature in heaven and on earth and under the earth and in the sea, and all that is in them' (5.13). To those living in the churches John was writing to, this all-encompassing image of worship offers a glimpse of the end result of their faithful endurance. In the new creation towards which the vision is heading, not only does every human acknowledge the Lamb, but also every living creature, every angelic being, and even every thing that exists in the underworld.[44]

There is an inherent tension present within the book of Revelation, between images such as that under consideration here, which seem to indicate a universal acceptance of the lordship of Christ as the end result of the faithful witness of the Church, and other images which indicate judgement on those forces that remain in opposition to the kingdom of Christ. It is worth contemplating this tension as it plays itself out over the remaining images for the people of God. 'Who are the people of God?' becomes the crucial question.

The two witnesses

This ecclesiological image occurs only in Chapter 11 of the Apocalypse. There is a complex history of interpretation for this image,[45] and even a cursory search of the Internet reveals countless contemporary attempts to continue the tradition of identifying the two witnesses.[46] There is, it seems, no shortage of candidates past, present or future and as with all attempts to correlate the imagery of Revelation with contemporary events, sufficient ingenuity on the part of the interpreter can generate a whole plethora of apparently plausible options.

The account of the two witnesses occurs as an interlude between the judgements of the sixth and seventh trumpets (9.13, 11.15). John has just consumed the scroll (10.10), the contents of which are then revealed in the narrative of the two witnesses that follows (11.3–13). Just as the scroll was bitter-sweet in its taste, so it is bitter-sweet in its message:

THE PEOPLE OF GOD

John sees the Church represented as two witnesses who faithfully carry out their task (11.3–6), die a martyr's death (11.7–10), and finally receive vindication from God in the sight of their enemies (11.11–13). The glory of the gospel proclaimed in the world and the ultimate destination of believers tastes sweet to John, but the suffering and martyrdom faced by the faithful in the meantime leaves him sick in his stomach.

The background for this image lies in the Jewish requirement that a single witness was insufficient in serious legal cases;[47] and so in John's vision the *two* witnesses therefore indicate the validity of the testimony of the Church. This is an image of the Church at work in the world, prophesying and witnessing to the gospel. The sackcloth worn by the witnesses contrasts with the white robes worn by those who have come through the great ordeal (7.14); the two witnesses are still wearing clothes of mourning and repentance,[48] indicative of the sorrow and tribulation that remain part of their present experience as they prophesy the need for repentance and turning to Christ.

The time of witnessing is limited to a symbolic 1,260 days. This number is variously expressed in Revelation, and is derivative of Daniel's description of the period of persecution experienced by the people of God at the hands of Antiochus Epiphanes ('a time, two times, and half a time', Dan. 7.25; 12.7; cf. Rev. 9.27). So three and a half years (12 months × 3½) = half of seven years = 42 months (30 days × 42) = 1,260 days. The following table illustrates the different uses John makes of this time-period.

11.2	42 months	The period during which the nations trample the holy city
11.3	1,260 days	The period during which the two witnesses prophesy wearing sackcloth
12.6	1,260 days	The period during which the woman is nourished in the wilderness
12.14	3½ years	The period during which the woman is nourished in the wilderness
13.5	42 months	The period during which the beast is allowed to exercise authority

It can be seen that the images invoked by John's use of this time-marker complement each other, and serve to indicate the Church's existence in a hostile world.[49] In John's scheme, the period during which the Church must endure and faithfully witness will not be without limit.

The two witnesses are also described as 'two olive trees' and 'two lampstands' (11.4). Lampstands have already been seen to function as an image for the Church (cf. 1.20), but the pairing of lampstands with two olive trees has a specific antecedent in the Old Testament. Zechariah reports a vision of a seven-branched lamp (a temple menorah) in the middle of two olive trees, from each of which comes a branch dripping oil to keep the lamps topped up (Zech. 4.2–3, 12–14). In Zechariah's context of the rebuilding of the temple, the two branches of the olive trees represent royalty (the governor Zerubbabel) and priesthood (the High Priest Joshua) as the two driving forces for the re-establishment of the temple. In John's reworking of this passage, the royal and priestly functions of the Church (cf. 5.10) are instrumental in the establishment of God's presence on the earth in the midst of his people (cf. 21.22). As the two witnesses seek to prophesy in the world, their words of truth overcome those who oppose their testimony (11.5),[50] and they have a Moses-like ability to call on plagues to lend their testimony still greater force as they seek to persuade the nations to repent (11.6).[51]

However dramatic and miraculous the signs, and however convincing the testimony, the bitterness of the scroll (10.10) is found in the persecution and martyrdom endured by the two witnesses, as they follow their saviour through suffering and death (11.7–10).[52] The ultimate act of prophetic witness required of the Church is that of faithfulness unto death. Just as Jesus' body lay in Jerusalem for three days, so the bodies of the two witnesses lie in the symbolic city for three and a half days. For John's congregations, facing the prospect of persecution and martyrdom, John's reworking here of what could so easily be construed as defeat is fundamental to his ongoing call to his churches to persevere through hardship. Death is not to be seen as defeat; rather it is the inevitable result of faithfully witnessing to the gospel. This point is reinforced through what comes next, for just as the Church must follow its Lord into the grave, so it will also rise with him to new life (11.11–13). The final glory of the witness, death and resurrection of the faithful is found in the glory given to God by the inhabitants of the city in 11.13. The earthquake and death of a tenth of the city is the final trigger for the repentance of the many. Just as Pharaoh remained hardened to the signs and plagues sent by Moses, only repenting at the plague of death (Ex. 11.4–10; 12.29–31), so the nations are oblivious to the signs and plagues performed by the witnesses, until the last sign, the plague of death, causes them to turn and give 'glory to the God of heaven'. In this way, the death of the faithful witnesses is transformed into the great sign that leads to the repentance of the nations.

The temple in Jerusalem

In Chapter 11 of Revelation, John is handed a measuring rod and instructed to measure the dimensions of the temple, the altar and those who worship there (11.1–2). Although elsewhere in Revelation 'the temple' is heavenly,[53] here John is measuring the earthly temple in Jerusalem. This is an image for the earthly Church, and in a scene that parallels the numbering of the 144,000 (7.3–8), John is invited to comprehend the size of the Church, and once again finds that it is a number that can be counted and measured.

The temple is then contrasted with the outer courtyard, which John does not measure, because it is 'given over to the nations' (11.2). Once again in John's scheme, the small and fragile nature of the Church in a large and hostile world is emphasized. John then records that the nations will trample over the 'holy city' for 42 months, a span that mirrors the length of time the two witnesses must prophesy (11.3). Here the point is again made that the period during which the Church must endure is limited. The 'holy city' is in this instance the earthly Jerusalem, and functions together with the 'outer court' of the temple, as an image for the context in which the Church must faithfully witness.[54]

The pregnant woman

The image of the pregnant woman (12.1–6, 13–17) is one that combines a variety of strands. There are a number of significant maternal figures from within the Judeo-Christian tradition who anticipate John's image to varying degrees: Mother Eve (Gen. 3.16, 20); Mother Israel (Isa. 26.17–18); Mother Jerusalem (Isa. 66.7–13); Mother Mary (Luke 1.30–3); and Mother Creation (Rom. 8.22). In addition to the Jewish background, there are also classical mythological echoes in John's image: such as the Greek myths of Gaia the earth-mother, and of Leto the wife of Zeus and mother to the twins Artemis and Apollo; and also the Egyptian myth of Isis the mother of Horus. In all of these traditions, the mother is threatened at the point of childbirth, not just through the natural dangers of delivery, but also through external forces seeking to endanger the child.[55] In John's story of this pregnant woman, once again the mother is endangered both by the pain of childbirth and by the forces of evil.

Within John's scheme, the pregnant woman is symbolic of the people of God down the ages, from ancient times to the present day. She is introduced in cosmological terms crowned with twelve stars symbolic of the twelve tribes of Israel (12.1).[56] Of particular significance to the interpretation of this image is the covenant made with Abraham:

God said to Abraham, 'As for Sarai your wife, you shall not call her Sarai, but Sarah shall be her name. I will bless her, and moreover I will give you a son by her. I will bless her, and she shall give rise to nations; kings of peoples shall come from her.' Then Abraham fell on his face and laughed, and said to himself, 'Can a child be born to a man who is a hundred years old? Can Sarah, who is ninety years old, bear a child?' And Abraham said to God, 'O that Ishmael might live in your sight!' God said, 'No, but your wife Sarah shall bear you a son, and you shall name him Isaac. I will establish my covenant with him as an everlasting covenant for his offspring after him ... my covenant I will establish with Isaac, whom Sarah shall bear to you at this season next year.' (Gen. 17.15—19, 21)

The image of the pregnant Sarah is thus integral to the fulfilment of the Abrahamic covenant that all the nations of the earth shall be blessed through their descendants (cf. Gen. 18.18), and John's image of the people of God as a pregnant woman giving birth to a son underscores his concept of the people of God as good news to all nations.

The child born to the woman is threatened by the dragon, but escapes to rule the nations with a rod of iron, and is taken to heaven to the throne of God (12.2–5). This story symbolically rehearses the birth of the Messiah to the people of Israel, together with a compressed summary of the life, resurrection and ascension of Jesus. The woman flees into the wilderness where she is nourished by God for 1,260 days (12.6). The use of this number ties the identification of the woman to that of the two witnesses from the previous chapter (11.2–3), and indicates that the time of difficulty experienced by the Church will not be unending. In John's vision, the Church finds itself in the wilderness, struggling to stay alive, utterly dependent on God for its ongoing existence as it seeks to survive the onslaught of the dragon (12.13–17). Using mythological terms, John has located the woman and her other children, the Church of John's day (12.17), in a situation of new exodus: on the path from slavery to the promised land, surviving on the divine nourishment of, not manna, but bread and wine.[57]

Those whose names have been written in the book of life, who are not marked with the mark of the beast from the sea, and who do not worship the image of the beast from the sea

This trilogy of images are related descriptors for the people of God, and they denote those who have made a positive choice to distance themselves from the forces of the beast, by resisting the mark of ownership so readily accepted by others, and by refusing to bow down and worship any other than the one on the throne in heaven. The way John sees it, almost the whole earth has bought into the lies of the beast, and it is only those whose names are written in the Lamb's book of life who can resist the idolatrous call to worship the beast (13.8; cf. 3.5; 21.27). This image for the Church paints a picture of an embattled minority, struggling to exist against almost overwhelming forces of opposition. It is in this context that the phrase, 'everyone whose name has not been written from the foundation of the world in the book of life of the Lamb' (13.8), needs to be heard. This should not be taken to imply specific predestination of the elect; rather it is written to assure the beleaguered congregations of the seven churches that their destiny is secure from eternity and to eternity. To ask questions about the doctrine of predestination of this image is to have unfair expectations of the text, for this is not a matter that it seeks to address. Rather, John's intention in using this imagery is to reassure those in his congregations that their experience of difficulty, as they seek to remain steadfast in witnessing to the gospel, is not a sign of their defeat. In fact such trials are to be expected as a sign of their faithfulness. This is reinforced when those who refuse to worship the image of the beast are killed (13.15),[58] and those who resist the mark of the beast face economic hardship (13.16–17). However, although the immediate future for the Church according to this image is one of trials and suffering, their eternal destination remains secure: those who conquer the beast and its image, and resist the mark of its name, are seen by John as the army of the Lamb, standing unharmed beside the sea (15.2–3).[59]

Those under the altar – the martyrs

The first-century reality of martyrdom presented a specific pastoral problem that John sought to address in his text.[60] Faithfulness and endurance under persecution and hardship is something which John sees as a universal calling for believers; but faithfulness unto death is, it seems, the ultimate fate of only a few. John does not outline a theology in which all believers should seek martyrdom, although he would have them all contemplate the possibility that they may be so called. John is writing to those who are the survivors; who have seen others martyred in the past, and who may have to face that same fate themselves in the future. Hence, the martyrs exist as a specific group within the scheme of Revelation, a distinct subset of the people of God, worthy of special consideration because of the level of sacrifice made by them in the service of their Lord.

The martyrs appear for the first time in Chapter 6, following the opening of the fifth seal. The souls of the martyrs are seen under the altar in heaven (6.9), an image that is reminiscent of the Levitical instruction to pour out the blood of the sacrificial animal at the base of the altar in the temple.[61] John here portrays the martyrs as sacrifices made in the tradition of the temple sacrifices of Judaism; they have followed the sacrificial Lamb through violent death on account of their testimony to the word of God. From the perspective of John's congregations, those who have been martyred have departed from the earth, and so it is that within John's vision their souls are seen resting under the altar,[62] from where they cry out for vengeance and justice (6.10). However, the time for the final vindication of the martyrs is not yet at hand, and so they are given white robes, symbolic of their ritual purity, and instructed to wait a little longer, 'until the number would be complete both of their fellow servants and of their brothers and sisters, who were soon to be killed as they themselves had been killed' (6.11). John is still, it seems, expecting martyrdom to occur among the churches, as they continue to witness faithfully to the word of God. However, the perspective of the congregations on martyrdom can now change. No longer is it to be seen as an experience of defeat; rather those who make this sacrifice have their eternal souls secure in the throne room of heaven.

At the pouring out of the third bowl, the judgement on the earth results in the rivers turning to blood as a fitting punishment for the shedding of the blood of the saints (16.4–6). This is followed by a voice from the altar, which proclaims the justice of God's judgement (16.7). The martyrs are here heard affirming the righteousness of the punishments being visited on the forces of evil.

The souls of those who have been martyred are next seen by John sitting on thrones with authority to judge, and are described as those who have been beheaded for their testimony to Jesus and the word of God (20.4–6). They are identified as a subset of those who had not worshipped the beast or its image, and had not received its mark on their foreheads or hands, indicating once again that while general tribulation may be the norm for those in John's churches, the specific fate of martyrdom is seen by him as something to which only a few are called. While the image of the millennium will be examined in more detail below,[63] it is sufficient to note at this point that it functions as a metaphor for the vindication of the martyrs. The moment of defeat, the death of a believer, is transformed into a moment of triumph, as the martyrs reign with Christ for a thousand years; the victory of the beast is transformed into the binding of the beast. This is heaven's perspective on martyrdom. John then refers to a complex scheme, mentioned in passing earlier in Revelation (2.11), of first and second death and resurrection. The following table may help to clarify his thinking:

[First death]	Not specifically mentioned	Physical death. Experienced either as martyrdom (cf. 6.9–11), or more usually as a result of the natural ending of life (cf. 14.13).

'First resurrection'	Rev. 20.4–5	Experienced by the martyrs at the start of the thousand years. The martyrs do not therefore take part in the second resurrection.
	Rev. 20.6	Those who experience the first resurrection are not subject to the power of the second death. Rather they are blessed and holy, as they both serve as priests and reign with Christ for a thousand years.
[Second resurrection]	Not specifically mentioned	Experienced by the rest of the dead (20.5, 12–13), and followed by the great judgement.
'Second death'	Rev. 20.14; Rev. 21.8	The Lake of fire into which are thrown: • The beast and the false prophet (19.20) • The Devil (20.10) • Death and Hades (20.14) • Anyone whose name was not found written in the book of life (20.15; 21.8). Not a physical death, but a spiritual burning of all that cannot exist within the new Jerusalem. There are some who are specifically excluded from the power of the second death: • Those who 'conquer' (2.11) • Those who have experienced the first resurrection (20.6) • Those whose names are written in the book of life (20.15).

To summarize, in Chapter 20 John combines the metaphor of the millennium with the image of the first resurrection, to portray the martyrs as safe and secure with God, fulfilling both royal and priestly functions in heaven just as the Church fulfils these same functions on the earth (20.6).[64] Heaven's perspective on the martyrs is that they minister in heaven on behalf of the Church, while waiting to be joined by their sisters and brothers from the congregations on earth. From the earth's perspective, the experience of martyrdom is thus transformed, and becomes a moment of great triumph over those forces that would seek to destroy the Church.

Those who have died in Christ

The corollary of the division of the faithful into those who are martyred and those who die by other causes, is that there is a much larger group of the dead known simply as 'the rest of the dead' (20.5). These are the departed souls of those who have died without being martyred. They are the subject of the second beatitude of Revelation (14.13), paralleling the martyrs who are the subject of the fifth beatitude (20.6).[65] Both the martyrs and the rest of the dead are described as 'resting' (6.11; 14.3), in contrast with the situation of those in the seven churches, who are still labouring (cf. 21.7). The non-martyred dead are brought to life at the second resurrection, and are judged according to their works (20.12–13; cf. 11.18).

The new Jerusalem, or 'the bride of the Lamb'

These two related images for the people of God occur almost exclusively in the final four chapters of Revelation. The only exception to this is in the letter to the Philadelphian church, where the congregation are promised: 'If you conquer ... I will write on you the name ... of the city of my God, the new Jerusalem that comes down from my God out of heaven, and my own new name' (3.12). Marking with a name is a symbol of ownership (cf. 7.3; 14.9), and here John records the promise that those who conquer will be marked with the name of the new Jerusalem (cf. 2.17; 19.12). This image of the new Jerusalem functions, together with the image of Babylon, to provide two alternative symbolic cities to which humans can give their loyalty. John's challenge is to come out of Babylon and assume citizenship of the new Jerusalem (cf. 18.4).[66]

To those living in the Roman Empire, the symbolic power of cities was manifest; in every city of the Empire, symbols of the power and might of Rome were to be found in art and architecture, poetry and prose. The propaganda of empire was everywhere. In this context, John invites his audience to see themselves as citizens of the coming city, the new Jerusalem. He fully recognizes that the present experience of his audience is one of difficulty and struggle, and so he pictures the holy city in the present as an embattled fortress assailed by the forces of Satan (20.7–9). However, John does not leave the image there. Rather, he provides heaven's perspective of the new Jerusalem descending to the earth, no longer a city under siege. To this end, the forces of Satan are seen as destroyed, along with the Devil, as they attack the holy city (20.9–10). Following the destruction of the forces of evil, the new Jerusalem descends from heaven in fulfilment of the prayer of the Church that the kingdom of God come to the earth (21.2).[67]

The extended descriptions of the architecture (21.11–21) and interior (21.22—22.5) of the new Jerusalem are complex, and combine imagery from numerous Old Testament texts.[68] The key point that John is making in his description is that the holy city exists as the antithesis to the satanic city of Babylon, as the place where the faithful saints find their ultimate security and residence. The message to John's audience is clear: the Church's true home is not Babylon, but is the new Jerusalem, and as the faithful people of God they are called to live as citizens of the coming city rather than as slaves of the present metropolis.

In Jewish tradition Jerusalem is often depicted as a woman,[69] and in Revelation the new Jerusalem is pictured as a bride prepared for her wedding day. The new Jerusalem is identified as the bride of the Lamb: 'Then one of the seven angels … said to me, "Come, I will show you the bride, the wife of the Lamb." … and [he] showed me the holy city Jerusalem coming down out of heaven from God' (21.9–10).[70] This combination of images offers John's recipients a tantalizing and hopeful series of pictures, designed to encourage them to remain faithful to the gospel while living in the midst of the satanic empire. As they conquer the forces of Babylon, their status is confirmed as the pure bride of the Lamb, destined for eternal union with their saviour.

The image of the marriage of the Lamb occurs for the first time in Chapter 19, when it is announced that, 'the marriage of the Lamb has come, and his bride has made herself ready' (19.7). The already confusing image of a slain yet living Lamb gets even more unusual as it emerges that he is about to marry. It is important when reading passages such as this to remain true to the symbolic world John is constructing, where the Lamb functions as an image for the crucified and risen Jesus. Just as the new Jerusalem and Babylon function as symbolic opposites, so do the bride of the Lamb and the whore of Babylon (17.1f.). The following table illustrates some of the key ways in which the descriptions parallel each other.[71]

Using these stark images, John invites his audience to understand that people have a choice as to whom they will seek union with: they can either participate in the corrupt and corrupting pleasures of the whore of Babylon, or they can seek the purity and faithfulness that is found through fidelity to Christ. In this way, the Church is in the process of becoming the bride of the Lamb as the faithful distance themselves ever further from the whore. The moment of the union of the Lamb with his bride is described in eschatological terms, as the wedding feast of the Lamb and the bride (19.7, 9). The marriage supper of the Lamb parallels the descent of the new Jerusalem to the earth, as the moment when the kingdom of God comes on the earth in fulfilment of the prayer 'your kingdom come' (cf. 11.15; 21.2).

The final union of Christ and Church is pictured by John as a wedding,

	new Jerusalem / Bride of the Lamb		Babylon / great whore
19.8	'clothed with fine linen, bright and pure' (cf. 21.2)	18.16	'clothed in fine linen, in purple and scarlet' (cf. 17.4)
21.2	'the holy city, the new Jerusalem, coming down out of heaven'	18.5	'her sins are heaped high as heaven'
21.9–10	'Then one of the seven angels	17.1	'Then one of the seven angels
	who had the seven bowls		who had the seven bowls
	came and said to me,		came and said to me,
	"Come, I will show you		"Come, I will show you
	the bride, the wife of the Lamb."		the judgement of the great whore"'
	And in the spirit he carried me away to a great, high mountain'	17.3	'So he carried me away in the spirit into a wilderness'
21.18	'the city is pure gold'	17.18	'adorned with gold
21.19	'adorned with every jewel'		and jewels
21.21	'the twelve gates are twelve pearls'		and pearls' (cf. 17.4; 18.12, 16)
21.24	'the kings of the earth will bring their glory'	17.18	'rules over the kings of the earth'
21.26	'People will bring into it the glory and the honor of the nations'	18.11	'the merchants of the earth weep and mourn for her, since no one buys their cargo anymore'
21.27	'nothing unclean will enter it' (cf. 21.8)	17.4	'full of abominations and the impurities of her fornication'
21.27	'only those who are written in the Lamb's book of life'	17.8	'[those] whose names have not been written in the book of life'
22.1–2	'the river of the water of life ... and the leaves of the tree ... for the healing of the nations'	18.24	'the blood of prophets and of saints, and of all who have been slaughtered on earth'

22.14	'Blessed are those who … may enter the city by the gates'	18.4	'Come out of her, my people, so that you do not take part in her sins, and so that you do not share in her plagues'
22.4	'his name will be on their foreheads'	17.5	'on her forehead was written a name, a mystery: "Babylon the great"'

and yet the language of weddings normally evokes, not so much endings, as beginnings. There is inherent *promise* in the image of a bride, an anticipation of what is to come. A wedding involves celebration of the possibility of new life coming into being as a result of the consummation of the relationship between bride and groom; all of which raises the question of who the offspring of the marriage between Christ and the Church might be. The Abrahamic covenant is predicated upon the barren Sarah becoming miraculously pregnant, thereby beginning the 'great nation' through whom all nations will be blessed (Gen. 15.5; 18.18).[72] It may be that John's image of the consummation of the relationship between Christ and the Church has in view the ultimate fulfilment of the promise made to Abraham. If this is the case, the marriage of the Lamb and the bride may not be so much the end of the story as the beginning. Rather than seeing the union of Christ and Church as the final goal of creation, the possibility arises that there is a much greater inheritance due to the Church as the Abrahamic covenant finds its completion in the proclamation of the gospel for 'every nation and tribe and language and people' (14.6).

The final appearance of the bride of the Lamb in Revelation is to be found just a few verses from the end, where the bride and the Spirit issue a call for everyone who is thirsty to 'come' and take the water of life (22.17; cf. John 7.37–8). This invitation forms the conclusion to the main drama of the Apocalypse,[73] and it is significant that the final act of the bride is to sound a note of universal summons.[74] If the bride is understood as the Church, the first fruits of the great harvest (14.4), then it is an act of supreme theological theatre for John to close in this liturgical way:

[Cantor]	The spirit and the bride say 'come.' And let everyone who hears say,
[7 Congregations]	*Come.*
[Cantor]	And let everyone who is thirsty come. Let anyone who wishes take the water of life as a gift. (22.17)

By this reading, the Church and the Spirit join their voices in calling the nations of the world, those beyond the gates of the new Jerusalem (cf. 22.15), to enter in and drink from the river of life which runs through the city (22.1–2). The Abrahamic covenant thus finds its fulfilment as the people of God become a source of blessing to all peoples, drawing them from the ruins of Babylon to their eternal destination in the new Jerusalem.

Draw your own conclusions

- Who are the 'people of God' in the book of Revelation?
- Why does John contrast the 144,000 with the 'great multitude'?
- Why does John portray the Church as a suffering minority?
- Why do you think John makes 'the martyrs' a special case?
- How do you understand John's image of the 'second death' in the lake of fire?
- Do you think John's vision of the new Jerusalem is ultimately 'inclusive' or 'exclusive'?

Notes

1 Cf. Rev. 2.20; 6.11; 7.3; 19.2, 5; 22.3, 6.

2 Cf. Matt. 6.24; Luke 16.13.

3 Rev. 1.3; 14.13; 16.15; 19.9; 20.6; 22.7, 14.

4 Rev. 2.7, 11, 17, 29; 3.6, 13, 22.

5 Wes Howard-Brook and Anthony Gwyther, 2001, *Unveiling Empire: Reading Revelation Then and Now*, New York: Orbis Books, pp. 183–4.

6 See the discussion of the new Jerusalem on pp. 110–14.

7 Cf. Rev. 7.17; Isa. 25.8.

8 Cf. Rev. 7.17; Isa. 49.10.

9 Cf. 2 Sam. 7.14.

10 Cf. Ex. 25.31–7; 37.17; Lev. 24.4; Num. 8.2–4.

11 Cf. 1 Kings 7.49; 1 Chron. 28.15; 2 Chron. 4.7, 20; 13.11.

12 Cf. Ex. 25.37; Num. 8.2.

13 Cf. Matt. 5.14; John 1.5; 8.12; 9.5; 11.9; 1 John 1.5.

14 A similar thought is expressed in 1 Enoch 104.2, 'But now you shall shine like the lights of heaven' Translated by E. Isaac in James H. Charlesworth (ed.), 1983, *The Old Testament Pseudepigrapha Vol. 1*, New York: Doubleday, p. 85.

15 Cf. Matt. 5.14; John 8.12; 9.5.

16 The following summary is drawn from Stephen S. Smalley, 2005, *The Revelation to John: A Commentary on the Greek text of the Apocalypse*, London: SPCK, p. 58.

17 Cf. Dan. 10.13–14, 20–1. The Ascension of Isaiah speaks of 'the angel of

the church which is in the heavens' (Asc. Isa. 3.15). Translated by M. A. Knibb in Charlesworth (ed.), *Pseudepigrapha Vol. 2*, p. 160.

18 G. R. Beasley-Murray, 1974, *The Book of Revelation*, London: Oliphants, p. 69.

19 Walter Wink, 1986, *Unmasking the Powers: The Invisible Forces That Determine Human Existence*, Philadelphia: Fortress Press, p. 70.

20 Wink, *Unmasking the Powers*, p. 73.

21 The two passages represented in the following table give evidence of divergent traditions. What is significant is the number 24, being twice 12, the number of the tribes of Israel:

The four generations descended from Levi 1 Chron. 23.6–24					The twenty-four courses of the Levitical Priesthood 1 Chron. 24.7–18	
Levi	Gershon	Ladan	1.	Jehiel	1.	Jehoiarib
			2.	Zetham	2.	Jedaiah
			3.	Joel	3.	Harim
		Shimei	4.	Shelomoth	4.	Seorim
			5.	Haziel	5.	Malchijah
			6.	Haran	6.	Mijamin
			7.	Jahath	7.	Hakkoz
			8.	Zina	8.	Abijah
			9.	Jeush	9.	Jeshua
			10.	Beriah	10.	Shecaniah
	Kohath	Amram	11.	Aaron	11.	Eliashib
			12.	Moses	12.	Jakim
		Izhar	13.	Shelomith	13.	Huppah
		Hebron	14.	Jeriah	14.	Jeshebeab
			15.	Amariah	15.	Bilgah
			16.	Jahaziel	16.	Immer
			17.	Jekameam	17.	Hezir
		Uzziel	18.	Micah	18.	Happizzez
			19.	Isshiah	19.	Pethahiah
	Merari	Mahli	20.	Eleazar	20.	Jehezkel
			21.	Kish	21.	Jachin
		Mushi	22.	Mahli	22.	Gamul
			23.	Eder	23.	Delaiah
			24.	Jeremoth	24.	Maaziah

22 Smalley, *Revelation*, p. 116.

23 Cf. Rev. 2.10; 3.5, 11, 18; 7.14; 14.2; 15.2.

24 Cf. Rev. 1.13; 2.1.

25 Cf. Rev. 15.7.

26 Cf. Rev. 5.8, 14; 11.16–18; 19.4.

27 Cf. Dan. 8.15–26.

28 For a detailed discussion of various suggestions as to how this image may be interpreted see G. K. Beale, 1999, *The Book of Revelation*, Carlisle: The Paternoster Press, pp. 416–23. See also Judith L. Kovacs and Christopher Rowland, 2004, *Revelation*, Oxford: Blackwell, p. 102.

THE BOOK OF REVELATION

29 Cf. Rev. 9.4; 13.16; 22.4. See also the discussion of the servants of God on pp. 91–2. John is here alluding to the practice of marking slaves or prisoners of war with a brand or tattoo to denote ownership. Cf. Ian Boxall, 2006, *The Revelation of St John*, London: Continuum, p. 196.

30 Cf. Rev. 22.4; Ezek. 9.4.

31 Cf. Rev. 1.11; 2.1.

32 Cf. Smalley, *Revelation*, p. 184.

33 For an analysis of John's presentation of the twelve tribes cf. Richard Bauckham, 1991, 'The List of the Tribes in Revelation 7 Again', *Journal for the Study of the New Testament*, vol. 42: 99–115.

34 Some, such as the Jehovah's Witnesses, regard this number as literally indicative of those who will reign with Christ during the millennium, with a wider number entering into the new Jerusalem. Cf. A. A. Hoekema, 1963, *The Four Major Cults*, Exeter: The Paternoster Press, pp. 261–2.

35 Cf. Ex. 8.22–4; 9.4–7, 26; 10.21–3.

36 See the discussion of tribulationism on p. 32.

37 For example, 'God's Word tells us that there will be one generation of believers who will never know death. These believers will be removed from the earth before the Great Tribulation'. Hal Lindsey and C. C. Carlson, 1970, *The Late, Great Planet Earth*, Grand Rapids: Zondervan, p. 127. Tina Pippin commented more recently that: 'In fundamentalist interpretations of the Apocalypse in the United States believers are told not to worry about or be responsible for the possible human ending of the world through nuclear accident or environmental pollution. The Rapture will occur first and all the believers will be taken up into the clouds with Jesus and will not suffer the tribulation on earth.' Tina Pippin, 1999, *Apocalyptic Bodies: The Biblical End of the World in Text and Image*, London: Routledge, p. 98. For a helpful discussion of pre-tribulationism as a 'misuse' of the book of Revelation, see Ian Paul, 2003, 'The End of Interpretation: Use and Misuse of the Book of Revelation', *The Bible in Transmission*. Retrieved from http://www.stjohns-nottm.ac.uk/html/images/revelation-misuse.pdf. Accessed 19.12.07.

38 See Kovacs and Rowland, *Revelation*, pp. 161–2, for a brief survey of the complex interpretative history of this image. Tina Pippin draws attention to the feminist concerns highlighted by an all-male virginal elect. Cf. Pippin, *Apocalyptic Bodies*, pp. 122–3.

39 Intriguingly, this tradition of celibacy before a battle is still current even in the UK: 'More than a third of male football fans abstain from sex the night before a big match, according to a survey.' Source: http://news.bbc.co.uk/sport3/worldcup2002/hi/other_news/newsid_2017000/2017239.stm. Accessed 2.8.2007. Additionally, 'Berti Vogts, the German football manager in 1994, banned his players from sex before games.' Source: http://news.bbc.co.uk/1/hi/magazine/3555734.stm. Accessed 2.8.2007.

40 Cf. Beale, *Revelation*, p. 746.

41 Cf. Rev. 5.11; 8.13; 22.8.

42 Cf. Gen. 2.9–10; 3.24; cf. Ezek. 47.12.

43 Cf. Isa. 60.11.

44 Cf. Phil. 2.10–11; Col. 1.20.

45 For a detailed discussion see Kovacs and Rowland, *Revelation*, pp.

126–30. The following is indicative of some of the suggestions they identify. The two witnesses have been variously identified as characters or themes as diverse as: Moses and Aaron; Enoch and Elijah; Elijah and Jeremiah; Peter and Paul; Matthew and John's Gospels; the Old and New Testaments; the law and the gospel; Francis of Assisi (AD 1181–1226) and Franciscan theologian Peter John Olivi (AD 1248–1298); Anabaptist leaders Jan Matthijs (d. AD 1534) and Caspar Schwenckfeld (AD 1490–1561); all Protestant preachers; the New Model Army of Cromwell's rebellion; William and Mary's reign of England after the Glorious Revolution (AD 1689–1694); Methodist founders Charles Wesley (AD 1707–1788) and George Whitefield (AD 1714–1770).

46 Typical examples include: two Jewish prophets who will proclaim the re-establishment of Israel's full territorial claims; or Great Britain and the United States of America.

47 Deut. 17.6; 19.15; cf. Matt. 18.16; 26.20; John 8.17; 2 Cor. 13.1; 1 Tim. 5.19; Heb. 10.28.

48 Cf. Ps. 30.11, Jonah 3.5–8.

49 Bauckham explores the complex relationship between these numbers, concluding that 12, 30, 42 and 1,260 are 'rectangular' numbers, to be compared with John's use of the 'square' number 144 (7.4; 14.1, 3; 21.17) representing the people of God, and the 'triangular' number 666 representing the beast (13.8). He concludes that, 'it may seem appropriate for the third class of number, the rectangular, to designate this ambiguous period in which the beast and the saints oppose each other.' Richard Bauckham, *The Climax of Prophecy: Studies on the Book of Revelation*, Edinburgh: T&T Clark, p. 401.

50 Cf. 1 Kings 18.38; Jer. 5.14.

51 Cf. Ex. 7.9–25.

52 Cf. Gal. 2.19; 6.17.

53 Cf. Rev. 3.12; 7.15; 11.19; 14.15, 17; 15.5–16.1; 16.17.

54 There is considerable discussion among scholars as to whether the 'holy city' of 11.2 is the earthly or heavenly Jerusalem. For an argument in favour of seeing it as the heavenly city see Beale, *Revelation*, p. 568.

55 Eve's children are promised the enmity of the Devil (Gen. 1.14–15); Israel's children face both the wrath of God and threats from surrounding nations (Isa. 26.20–21); Jerusalem and her children remain under continual threat both from their own unfaithfulness and from surrounding nations (Isa. 65.2–7); Mary's child is faced with fleeing to Egypt to escape Herod's attack (Matt. 2.14); Creation's children are held in bondage waiting for redemption (Rom. 8.23); Gaia's children by Uranus are hidden in Tartarus; Leto is pursued by Python the dragon; and Isis has to hide in the papyrus marshes to protect Horus from his evil uncle Seth.

56 Cf. Gen. 37.9; cf. Gen. 15.5.

57 Cf. Ex. 16.35; cf. 1 Cor. 11.26.

58 Cf. Dan. 3.6.

59 See the discussion of the 144,000 on pp. 96–8.

60 While it is unlikely that martyrdom was the current experience of the churches in Asia Minor at the time John was writing, nonetheless persecution under Nero was still within living memory, and the low-level harassment experienced by those in the churches would have left them alert to the possibility that state-orchestrated murder of believers might reoccur.

61 Lev. 4.7, 18, 25, 30, 34; 5.9; 8.15; 9.9; cf. Ex. 29.12; Lev. 1.15; 17.6.

62 This image has been used by those who have sought to develop a doctrine of an intermediate heavenly state for martyrs. However, this is to misunderstand the time frame of Revelation. John is seeking to present the heavenly perspective on the earthly situation, hence from heaven's viewpoint the souls of the martyrs are safe from the moment of death to all eternity.

63 See the discussion of the millennium on pp. 224–31.

64 Cf. Rev. 5.10; 11.4. It should not be thought that there is a contradiction here between the image of the martyrs reigning and serving as priests, and the image from Chapter 6 of them resting under the altar. These two images function in a complementary way, each conveying an important pastoral perspective on martyrdom (reigning with Christ, secure with God). It is only if they are treated literally that confusion arises.

65 Cf. Rev. 1.3; 16.15; 19.9; 22.7, 14.

66 See the further discussion of the new Jerusalem on pp. 231–6.

67 Cf. Matt. 6.9–10; Luke 11.2–4.

68 Particularly 1 Kings 6—7; Isa. 35, 54, 58—60; Ezek. 40—48. For a meticulous analysis of the background to John's imagery, see Beale, *Revelation*, pp. 1066–121. For a more light-hearted analysis of 21.16–17 consider the following: 'Few religions are definite about the size of Heaven, but ... the Book of Revelation ... gives it as a cube about 12,000 furlongs on a side. This is somewhat less than 500,000,000,000,000,000,000 cubic feet. Even allowing that the Heavenly Host and other essential services take up at least two thirds of this space, this leaves about one million cubic feet of space for each human occupant – assuming that every creature that could be called "human" is allowed in, and that the human race eventually totals a thousand times the number of humans alive up until now. This is such a generous amount of space that it suggests that room has also been provided for some alien races or – a happy thought – that pets are allowed.' Terry Pratchett, 2001, *The Last Hero*, London: Gollancz, p. 18.

69 Cf. Isa. 1.8; Jer. 4.31.

70 Cf. Rev. 21.2; Isa. 54.1–6; Jer. 31.32; Ezek. 16.8; Hos. 2.1–23.

71 This table is based on Beale, *Revelation*, pp. 1063–4, 1118–9; cf. also Richard Bauckham, 1993, *The Theology of the Book of Revelation*, Cambridge: Cambridge University Press, pp. 131–2.

72 See the discussion of the Abrahamic covenant in relation to the image of the pregnant woman on pp. 105–6.

73 Beyond this point is found only the concluding warnings (22.18–19), a final liturgical prayer (22.20) and the grace (22.21).

74 Boxall suggests that the prayer 'Come!' is here addressed to Christ alone, thereby paralleling the 'maranatha' ('Come, Lord Jesus!') prayer of 22.20. While this neatly sidesteps the issue of ending the Apocalypse on a note of universal invitation, it is problematic in requiring the first and second parts of 22.17 to function separately to each other. Cf. Boxall, *Revelation*, pp. 318–19.

6

The Inhabitants of Heaven and Earth

The inhabitants of heaven

The heavens in John's vision are populated with a panoply of angelic beings, who fulfil a number of functions within the heavenly realm.[1] This feature is far from unique to Revelation, and the profusion of angels is a common element found throughout apocalyptic literature. At one level, angels are intermediaries between God and humanity, described by Russell as 'celestial postmen'.[2] At another level, the angels fulfil the task of heavenly tour guide, ensuring that the visionary doesn't miss any of the important action.[3] It is when these two aspects combine, postman and tour-guide, that the angelic role becomes that of revealer of mysteries; explaining the events that the visionary is experiencing and imparting the secrets of the heavens.[4]

The archangels

The seven spirits of God, who are the eyes of the Lamb in the world

The opening vision of God on the throne in heaven evokes the image of a busy temple scene, with various characters occupied with different tasks, and it is in this context that the seven spirits of God are seen.[5] The description of them as 'seven flaming torches' in front of the throne (4.5) suggests Zechariah's vision of seven flaming lamps before the throne of God symbolizing the eyes of the Lord looking at the whole earth (Zech. 4.2, 10). In John's vision this image is adapted slightly, with the seven spirits described as the seven eyes of the Lamb sent out into the world (5.6). Whether functioning as the eyes of God, or the Lamb, or both, the seven spirits represent a personification of the all-seeing, all-knowing nature of the one seated on the throne. It is in this capacity that the seven spirits feature in the opening greetings of both the whole Apocalypse (1.4), and also the letter to the church in Sardis (3.1); the message comes from the one who knows, the one who sees, the one who understands.

It is likely that in his description of the seven spirits, John is drawing on the Jewish tradition of angelology, which identified angels of various ranks.[6] At the élite end of the ordering were two groups: the seven archangels,[7] and the 'angels of the presence'.[8] John combines these in his description of not only the seven spirits of God, but also the seven trumpet-angels and the seven bowl-angels.

The seven trumpet-angels

John sees seven angels before the throne, and they are handed seven trumpets following the opening of the seventh seal (8.1–2). As suggested above, the seven angels may be synonymous with the seven spirits of God, representing John's reworking of the Jewish traditions of seven archangels and 'angels of the presence'. Following the offering of the incense of the prayers of the saints, the seven angels make ready to blow their trumpets (8.6).

The background to trumpets being used as weapons of mass destruction is found in the narrative of the fall of Jericho (Josh. 6.1–20), where they are instrumental in the downfall of the city. Also, within the early Christian tradition the return of Christ was expected to be heralded with a trumpet's cry (Matt. 24.31), as the archangel (1 Thess. 4.16) sounds the 'last trumpet' (1 Cor. 15.52). In John's vision, the sounding of the first six trumpets begins the process of the judgement of God coming on the earth (8.7, 8, 10, 12; 9.1, 13). However, the angel of Jesus Christ proclaims that it will not be until the sounding of the seventh and last trumpet that 'the mystery of God will be fulfilled' (10.7). So it is that when the seventh angel blows his trumpet, voices are triggered in heaven proclaiming that: 'The kingdom of the world has become the kingdom of our Lord and of his Messiah, and he will reign forever and ever' (11.15). The seven trumpet-angels thus herald the judgements of God on the forces of evil in the world, as the kingdom of God breaks in upon the nations of the earth through the faithful witness of the followers of Jesus Christ.

The seven angels with seven bowl-plagues

The seven angels who will bring the last seven plagues upon the earth are introduced at the beginning of Chapter 15. The sequence of seven trumpets concluded some chapters earlier with the blowing of the seventh trumpet (11.15), and John returns to his series of sevenfold judgements on the earth with the seven bowl-plagues. It is unclear from the text as to whether the angels who pour out the bowls are the same archangels who blew the trumpets, but there is no reason to think that they are not. This would identify them as a further appearance of the seven archangels, yet they are examined separately here, because although they may be synonymous with the trumpet-angels, they also have their own dramatic identity within John's scheme.

The bowl-angels emerge from the temple wearing clothes appropriate to a priestly role (15.6),[9] and are given seven bowls filled with the wrath of God (15.7).[10] The bowls are seven of the 28 held by the elders and the living creatures in the opening vision of the throne room, where they contain the prayers of the saints (5.8).[11] The prayers of the churches have ascended to heaven, been burned on the altar, and now the fire of their burning is thrown back to the earth as judgement on evil and a vindication of the righteous. The seven bowl-angels accordingly pour the contents of their bowls out on the earth, and judgement comes on the forces of the beast (16.2; 16.3; 16.4; 16.8; 16.10; 16.12; 16.17) in a series of plagues reminiscent of those of the exodus.

Six of the bowl-angels pass from view at this point in the text, but one of them assumes the new role of interpreting angel. In this role as revealer of mysteries, this angel first invites John to witness the judgement of the whore, and then explains the mystery of the whore to John (17.1, 7). The same angel tells John to write a blessing on those invited to the marriage supper of the Lamb (19.9), and resists John's attempt to worship him, saying he is a fellow servant with John (19.10). The bowl-angel tells John to follow him so he can be shown the bride of the Lamb (21.9), and then measures the new Jerusalem (21.15). The angel tells John that the words of the book are trustworthy and true (22.6), and once again has to deflect John's attempt to worship him, repeating the fact that he is a fellow servant and directing John's worship to God (22.9). In this angel's final appearance, he tells John not to seal up the words of the prophecy (22.10).

The identity of this angel is not spelled out in Revelation. However, if it is correct that the bowl-angels, the trumpet-angels and the seven spirits of God are all different characterizations of the seven archangels, it becomes reasonable to identify the interpreting bowl-angel with Michael the chief archangel.

The mighty angel of Jesus Christ who speaks with a loud voice, takes a stand on the sea and the land, passes the scroll to John, destroys Babylon, and may be called Michael

It is in the role of intermediary that the angel of God first appears to John at the beginning of the Apocalypse, where the angel is the final link in the chain of revelation which runs: God → Jesus → angel → John (1.1). It is unclear from the Greek at this point διὰ τοῦ ἀγγέλου αὐτοῦ ('through his angel') as to whether this angel is the angel of God or the angel of Christ. However, identification as 'the angel of Jesus Christ' is subsequently indicated by his further appearances.

This angel next appears in Chapter 5, when he enquires with a loud voice as to who is worthy to open the scroll (5.2). This begins an association between this angel and the scroll, which continues in Chapter 10 where he once again functions as an intermediary or messenger for Jesus. In this instance, he delivers the scroll from the hand of Jesus to John (cf. 5.1–9). The transfer of the scroll exactly mirrors the sequence of revelation identified in Chapter 1: it starts in the hand of the one seated on the throne (5.1), passes to the Lamb (5.7), then to the angel (10.2), then finally to John (10.9–10). In this way, although the mediatorial role of this angel breaks down in Chapter 1 as John is addressed directly by the 'son of man' figure (1.17), nonetheless the chain of revelation is fulfilled through the delivery of the scroll.

The physical appearance of the angel bears a strong similarity to the description of the 'one like a son of man' (10.1; cf. 1.13–16), and is indicative of the fact that this is no mere angelic intermediary; this is the angel of Jesus Christ himself.[12] He is seen by John descending from heaven, in a dramatic reversal of the ascension of Jesus,[13] as he brings the scroll of Revelation to the earth. Having reached the earth he takes a stand on both the land and the sea (10.2), like a giant Colossus of Rhodes.[14] When he speaks, his voice is similarly impressive (10.3; cf. 5.2) and triggers the seven thunderclaps (10.3–4). The mediatory role for this angel then continues, as he raises his hand to heaven to receive the scroll from the Lamb. At this point, the angel is touching land, sea and sky in a demonstration of the universal dominion of Jesus over the entirety of creation (10.5–8). The angel proclaims that the mystery of God will be fulfilled when the seventh angel blows his trumpet (cf. 11.15), and then passes the scroll to John, warning him that it will taste sweet but will make his stomach bitter (10.9–10).

Smalley offers the compelling suggestion that this angel should be identified as the archangel Michael, who leads the angelic onslaught against the dragon (12.7–9).[15] If this is correct, then the actions of Michael in throwing the dragon to the earth parallel those of the mighty angel at the downfall of Babylon, where he violently throws the evil city into the sea (18.21).[16] This identification would also make the angel of Jesus one of the seven archangels of Jewish mythology, and therefore identify him as being both a trumpet-angel (8.1–2f.) and a bowl-angel (15.1f.; cf. 17.1f.). The angel of Jesus Christ makes his final appearances in the final chapter of the Apocalypse, where once again his mediatory function is stressed: 'It is I, Jesus, who sent my angel to you with this testimony for the churches' (22.16; cf. 1.1; 22.6).

A voice from the throne

On two occasions, an otherwise unidentified voice is heard coming from the throne of God. Although it is tempting to equate this voice with that of God or the Lamb, the context in both cases makes it clear that this cannot be the divine voice: in 19.5 the voice exhorts the servants of God to praise him, and in 21.3 it proclaims that God has made his home among people. In both cases, God is spoken of in the third person, indicating that this is not the voice of God. Rather, this is the voice of an angelic mediator. It is not possible positively to identify this angel, but his presence before the throne may indicate that, once again, this is Michael the archangel.[17]

Other angels

Two loud voices

There are two instances where an otherwise unidentified 'loud voice' calls from heaven. In the first of these, the voice calls the two witnesses up to heaven (11.12), thereby initiating the events surrounding the seventh trumpet (11.15); in the second, the voice provides an interlude in the story of the woman and the dragon, and proclaims the coming of the kingdom of God (12.10–12). It is impossible to identify these angelic voices with any accuracy, and suggestions as to their identity include God, Christ, an angel, or the heavenly multitude.[18]

The many angels surrounding the throne

While John's attention in the Apocalypse is usually given to specific characters and their actions, the whole drama is played out against a background of worship being offered by the countless multitude of other heavenly beings (5.11; 7.11).[19] The angelic multitude appear twice in Revelation, both times singing songs of devotion. In Chapter 5 they sing praise to the Lamb (5.11–12). This worship of Jesus is a significant feature of Revelation's Christology, as Jesus is worshipped alongside God (cf. 5.13–14). They are heard singing again in Chapter 7, and their song of praise is this time directed at God himself (7.11–12). In a direct challenge to the cult of emperor worship, in John's vision praise can only be offered to God and to the Lamb.

The four angels who restrain the four winds

Following the opening of the sixth seal, John sees four angels standing at the four corners of the earth, holding back the four winds of the earth

(7.1). The background to this image is found primarily in Daniel's vision of the four winds of heaven stirring up the sea and triggering the rising from the sea of four terrible beasts (Dan. 7.2–3).[20] Some have suggested identifying the four winds as the four horsemen (6.1–8),[21] but the text does not naturally lead to this conclusion. It is more straightforward to see the four winds, held back by the angels, as the agents of God's judgement.[22] The winds are restrained by the four angels, and the judgement sequence of the preceding chapter is temporarily interrupted, until the numbering of the 144,000 is complete (7.3). The pastoral impact of this image on John's audience is to assure them that the winds of judgement are within the control of God, and that the eternal security of the Church will not be put in jeopardy by the coming judgements on evil. Once the 144,000 are numbered, the destruction of the satanic forces begins again (8.5).

The angel who ascends from the rising of the sun

At the beginning of Chapter 7 four angels restrain the four winds from blowing on the earth, sea and trees (7.1). This unusual triad is repeated almost immediately by an angel who rises like the sun in the east, commanding the four angels not to harm 'the earth or the sea or the trees' until the 144,000 have been sealed (7.2–3). One might more naturally expect a fourfold designation of creation at this point, to match the four angels and the four winds.[23] However, in a parallel passage the scorpions from the pit are similarly told not to damage any tree, grass or green growth, while sparing those who have the seal of God on their foreheads (9.4). This association of trees with grass seems to indicate that what John has in mind here is the judgement of the first trumpet which occurs after the numbering of the 144,000, during which a third of the earth, trees and all the grass are burned up (8.7). This trumpet-judgement is a parallel of the Egyptian plague of hail and fire where all the trees and vegetation are burned up (Ex. 9.22–5). In this context of forthcoming plagues of judgement, the angel from the east fulfils a protective function for the servants of God in the churches. He has the seal of God with him (7.2), and uses this seal to mark the 144,000 on their foreheads (7.3).[24] The unleashing of judgement on the earth is delayed at his command until the Church is sealed. This should not be understood as indicating that the Church is removed from the earth before the judgement-plagues arrive; the faithful are still on the earth during the sounding of the trumpets, as the Israelites were still in Egypt during the plagues. The purpose of this image, for John's recipients, is to reinforce to them that in spite of the terrible judgements they have to live through on the earth, from heaven's perspective the winds of justice are under the control of God's angel, and the future of the faithful is secure because they have been marked with the seal of God (cf. Ex. 9.26).

The angel with a golden censer, who has authority over fire

Following the opening of the seventh seal and the sounding of the seven trumpets, there appears another angel carrying a golden censer[25] from which he pours incense onto the prayers of the saints on the altar before the throne (8.3).[26] The prayers and the incense burn, and the smoke rises before God (8.4).[27] This image of the prayers of the saints before the throne of God is intended to provide pastoral comfort to those in John's churches, who must on occasions have felt that their prayers were futile, given the overwhelming nature of the beast they were called to oppose. However, the image is not complete as a metaphor of mere assurance that prayers are heard. The angel then takes the censer, fills it with fire from the altar, and throws it back to the earth (8.5). This is then the trigger for the sounding of the seven trumpets and the series of judgements on evil that follow (8.6f.). It seems that, according to John's scheme, the prayers of the saints play a crucial role in the coming of divine judgement on the earth.

This angel reappears in Chapter 14, where he fulfils a similar function. He is described as 'the angel who has authority over fire' (14.18), and he commands the angel with the sickle to reap the vintage of the earth, an image for judgement on evil (14.19–20). Once again, this angel is instrumental in the outworking of the judgement of God on the earth in response to the prayers of the faithful (cf. 14.12).

Michael's heavenly army

The ongoing battle between good and evil that the seven churches saw themselves as participating in on a daily basis is presented by John as the earthly outworking of a similar battle in the heavenly realm. The difference between the two is that in heaven the decisive battle has already been won, whereas on earth the end to hostilities is yet to come, as evil will be conquered through the faithfulness of the saints. John expresses this tension in the story of the battle between Michael's heavenly army and the dragon and his satanic hordes (12.7–9). The dragon and his forces are thrown from heaven to the earth (cf. 8.8; 18.21), providing an explanation to John's audience of why it is that the battle now seems to be raging around them, while simultaneously assuring them that the forces of God are superior to those of the dragon. Michael has already been identified as the mighty angel (1.1), but the concept of the armies of heaven is also significant.[28] The background to this idea is found in Daniel's vision of Michael battling the angels of Persia and Greece (Dan.

10.13–21), although in Revelation Michael doesn't fight alone, but is joined by an army of angelic beings resembling the heavenly 'army of the Lord' who are seen in the Old Testament fighting alongside Israel.[29] John is not specific about who this angelic army are, but the image is constructed to assure the people in his congregations that they are fighting alongside Michael's army in the battle against evil.

The angel of the waters

The third bowl-angel pours his plagues into the rivers and springs thus causing them to turn to blood. This then elicits a response from an angel known as 'the angel of the waters' (16.5–6). However, rather than complaining at the divine justice affecting his realm, this angel instead offers an affirmation that the judgement of God is right and just. The angel of the waters interprets the plague of water that turns into blood as a fitting response to the persecution of the martyrs: as their blood has been shed, so those who have performed this persecution will be made to drink blood. This interpretative statement is helpful in understanding the scope of the bowl-plagues. It can appear on an initial reading that they represent a total judgement on the entire earth. However, the angel of the waters makes it clear that these are still sequences of judgement against those earthly forces that have sought to persecute, oppress and oppose the people of God. Those who tyrannize the Church are equated with the Egyptians oppressing the people of Israel, with the third bowl-plague recalling the Nile turning to blood at the command of Moses and Aaron (Ex. 7.17–21). In this way the faithful followers of the Lamb symbolically assume the role of Israel on the way from slavery to exodus, as the oppressive empire becomes subject to divine judgement.

The shining angel from the sun

This angel appears on two occasions, in both cases announcing the downfall of evil with a loud voice.[30] In the first instance the angel comes from heaven and makes the earth 'bright with his splendour', while announcing the downfall of Babylon (18.1–2). In the second instance, the angel is standing in the sun, announcing the downfall of the forces of Babylon (19.17–18). This image of a figure shining with the brightness of the sun is reminiscent of Moses' experience after coming down from Mount Sinai, where contact with God left his face so bright that others were afraid to look at him (Ex. 34.29–35). The idea of brightness as a symbol for the reflected glory of God is not unique to this image: there are a number of other places in Revelation where the sun is used as a descriptor for righteous figures,[31] and in Jewish mythology there is a tradition of an angel who lives in the sun.[32] In John's presentation of the shining angel from the sun, the divine glory reflected by this angel is rhetorically contrasted with the darkness of Babylon, whose end is being proclaimed.[33]

Six angels

Following the vision of the Lamb and his army standing on Mount Zion (14.1–5), there is a series of images of judgement featuring six angels. The first is seen flying in mid-heaven, proclaiming 'an eternal gospel' for 'every nation and tribe and language and people', and announcing the coming of God's judgement (14.6). This is the only instance in the New Testament of a flying angel,[34] and also the only occurrence in the Johannine writings of the term εὐαγγέλιον ('a gospel').[35] The flying angel's gospel should not be confused with 'the gospel' found in the Pauline writings, which refers to the death and resurrection of Jesus.[36] Rather the good news ('gospel') proclaimed by the angel is something else: its content is explicated in the following verse (14.7) where it becomes clear that the angel's 'eternal gospel' is the arrival of the hour of the judgement of God.[37] This good news for 'every nation' is thus their release from the satanic forces which have been oppressing them, as divine judgement comes upon all those structures and powers which oppose and distort the kingdom of God. The nations are thereby freed by the 'eternal gospel' to make their journey from Babylon to the new Jerusalem (21.24–6), in a new exodus from slavery to freedom.[38] The proclamation of the gospel thus results in the ingathering of the nations, in fulfilment of the divine promise to Abraham that his descendants, the people of God, will be good news to all nations.[39]

The second angel is then seen flying behind the first, proclaiming the fall of Babylon who has made the nations drink the wine of her corruption (14.8).[40] The third angel follows the first two, proclaiming God's wrath on those who worship the beast and its image and receive its mark on their foreheads or hands (14.9–11; cf. 19.11–20.15). The fourth angel comes out of the temple, passing to the 'one like a son of man' the divine instruction to use his sickle and reap the harvest of the earth (14.15; cf. 14.4). The fifth angel also comes out from the temple carrying a harvesting sickle which he uses to gather the vintage of the earth (14.17, 19–20). The sixth angel comes from the altar and is one who has been met before. He is described as having 'authority over fire' (14.18) and is to be identified as the angel with the golden censer who bears the prayers of the saints (cf. 8.3–5), which are answered as he instructs the fifth angel to gather the vintage of the earth in an image of judgement on the beast and its forces.

The angel with the key to the bottomless pit

At the sounding of the fifth trumpet, John witnessed a star that had fallen from heaven to earth being given the key to the bottomless pit, which he opened to release the plague of locusts (9.1–3). However in a dramatic reversal of this image, in Chapter 20 John sees an angel coming from heaven holding the key to the bottomless pit. The angel seizes the dragon and locks him in the pit for a thousand years (20.1–2). Clearly these two beings are not the same; the former is satanic, whereas the latter is divine. Here John presents the conclusion of the story that began at the sounding of the fifth trumpet. The time for plagues on the earth is limited, and once that time has expired, the one who opened the pit will be consigned to the pit. The angel holds not just the key to the pit, but also a great chain that he uses to bind the dragon. Judgement has been passed on the dragon, and the angel from heaven executes the prescribed punishment.

Heavenly creatures

The four living creatures

The four living creatures that John sees around the throne are his re-working of the living creatures from the visions of Ezekiel and Isaiah (Ezek. 1.5–12; Isa. 6.2). They are seen by John surrounding the throne (4.6), and are 'full of eyes' (4.6, 8).[41] Where Ezekiel's creatures each had four faces (human, lion, ox and eagle; Ezek. 1.10), John's living creatures each take the form of just one of these (4.7).[42] The function of the four living creatures is to sing praise to God, day and night without ceasing (4.8), and their singing causes the twenty-four elders to fall before the throne (4.9–10). The living creatures worship the Lamb together with the elders (5.8; 7.11; 19.4; cf. 14.3), and they articulate the great 'amen' to the song offered by the whole of creation (5.14).

The interpretation of these creatures is much debated, with a prominent early interpretation being to equate the four creatures with the four Gospel-writers.[43] However helpful some have found this, and however influential it has been on art and sculpture, it is certain that this was not John's original intention.[44] More likely is that the four living creatures represent the created order of humans, wild animals, domesticated animals and birds, all present before the throne in worship.[45]

The four living creatures have a role to play in the opening of the first four seals, when each in turn calls 'come!', thereby triggering the arrival of the four coloured horses and their riders (6.1–8). Similarly, at the inauguration of the bowl-plagues, one of the living creatures hands the seven angels the seven golden bowls containing the wrath of God (15.7). The effect of these images is to signify creation itself crying out for the coming judgement of evil.[46]

The birds of mid-heaven

One of the four living creatures announces the opening of the first four seals (6.1–8), and it is possible that another plays a similar role with the last three trumpets.[47] An eagle, flying in mid-heaven, cries three woes on the inhabitants of the earth, approximating to the fifth, sixth and seventh trumpets (8.13).[48]

The location 'mid-heaven' recurs when the angel from the sun calls the birds of mid-heaven to gather for the great supper of God (19.17–18). What is in view here are those large birds of prey such as the eagle and vulture, which circle high in the sky before descending to feed. Accordingly, once summoned by the angel, the birds descend from mid-heaven and, in a parallel to the marriage supper of the Lamb (19.9), consume the flesh of the forces of evil that have been defeated by the rider on the white horse (19.21).[49] The consummation of the relationship between Christ and the Church therefore finds its counterpart in the destruction of those forces which destroy the divine-human relationship. As the Lamb and his bride are joined, so the satanic forces which oppress the nations are consumed.

The voice from the horns of the altar

At the sixth trumpet blast John hears a voice coming from the four horns of the golden altar in the heavenly throne room (9.13–14). The voice commands the release of the four demonic angels who are bound at the Euphrates. There have been various attempts to identify this voice. Clearly it is not the voice of God himself, as it comes from the altar that is 'before God'. Some have sought to identify the voice with those of the martyrs under the altar (6.9–10), but the active command issued by the voice is at variance with the 'resting' of the martyrs (6.11). Other suggestions include the voice of the Lamb (cf. 6.6), and the voice of the angel with the golden censer (cf. 8.3).[50] A more satisfying solution is found in equating the role of the voice from the altar who releases the four angels, with the role of the four living creatures who release the four riders (6.1–8);[51] and in noting its similarity to that of the eagle flying in mid-heaven (8.13). The fact that the voice comes from the 'horns' of the altar is also suggestive of animal characteristics.[52] This evidence leads to the conclusion that once again here is the voice of one of the four living creatures, heralding the judgement of God on the earth.

The inhabitants of the earth

Within John's visionary scheme, the Church consists of those who are the followers of Jesus Christ. As such, they form a sub-set of a wider humanity since in addition to the images that John uses to describe the people of God, there is also a number of references to other human groups. These are the inhabitants of the earth, and they represent those with whom the people of God must deal on a daily basis. The seven congregations of Asia Minor, to whom the Apocalypse is addressed, existed as small and struggling communities within the wider world of Graeco-Roman culture, philosophy and religion. As such, they faced constant pressure to conform to the society surrounding them. It is various aspects of this wider society that are in view in John's imagery for the inhabitants of the earth.

The Nicolaitans

The Nicolaitans appear in two of the seven letters: in the letter to Ephesus, where they are hated by both the Ephesians and by Jesus (2.6), and apparently posing a problem in Pergamum, where some in the church are following their teaching (2.15). The evidence suggests a group, with a presence in at least two of the cities addressed by John, which is making inroads into the Christian congregations by offering some alternative or distorted philosophy. At the time of John's writing, those in the Ephesian church are clearly being more successful at holding the Nicolaitans at bay than those in Pergamum.

The best clue as to the teaching of the Nicolaitans is found in the letter to Pergamum, where it is said, 'you have some there who hold to the teaching of Balaam, who taught Balak to put a stumbling block before the people of Israel, so that they would eat food sacrificed to idols and practice fornication' (2.14; cf. 1 Cor. 8.1–13; 10.19). This is a reference to Balaam's prophecy before Balak, which resulted in the Israelites having sexual relations with the women of Moab, and making offerings of worship to the Moabite gods (Num. 24.25—25.3). Thus it seems that the Nicolaitan teaching was a form of syncretism, combining the following of Christ with pagan behaviour and belief. Some have suggested that early Gnostic influence can be detected here, prefiguring the great gnosticizing debates that beset the Church in the second century.[53]

Jezebel

The teaching of the proto-gnostic Nicolaitans may also lie behind the references to Jezebel, a female false prophet mentioned in the letter to

Thyatira (2.20–3). It is reported that she has been beguiling those in the church into fornication and eating food offered to idols. She is unrepentant of her activities, and a severe warning is given as to the fate of those who join her: her children will be struck dead. Again false belief and false practice combine to produce a philosophical outlook that is threatening to the stability of John's congregation.

This false teaching is referred to as 'the deep things of Satan' (2.24; cf. 2.9; 3.9), and is reminiscent of the tendency of the Gnostics to seek deep knowledge. John clearly has in mind here a particular individual in Thyatira, who is a proponent and practitioner of the philosophy, whom he characterizes as 'Jezebel', thus recalling the wife of Ahab who killed the prophets of the Lord and introduced the worship of Baal into Israel (1 Kings 16.31; 18.4). The image of Jezebel occurs again later in Revelation, where the story of Jezebel's gruesome demise is used to frame the description of the destruction of the great whore (17.16; cf. 1 Kings 21.23–4; 2 Kings 9.10, 36–7).

The nations of the earth

It has already been noted that the Church exists as a sub-set of humanity. When John speaks of the nations of the earth, he is referring to that vast swathe of humanity beyond those who make up the followers of Jesus. The nations in Revelation are those who are deceived by Satan, and who are subject to judgement for their evildoing. They are not to be confused with the systems of evil which oppress them, neither are they people who make a conscious decision to act as agents of the beast. Rather, they represent the homogeneous mass of humanity who fall under the influence of the beast, and so fail to resist the empire of the beast in which they find themselves. The judgements that come upon them are warnings and are designed to produce repentance.

The relationship between the nations and the Church is explored in the story of the two witnesses, where it is said that the nations trample the holy city for 42 months, and gaze at the dead bodies of the two witnesses, gloating and celebrating over their deaths (11.2, 9–10).[54] By John's understanding, for as long as the Church seeks to give faithful witness in the world (i.e. 1,260 days),[55] the world will seek to oppress and destroy the Church (i.e. 42 months), and those who face martyrdom will do so to the ridicule of the nations. This is because the nations have been deceived and intoxicated into worshipping the beast, the dragon and the whore by the great and terrifying signs that they perform.[56] Even the sign of martyrdom, which temporarily breaks the power of Satan over the nations, fails to make them aware of the deceptions of the beast (20.3, 8).

As a result of their susceptibility to the beast's deception, the nations capitulate to the evil empire and so bring upon themselves judgement for their compromise. The purpose of these judgements is to bring the nations to repentance (9.20–1; 16.9, 11), but the plagues fail to produce repentance, and instead generate only fear and hard-heartedness.[57] Rich and poor alike hide in caves and among rocks on the mountains in response to the cosmically cataclysmic events of the sixth seal (6.15), and they plead for the rocks to fall on them and hide them from the one seated on the throne, and from the wrath of the Lamb (6.16). However instead of turning to the Lamb in repentance, they turn away in fear. The only example in Revelation of people turning to God as a result of the judgements is found following the earthquake in 11.13, a significant passage that emphasizes the intention of the series of judgements.

It is ironic that when Jesus eventually engages in battle, his only weapon is the word of God (19.21) and because the nations cannot bear the truth of the gospel, when faced with the warning judgements they would rather run to the hills in fear than towards the Lamb. Of significance here also is the mention of both rich and poor among those who are deceived and face judgement; this sets John's designation of 'the nations' apart from 'the kings of the earth' who are judged not as those who have been deceived, but as those who have willingly capitulated and benefited from the empire of the beast. The nations, on the other hand, are made up of all ranks of society who are enslaved to the beast and so work to support his kingdom (cf. 17.1, 15). The image here is of a people in bondage, working for a tyrannical king, brainwashed to such an extent that they are unable to see any way to freedom, and who therefore interpret the plagues of judgement as yet further oppression, rather than as a path to freedom opening before them. The parallel with the Israelites in Egypt is once again striking (cf. Ex. 5.20–1).

So it is that the nations are the recipients of divine judgement, and their response to this is a mixture of anger and fear (11.18; 16.19–21). The final judgement on the nations however does not occur until after the thousand years. Still unconvinced, even by the sign of martyrdom, the nations are once again deceived by the released Satan, and are described as 'Gog and Magog', the traditional enemies of God's people (20.8; cf. Ezek. 38.2–3). The nations gather for battle, and in a parallel to the fecundity promised to the descendants of Abraham, are described as being as numerous as the sands of the sea (20.8). The divine promise to Abraham was that:

> I will indeed bless you, and I will make your offspring as numerous as the stars of heaven and as the sand that is on the seashore. And your offspring shall possess the gate of their enemies, and by your offspring

shall all the nations of the earth gain blessing for themselves. (Gen. 22.17–18)

For a time it looks as if the fulfilment of the Abrahamic covenant is threatened. The nations who have placed themselves in opposition to the people of God dominate the earth, marching to surround the encampment of the saints.

This time, however, there are no more warning judgements, but neither is there any battle. The nations are simply consumed with fire from heaven (20.9).[58] Everything from among the nations that cannot endure into the new Jerusalem is thus burned away, and the way is cleared for the people of God to become a blessing to 'all the nations of the earth'. All is not as bleak as it might seem for the nations of the world and in spite of their experience of the judgement and fire of God, there is a strand of hope for the nations running through Revelation. So it is that the 144,000 sing that God is the true king of the nations, and that all nations will one day come and worship God (15.3–4).

Revelation speaks of the nations being ruled with an iron rod three times (2.26; 12.5; 19.15). This image has its origin in Psalm 2 (cf. Isa. 11.4), which is frequently given a Christological interpretation within the New Testament.[59] The psalm addresses the question of why it is that the nations of the world fail to acknowledge the dominion of the Lord (Ps. 2.1–3). In answer, the universal might of the Lord over the nations is asserted (Ps. 2.4–6). To the people of Israel the Lord says: 'Ask of me, and I will make the nations your heritage ... You shall break them with a rod of iron, and dash them in pieces like a potter's vessel' (Ps. 2.8–9). The psalm exhorts the rulers of the nations to serve the Lord with fear and trembling in order to avoid his wrath (Ps. 2.10–12), and concludes with the promise that: 'Happy are all who take refuge in him' (Ps. 2.12).

John evokes this psalm when he says that everyone who conquers will receive authority to rule the nations with a rod of iron (2.26–7).[60] As they ponder the opposition of the nations to the word of God, John offers to the oppressed people of God the hope that the nations will become the inheritance of the Church, that their faithful witness to the world will ultimately prove fruitful. In this image, the present situation of persecution is reversed as those powers that currently tyrannize are themselves destroyed with a rod of iron. The hope here, as in Psalm 2, is that the nations will heed the warning, and turn to God and serve him, taking refuge in him so that they may avoid the judgements.

In the second and third references to the nations being ruled with an iron rod, it is not the Church but Christ himself who wields the staff (12.5; 19.15). The waywardness of the nations is not to be allowed to continue for ever, and Christ and his Church share the task of guiding the nations back to God. In view here is the role of a shepherd with an iron crook, shepherding the nations who are so easily led astray, directing them towards their ultimate destination (cf. 7.17).

In fulfilment of the Abrahamic covenant, the nations reappear after their consumption by the fire of heaven (20.9), and are seen walking by the light of the glory of God in the streets of the new Jerusalem (21.24).[61] With the final destruction of the beast, the nations are freed from the satanic deception that has consistently led them into conflict with the Church, and the prophecy of the 144,000 is fulfilled as the nations worship God (15.3-4). The glory and honour of the nations are carried into the new Jerusalem in a scene reminiscent of returning with the spoils of war (21.26).[62] No longer do the nations pay tribute to Babylon, sending their treasures to the evil city; rather they give homage to God himself. This is the liturgical response on the part of the nations to the invitation issued by the Spirit and the bride to 'come' into the new Jerusalem.[63] The final vision of the nations in Revelation is therefore one of profound hope, as fractured human society is finally healed, and all nations are united in the praise and adoration of God. In a symbolic reversal of the relationships of Eden (Gen. 2.9; 3.13-24), the tree in the centre of the new Jerusalem is 'for the healing of the nations' (22.2). The purpose of Israel is thus fulfilled, as the people of God finally and definitively become a blessing for all the nations of the earth.

Those people who do not have the seal of God on their foreheads

The phrase 'the nations of the earth' functions as a catch-all used by John to describe the mass of humanity who are deceived, judged and ultimately restored. But there are a number of further images that he also utilizes to describe those who are not followers of Jesus. Having defined the 144,000 as those who are marked with the seal of God on their foreheads (7.3),[64] John speaks of those who do not have the seal of God on their foreheads (9.5). There is a striking parallel between these two passages, as the following table illustrates.

Revelation 7.2-4	Revelation 9.1b-6
I saw another angel ascending from the rising of the sun,	I saw a star that had fallen from heaven to earth,
having the seal of the living God,	and he was given the key to the shaft of the bottomless pit;

and he called with a loud voice to the four angels who had been given power to damage earth and sea, saying,	he opened the shaft of the bottomless pit, and from the shaft rose smoke like the smoke of a great furnace, and the sun and the air were darkened with the smoke from the shaft. Then from the smoke came locusts on the earth, and they were given authority like the authority of scorpions of the earth.
'Do not damage the earth or the sea or the trees,	They were told not to damage the grass of the earth or any green growth or any tree,
until we have marked the servants of our God with a seal on their foreheads.'	but only those people who do not have the seal of God on their foreheads.
And I heard the number of those who were sealed, one hundred forty-four thousand	They were allowed to torture them for five months, but not to kill them, and their torture was like the torture of a scorpion when it stings someone. And in those days people will seek death but will not find it; they will long to die, but death will flee from them.

In both passages, an angelic being utilizes an implement (a seal or a key) to effect an action upon humanity. The seal placed on the foreheads of the 144,000 marks them as belonging to God on the throne in heaven, and signifies that it is to him alone that their allegiance lies. The result of this sealing is that they are protected from the worst extremes of the judgements that come upon those who are not marked in this way. John's concern here is to indicate that those who have not taken the seal of God upon themselves are inevitably aligned with the empire of the beast and all the judgements that it inevitably suffers. This category of those who are 'not marked' is therefore an inclusive category – it is everyone who is not part of the 144,000.

The judgement of locusts with scorpion stings, which comes upon those who are 'not marked', is limited in both time and scope, leaving the way open for those receiving it to repent and turn to God (9.5–6). The plague of locusts clearly echoes the similar plague in Egypt at the time of the exodus (Ex. 10.4–15), a further indication of John's understanding of humanity embarking on a second exodus whereby the judgements of God lead ultimately to freedom from slavery and entry to the promised land. It is significant that in John's vision, the trees, grass and plants are excluded from harm (7.3; 9.4), in direct contrast to the result of the locust plague in Egypt where 'nothing green was left, no tree, no plant in the field' (Ex. 10.15). Within John's scheme, the core of the food chain is left intact (cf. 8.7), indicating that however severe the suffering of those who are 'not marked', God's intention is not to destroy them utterly.

Those who bear the mark of the beast from the earth

An alternative way of describing those who are 'not marked' with the seal of God, is to speak of those who 'are marked' with the mark of the beast. The key issue for John here is one of idolatry, as he sees the majority of the inhabitants of the earth giving worship to the beast, rather than to the one on the throne in heaven. John is uncompromising, and has no middle ground for humanity in terms of idolatry and worship. Within his theological scheme, a person must either recognize the dominion of God or worship the beast. Hence, those who are 'not marked' with the seal of God are inevitably also those who are 'marked' with the mark of the beast.

For John, this bleak categorization of human spiritual allegiance includes people of all social classes; it is not something that is confined to the rich and powerful, neither is it something that is the preserve of the obviously wicked and evil. As with his understanding of 'the nations of the world', those who take the mark of the beast are deceived into doing so: '[The beast] causes all, both small and great, both rich and poor, both free and slave, to be marked on the right hand or the forehead' (13.16).[65] The seductive power of the beast thus draws everyone into its web of deceit, compromising and oppressing in equal measure. The tragedy for John is that this category of those 'marked' by the beast includes blameless people, with the poor and exploited becoming the victims of the beast at least as much as the wealthy and influential.

By John's understanding, the only way to stand against the deceptively idolatrous lure of the beast is to switch allegiance to Christ, and to take the seal of God in place of the mark of the beast. However, there is a cost to be paid, as those who capitulate to the satanic empire benefit economically from so doing, while those who resist must count the financial cost of their resistance. Just as some individuals would sell themselves into slavery for financial or social gain,[66] so economic promises are part of the deception of the beast, with those who take its mark selling themselves into the corrupt and exploitative economic ideologies of empire (13.17).

However, the good times offered to those who take the mark of the beast are short-lived. John understands that the practices of the satanic empire are ultimately self-destructive, bringing judgement upon those who have worshipped the beast. In this way, those who are marked with the mark of the beast are said to drink the wine of God's wrath, being tormented with fire and sulphur (14.9–11). The extremity of this portrayal of the judgements awaiting those marked by the beast is indicative of John's passionate concern that those in his churches take every possible step to avoid the powerful seductions of the beast. He knows how attractive the ideology of empire can be, seeing how easily it leads to idolatry, and he wants his audience to be in no doubt as to the catastrophic results of yielding to the temptation to compromise with the beast. He says that 'the smoke of their torment goes up forever and ever' (14.11), describing a lasting memorial to the futility of directing worship anywhere other than towards God himself. The pain that humanity brings upon itself through its idolatrous folly cannot be minimized or glossed over.

The pouring out of the bowls of God's wrath in response to the prayers of the saints provokes a series of dramatic judgements against those who bear the mark of the beast. They develop foul and painful sores (16.2); they are scorched with fire from the sun (16.8–9) and then plunged into darkness, gnawing their tongues in agony (16.10–11); and they are pelted with huge hailstones (16.21). These plagues, which are derivative of the plagues of Egypt (Ex. 9.11, 23–5; 10.22), are intended to produce repentance, and are seen as a direct consequence of persistent idolatry on the part of those marked by the beast. However, those who have given their allegiance to the beast fail to recognize the extent of their idolatry, and instead they curse God (16.9, 11, 21), thus compounding their idolatry with blasphemy.[67]

As with John's portrayal of 'the nations of the world', his presentation of those marked with the mark of the beast ends on a hopeful note. The beast and the false prophet, who had deceived those who took the mark of the beast, are consigned to the lake of fire (19.20), and thus the source of deception is finally removed. Throughout his use of this imagery, John seeks to provide his audience with an understanding of the insidious nature of idolatry, which promises much but delivers only disaster. John's point is clear: until final judgement is passed on the satanic forces of empire, the only alternative to idolatry to the beast is allegiance to Christ.

Those whose names have not been written in the book of life

The book of life is an image that occurs a number of times in Revelation.[68] It is used in the context either of those whose names are included in the book of life (3.5; 20.12; 21.27), or those whose names are excluded from it (13.8; 17.8; 20.15).[69] The positive instances remind John's audience that their destiny is secure for all eternity, with their names recorded in heaven. The negative occurrences of the image are followed by very vivid images, with those whose names are not found in the book being cast into the lake of fire which is the second death (13.8; 20.14–15). This second group are those people who have been deceived into offering idolatrous worship to the beast (17.8).

Clearly the image of the second death is intended at one level as a stark warning to those who might be tempted to turn their backs on Christ and renew their association with the beast. However, at another level it raises the broader theological question of the identity and ultimate destination of those whose names are not to be found recorded in the Lamb's book of life. Those who are thrown into the lake of fire are listed as: the beast and the false prophet (19.20); the Devil (20.10); Death and Hades (20.14); and anyone whose name was not found written in the book of life (20.15). This final group is then revealed to be 'the cowardly, the faithless, the polluted, the murderers, the fornicators, the sorcerers, the idolaters, and all liars' (21.8).[70] Similar lists of sinners are found in 21.27 and 22.15, where they are spoken of as being 'outside' the new Jerusalem rather than in the lake of fire, indicating once again the non-literal nature of John's imagery. These lists of vices are so comprehensive that it is impossible to imagine any human escaping, suggesting that John has in mind once more the vast swathe of humanity that has given its idolatrous allegiance to the beast. The universal nature of the condemnation suggests that if everybody is indicted then nobody is specifically targeted, conveying the universal human need to receive mercy.

John has already indicated that the martyrs (20.6), those who 'conquer' (2.11), and those whose names are written in the book of life (20.15) are excused the suffering of the lake of fire, which raises the question of the fate of those beyond the Church, elsewhere symbolized as 'the nations',[71] those 'not marked' by the seal of God,[72] and those 'marked' with the mark of the beast.[73] John's concern here is to emphasize that evil in all its forms has no place within the renewed creation, as well as to discourage those in his congregations from taking part in practices that are ultimately futile and bound for destruction. The second death in the lake of fire represents the purification of creation, a burning away of all that cannot endure into the new Jerusalem. The hopeful and inclusive image of the nations streaming into the new Jerusalem (21.24) suggests that John's language of exclusion from the book of life and of the second death in the lake of fire indicates the purificatory obliteration of evil and all its works from the nations of the earth; from those who have not participated already in the purificatory sacrifice of the Lamb.[74]

In this way, while all those indicted by the vice list go into the lake of fire, only the vices are actually consumed by the flames (20.15; 21.8).[75] The reappearance of these same people outside the gates of the new Jerusalem in 22.15 reinforces this observation. This group are contrasted with those who have washed their robes clean, indicating once again John's division of humanity into two groups: those who follow the Lamb, and everyone else. The Spirit and the Bride then invite those outside the gates to come in (22.17).[76] It is significant that those outside the new Jerusalem are referred to as 'dogs' at this point (22.15), the only occurrence of this term in Revelation. Typically, 'dogs' was used by Jews as a derogatory description of the Gentile nations,[77] and its use here by John highlights again the contrast between the people of God who are already inside the new Jerusalem, and the nations of the world to whom the invitation 'come' is extended. In view here once again is the fulfilment of the Abrahamic covenant that the people of God should become a blessing to all the nations of the earth.[78]

The kings of the earth

John uses the phrase 'the kings of the earth' as a symbolic representation of those powerful humans who participate in and benefit from the kingdom of the beast. They are seen as the rulers of the nations of the earth, and as such they bear some responsibility for the deception of the nations. The kings of the earth are not themselves deceived, but they choose to enter into an alliance with the satanic kingdom for their own benefit. The background to this image is found in the repeated assertion in the Old Testament that the kings of the earth, however powerful they may appear to be, are actually under the authority of the Lord.[79]

The first occurrence of the kings of the earth is found in the opening verses of the Apocalypse, where Jesus is affirmed as their ruler. While the kings may choose to pay tribute to Babylon, the way John sees them their authority derives from none other than Jesus himself, to whom they are ultimately accountable (1.5). However, their persistent idolatry in worshipping and following the beast attracts the judgement of God, and they are seen with the rest of humanity hiding from the wrath of the Lamb in the mountains, as the world in which they have invested their lives and wealth comes crashing down around them (6.15).

There is considerable discussion as to whether the 'kings from the east' who come from beyond the Euphrates river should be identified with the 'kings of the earth' (16.12).[80] Here it is assumed that they can be identified in this way, thereby giving a vision of the kings of the earth as oppressive powers, in league with the empire of the beast, marching against the people of Christ. The kings assemble for the great battle of Harmagedon, at which they attempt to destroy the army of the faithful and take ownership of the world for themselves (16.14–16). This self-promoting attitude of conquest and acquisition adopted by the kings puts them in direct opposition to the faithful witness of the Church, which continues to testify that supreme authority resides only with the one seated on the throne. It is a measure of the arrogance of the kings that they believe the world is theirs for the taking. They have convinced themselves that joining with the forces of empire will lead to victory.

The kings are seen as those who have committed fornication with the great whore of Babylon (17.2a), having sold their moral and spiritual integrity for the earthly pleasures offered by the seductive forces of the beast. But worse than this, the result is that the inhabitants of the earth have in turn become intoxicated with the wine of the kings' fornication (17.2b). This image provides a searing critique of the economic systems and ideologies of empire, that seduce both kings and people into their webs of deceit and corruption.

It is possible that the ten horns of the scarlet beast are a further representation of the kings of the earth (17.12–17).[81] The kings have given their allegiance to Babylon, who rules over them (17.18), and they have grown powerful as a result (18.3). So it is that when the judgement of God comes upon Babylon, the kings weep and wail as they see the smoke of the burning city (18.9–10). In anger at their loss, the kings and their armies join forces with the beast to make war on the rider on the white horse and his army (19.19). They are, however, killed by the sword that comes from the mouth of the Messiah, and the birds consume their flesh (19.21).[82] In this way, the earthly agents of the beast who put themselves in direct opposition to the lordship of Christ for their own gain are seen to be defeated by the word of God. However, as with the nations of the world, this is not the end of the story for the kings of the earth. Clearly the judgement visited upon them by the rider on the white horse did not involve the eternal destruction of the individuals involved, as they soon reappear bringing their glory into the new Jerusalem (21.24).[83] Their time of self-interested idolatrous devotion to Babylon is over, and they finally acknowledge God and the Lamb as having the true authority over the earth.

Merchants, seafarers and traders

The merchants, seafarers and traders function in a similar fashion to the kings of the earth, with the difference being that where the kings compromised with Babylon in exchange for power, the merchants are seduced by the ideology of acquisition and the promise of financial gain (18.3). Consequently, they join with the kings of the earth in mourning the loss of the great city (18.11–19). The list of goods in which the merchants trade is evidence of the extent to which they have embraced corruption, including not only luxury goods from every part of the known world, but also human lives (18.12–13).[84] The system of imperial international economics portrayed here is damning, as it highlights that it is revealed to be predicated on the consumption not just of necessities, but of luxuries at any cost.[85] The system of slavery was the backbone of the economic success of the Empire, and ranged from the bonded slaves of individual households in Rome, to the economic slaves in distant countries working to produce goods for the Empire to consume. Once the great city has gone, the merchants complain that there is no one to buy their goods, indicating that the trade structures of the world have entirely focused themselves on the conspicuous and gratuitous consumption of the élite at the centre of the Empire. It is the poverty and oppression of those at the fringes that support the lifestyles of those at the centre, and the merchants are the conduits for this one-way traffic of goods. An alternative economic model is offered in the vision of the new Jerusalem, where the nations bring their wealth as an offering to God, rather than selling them to the emperor (21.26).

The third of humankind who are killed

Even a cursory review of the history of humanity reveals incalculable deaths due to both human activity and natural disaster. John reflects this in his image of the death of a third of humankind in the plagues of fire, smoke and sulphur that come from the four angels who were bound at the Euphrates (9.18). The designation of 'one third' should not be taken literally, but rather as a symbolic representation of the fact that when humanity aligns itself with the beast, the inevitable result is that death on a grand scale is visited back upon the inhabitants of the earth. However, those who survive still remain enthralled by the deception of the satanic empire, and so even in spite of witnessing the results of their actions, they still fail to repent of their idolatry to the beast (9.20–1).[86]

All who have died

Although some may die premature deaths as a result of the judgements that come upon humanity for its adoption of the practices and ideology of the beast, nonetheless the truth remains that all humans must one day die. It is this category that John refers to when he speaks of 'the dead, great and small' (20.12). They are seen standing before the throne in heaven, and are judged according to their works as recorded in the book of life. There is no distinction here, making this a universal vision of humanity, incorporating both the followers of the Lamb and those enslaved to the beast. The martyrs have already experienced resurrection, and they are now joined by the rest of the dead at this second resurrection (cf. 20.5). Even those who have gone to Death, Hades and the sea are present at this final judgement (20.13).

Judgement is then passed on the 'deeds' and 'works' that have been performed by the assembled mass of humanity.[87] No detail, good or bad, has been omitted from the book of life. Contrary to popular mythology, there is no hint here that what is in view is a pair of divine weighing scales, whereby if one's righteous deeds outnumber one's unrighteous deeds, then heaven awaits, whereas if the opposite is the case, hell is one's destination.[88] Rather, this is a scene where judgement is passed on all the deeds of all humans,[89] with a view to purifying humanity prior to their entry into the new Jerusalem.

The preceding chapter has shown how John interprets those in his congregations to be the people of God who are the fulfilment of the Abrahamic covenant. They are those who proclaim a gospel which is good news for all nations, and who pave the way for the eventual ingathering of all those who pass through judgement. In this way, the burning of the nations in the lake of fire and by the fire which comes from heaven is cast as a purificatory process, preparing the nations for their eventual entry into the new Jerusalem. All nations are therefore blessed through the faithful witness of the people of God.

Draw your own conclusions

- How would you characterize the understanding of 'angels' in contemporary culture?
- How do you respond to John's imagery of angelic beings?
- In what ways might John's visions of heavenly worship affect the worship offered by those in earthly Christian congregations?
- What might it mean for 'the nations' to become the inheritance of the Church?
- What contemporary parallels can you think of to people being 'marked' with the mark of the beast?
- Who might comprise modern day 'kings of the earth', 'merchants', 'seafarers' and 'traders'? What does Revelation say to them?

Notes

1 For a detailed overview of angels in Revelation see Stephen S. Smalley, 2005, *The Revelation to John: A Commentary on the Greek Text of the Apocalypse*, London: SPCK, pp. 28–30.

2 D. S. Russell, 1992, *Divine Disclosure*, London: SCM Press, p. 77.

3 See for example 1 Enoch 72.1, 'Uriel, the holy angel who was with me, and who (also) is their guide, showed me ... the nature of the years of the world unto eternity, till the new creation which abides forever is created.' Translated by E. Isaac in James H. Charlesworth (ed.), 1983, *The Old Testament Pseudepigrapha Vol. 1*, New York: Doubleday, p. 50.

4 An example of this from within the Jewish apocalyptic tradition is found in the Book of Jubilees 4.21, 'And he was therefore with the angels of God six jubilees of years. And they showed him everything which is on earth and in the heavens, the dominion of the sun. And he wrote everything.' Translated by O. S. Wintermute in James H. Charlesworth (ed.), *The Old Testament Pseudepigrapha Vol. 2*, New York: Doubleday, p. 62. Cf. James C. VanderKam, 2001, *The Book of Jubilees*, Guides to Apocrypha and Pseudepigrapha, Sheffield: Sheffield Academic Press, pp. 118–19.

5 Beale and Smalley follow Caird here in identifying the seven spirits with the Holy Spirit. Cf. G. K. Beale, 1999, *The Book of Revelation*, Carlisle: Paternoster Press, p. 189; Smalley, *Revelation*, pp. 33–4; G. B. Caird, 1984, *The Revelation of St John the Divine*, London: A & C Black, p. 15. However, Boxall rightly notes that this may be assuming a too highly developed Trinitarian theology. Cf. Ian Boxall, 2006, *The Revelation of St John*, London: Continuum, pp. 31–2. Waddell provides a helpful survey of different opinions as to whether these spirits should be seen as representing the Holy Spirit. Cf. Robby Waddell, *The Spirit of the Book of Revelation*, Blandford Forum: Deo Publishing, pp. 1–21. For a discussion on the characterization of the Holy Spirit in Revelation, see pp. 81–3.

6 Boxall, *Revelation*, p. 132.

7 1 Enoch 20.1–8 names the seven archangels as: Uriel, Raphael, Raguel, Michael, Saraqa'el, Gabriel and Remiel. Cf. Charlesworth (ed.), *Pseudepigrapha Vol. 1*, pp. 21–2.

8 These are found primarily in the book of Jubilees, a late second-century BC text, and represent superior angelic beings, above the lesser 'angels of sanctification'. The phrase 'angels of the presence' can also be translated as 'angels of the face', indicating that these are the angels before the 'face' of God. Cf. VanderKam, *The Book of Jubilees*, pp. 87–8.

9 Cf. Ex. 28.39–43.

10 Cf. Ex. 25.29.

11 The Greek is ambiguous as to whether only the twenty-four elders, or the elders plus the four living creatures, are actually holding bowls. See Boxall, *Revelation*, p. 99. Although only the bowl-plagues are explicitly mentioned as having their origin with the bowls of 5.8, it is nonetheless tempting to see the twenty-eight bowls as resulting in the four series of seven judgements described in the sequences of trumpets, seals, bowls and thunders (4 × 7 = 28). This suggestion may help to account for the presence within the text of the seven thunders, which are otherwise unnecessary to John's scheme (10.3–4).

12 There is considerable debate as to whether this angel should actually be seen as Christological. Smalley provides a helpful summary of the arguments. See Smalley, *Revelation*, pp. 257–8.

13 Cf. Acts 1.9; cf. Ex. 19.9; Dan. 7.13.

14 The Colossus of Rhodes was one of the seven wonders of the ancient world, a giant (30m) statue of the Greek god Helios erected in the third century

BC. See George H. van Kooten, 2007, 'The Year of the Four Emperors and the Revelation of John: The "Pro-Neronian" Emperors Otho and Vitellius, and the Images and Colossus of Nero in Rome', *Journal for the Study of the New Testament*, vol. 30.2: 205–48.

15 Smalley, *Revelation*, p. 258.

16 Cf. Jer. 51.63–4.

17 Cf. Beale, *Revelation*, p. 930.

18 Beale, *Revelation*, p. 657

19 Cf. Deut. 33.2; Dan. 7.10.

20 Cf. Jer. 49.36; Ezek. 37.9; Dan. 8.8; 11.4; Zech. 2.6; 6.5.

21 Boxall, *Revelation*, p. 121; Beale, *Revelation*, p. 406.

22 So Smalley, *Revelation*, p. 180.

23 Such as: earth, sea, rivers and heavens (cf. 14.7).

24 See the discussion of the 144,000 on pp. 96–8.

25 A censer is a vessel used in worship to hold incense.

26 Cf. Rev. 5.8; 1 Kings 7.50.

27 Cf. Ps. 141.2.

28 Although the phrase 'armies of heaven' appears also in 19.14, 19, this does not denote the same group. In Chapter 19 this term refers to the 144,000, the army of the Lamb, rather than to angelic warriors.

29 Josh. 5.14; 2 Kings 6.17. Cf. Smalley, *Revelation*, p. 323.

30 On identifying these two as the same angel, see Beale, *Revelation*, p. 965; Smalley, *Revelation*, p. 496.

31 Rev. 1.16; 7.2; 10.1; 12.1; cf. 21.23; 22.5. Cf. Jonathan Knight, 1999, *Revelation*, Sheffield: Sheffield Academic Press, p. 129.

32 For an analysis of the Jewish and Syrian background to this image, see David E. Aune, 1998, *Revelation 17–22*, Word Biblical Commentary, vol. 52C, Nashville: Thomas Nelson Publishers, p. 1063.

33 Cf. Rev. 16.10; 21.25; 22.5.

34 Cf. Rev. 4.7; 8.13; 19.17.

35 Although see 10.7 where the verb form εὐηγγέλισεν ('he preached') is found.

36 e.g. 1 Cor. 9.12; 2 Cor 9.13; Gal. 1.7; Phil. 1.27; 1 Thess. 3.2; cf. Mark 8.35.

37 Rev. 15.5–16.21. Cf. Smalley, *Revelation*, p. 361.

38 For more on the nations making a new exodus, see the discussion on pp. 189–90.

39 Cf. Gen. 18.18; 22.18; 26.4.

40 Cf. Isa. 21.9; Jer. 51.7–8; Rev. 17.1–19.10.

41 Cf. Ezek. 1.18; 10.12.

42 Compare the following passage from the Apocalypse of Abraham 18.3–4, 8, 'I saw under the fire a throne of fire and the many-eyed ones round about, reciting the song, under the throne four fiery living creatures, singing. And the appearance of each of them was the same, each having four faces. And this (was) the aspect of their faces: of a lion, of a man, of an ox, and of an eagle ... And when they finished singing, they would look at one another and threaten one another.' Translated by R. Rubinkiewicz in Charlesworth (ed.), *Pseudepigrapha Vol. 1*, p. 698.

43 This interpretation originated with Irenaeus, and was adopted by Victorinus. Judith L. Kovacs and Christopher Rowland, 2004, *Revelation*, Oxford Blackwell, p. 66. Cf. Richard A. Burridge, 2005, *Four Gospels, One Jesus? A Symbolic Reading*, 2nd edn, London: SPCK.

44 It becomes impossible if a date of composition for Revelation during the reign of Vespasian is accepted, as this would place Revelation prior to the composition of at least two of the Gospels. See the discussion of dating on pp. 15–16.

45 Boxall, *Revelation*, p. 87. John Sweet quotes *Midrash Shemoth* R.23. 'Man is exalted among creatures, the eagle among birds, the ox among domestic animals, the lion among wild beasts; all of them have received dominion ... Yet they are stationed below the chariot of the Holy One'. John Sweet, 1979, *Revelation*, London: SCM Press, p. 120.

46 Cf. Rom. 8.22.

47 Although this eagle is not positively identified as one of the four living creatures, it is likely that this is the case. The only other occurrence of an eagle in Revelation is where the woman is given an eagle's wings to escape the serpent (12.14).

48 Cf. Rev. 4.7; 9.12; 11.14; 12.12.

49 Cf. Ezek. 39.4b; 17; Matt. 24.28.

50 Smalley, *Revelation*, p. 235.

51 Boxall notes that there is a variant reading of the text which could give, 'a voice from the four living creatures which were before the altar of God'. See Boxall, *Revelation*, pp. 146–7.

52 Smalley, *Revelation*, p. 236.

53 See Stephen S. Smalley, 1994, *Thunder and Love: John's Revelation and John's Community*, Milton Keynes: Nelson Word, pp. 87–9 for a detailed survey of the source material relating to the Nicolaitans. For a useful article on Gnosticism see D. M. Scholer, 1997, 'Gnosis, Gnosticism', in Ralph P. Martin and Peter H. Davids (eds), *Dictionary of the Later New Testament & Its Developments*, Leicester: InterVarsity Press.

54 For further discussion of the two witnesses, see pp. 102–4. Cf. Caird, *Revelation*, p. 132.

55 See table and explanation on p. 103.

56 Cf. Rev. 13.3–4, 7–8, 12, 14–15; 14.8; 17.2; 18.3, 23.

57 Cf. Ex. 7.22.

58 Cf. 2 Kings 1.10; Ezek. 38.21–2; 39.6.

59 The declaration of the Psalm that the king enthroned in Zion is the son of God is applied to Jesus (Ps. 2.6–7; cf. Mark 1.11; 9.7; Acts 4.25–30; 13.33; Rom. 1.4; Heb. 1.5; 5.5; 2 Peter 1.17; Rev. 2.18). See James L. Mays, 1994, *Psalms*, Interpretation: A Bible Commentary for Teaching and Preaching, Louisville: John Knox Press, pp. 49–51.

60 Cf. Matt. 19.28.

61 Cf. Isa. 60.3.

62 Cf. Isa. 60.5.

63 See the discussion of this passage on pp. 113–14.

64 See the discussion of the 144,000 on pp. 96–8.

65 Cf. Rev. 6.15; 13.3–4.

66 S. S. Bartchy, 1997, 'Slave, Slavery', in Ralph P. Martin and Peter H. Davids (eds), *Dictionary of the Later New Testament & Its Developments*, Leicester: InterVarsity Press, pp. 1098–9.

67 Cf. Rev. 13.1, 5; 17.3.

68 Cf. Ex. 32.32–3; Ezek. 13.9; Ps. 69.28; Dan. 7.10; 12.1; Luke 10.20; Phil. 4.3.

69 For further discussion of the image of the book of life, see pp. 73–4, 106.

70 See the table on pp. 108–9 for more information on the first- and second-deaths and resurrections.

71 For a discussion of 'the nations' see pp. 131–4.

72 For a discussion of those 'not sealed' see pp. 134–6.

73 For a discussion of those 'marked' with the mark of the beast see pp. 136–7.

74 Cf. Rev. 3.18; 7.14; 1 Cor. 3.15.

75 In popular Roman mythology, the complete consumption of a body in the flames of a funeral pyre, or *bustum*, was required for the soul to make the transition to the afterlife successfully. There was a fear of only being half-burned, as this would compromise the effectiveness of the purificatory flames. For example, the ghost of the Emperor Caligula (AD 12–41) was believed to haunt the Lamian Gardens until his remains were re-burned by his sisters and totally consumed in the flames. See David Noy, 2002, '"Half-Burnt on an Emergency Pyre": Roman Cremations Which Went Wrong', *Greece & Rome*, vol. 47, no. 2: 186–96, p. 192.

76 For this interpretation of 22.17 see pp. 113–14.

77 Cf. Matt. 15.26–7; Mark 7.27–8; Phil. 3.2.

78 Cf. Gen. 18.18; 22.18; 26.4.

79 Cf. Ps. 2.10–11; 76.11–12; 89.27; 102.15; 138.4; 148.11; Isa. 24.21.

80 Two of these options for the identification of the 'kings from the east' are that they represent Cyrus who diverted the river to allow his army across; or Parthian invaders led by a resurrected Nero. However, these historical interpretations necessitate an understanding of the 'kings from the east' as being distinct from the 'the kings of the earth', which undermines the symbolic power of John's vision of the kings. See the helpful and detailed discussion in Smalley, *Revelation*, p. 408.

81 See the discussion of the ten horns of the scarlet beast on pp. 167–8.

82 This consumption by birds means the bodies of the kings go unburied (cf. Deut 28.26).

83 Cf. Isa. 60.5, 11.

84 Six thousand ships per year would arrive at Rome's port to feed the population with grain alone, indicating an unsustainable level of consumption on the part of those at the centre of the Empire. Aelius Aristides (AD 117–181) said of Rome: 'Produce is brought from every land and every sea, depending on what the seasons bring forth, and what is produced by all lands, rivers and lakes and the arts of Greeks and barbarians. If anyone wants to see it all he must travel over the whole earth to see it in such a way or come to this city. For what grows and is produced among individual people is necessarily always here, and here in abundance' (*Eulogy to Rome* 11). Quoted in Wes Howard-Brook

and Anthony Gwyther, 2001, *Unveiling Empire: Reading Revelation Then and Now*, New York: Orbis Books, p. 99.

85 See the section 'Heaven's Perspective on Economics', pp. 212–16.

86 Although cf. Rev. 11.13. Beale notes that the theme of deception is present in the judgements which follow the sixth seal. Beale, *Revelation*, pp. 513–15.

87 For images of final judgement elsewhere in the New Testament see Matt. 10.15; 11.22–5; 12.36–7; 25.31–46; John 5.28–9; Rom. 2.5–11; 14.10; 2 Cor. 5.10; Heb. 10.26–7; 2 Peter 2.9; 3.7; 1 John 4.17; Jude 1.6. Cf. Kovacs and Rowland, *Revelation*, p. 214.

88 The position of Lactantius (AD *c.240–c.320*) for example was that there comes a critical point where the balance is tipped between righteous and unrighteous deeds. See Kovacs and Rowland, *Revelation*, p. 215.

89 Cf. Job 34.11; Ps. 62.12; Prov. 24.12; Jer. 17.10.

7

The Forces of Evil

There are four key images utilized in Revelation to denote the evil one: the Devil and Satan are spoken of in the first part of the book up to Chapter 12, before disappearing from the narrative until Chapter 20 when in their place John depicts the great red dragon, also known as the ancient serpent. There are two key verses that serve to tie these different images together. In Chapter 12 John describes the casting of the dragon from heaven in the following terms: 'The great dragon was thrown down, that ancient serpent, who is called the Devil and Satan, the deceiver of the whole world' (12.9). This is almost exactly mirrored in Chapter 20, where John describes the binding of the dragon and his casting into the bottomless pit: 'He seized the dragon, that ancient serpent, who is the Devil and Satan, and bound him for a thousand years' (20.2). The key to understanding the character of Satan in the book of Revelation is found in his capacity to mislead people (12.9; 20.3, 8–10). The dominant power that John ascribes to him is that of deception, leading the nations of the world away from the one seated on the throne in heaven into idolatrous worship.

In addition to the imagery that symbolizes the evil one, there are a significant number of characters within the narrative scheme of Revelation that represent the forces loyal to Satan or the dragon. These are to be distinguished from those humans who are deceived into offering their allegiance to the beast. Rather, the forces of the evil one are either depicted as satanic angelic beings, or as earthly power structures. In either case, they function on behalf of Satan to bind, oppress and mislead the nations of the world into worshipping the beast, and into persecuting and opposing the army of the Lamb.

Satan/'The Devil'

The first use of the name Satan in the book is found in the letter to the church in Smyrna where those 'who say that they are Jews and are not' are described as 'a synagogue of Satan' (2.9)[1] – language which is also in the letter to the Philadelphian church (3.9). These 'synagogues of Satan' clearly pose a threat to the Christian communities to which John is writing. Although their precise identity remains uncertain,[2] John's intent in describing them using such strong polemic is clear; they are those who have sold their souls to Satan, who have bought the satanic deception, and who are thus in opposition to the faithful witnesses of the Church. The nature of this opposition in Smyrna is seen in the following verse, when John predicts imminent and severe persecution for those in the church, identifying this as the work of the Devil (2.10). In this way, those who act against the Christians are once again cast as the agents of the Devil. In the Philadelphian letter, John assures his audience that those in the 'synagogue of Satan' will one day realize that it is actually the Church who enjoys God's true approval (3.9).

Satan's next mention is found in the letter to the church in Pergamum. The city is described as being 'where Satan's throne is' (2.13), and the congregation there are commended for their faithfulness to God despite the satanic context in which they live. Given the nature of Satan as the one who lures people away from worshipping the one on the throne in heaven, it is significant that John speaks here of Satan's throne.[3] He clearly has in mind the temptation to offer idolatrous worship, and is concerned to encourage those in the congregation to remain faithful in their devotion to the one seated on the throne in heaven alone.

In the letter to Thyatira, John accuses those who have followed the teaching of 'Jezebel' (2.20) as having 'learned what some call "the deep things of Satan"' (2.24). This language is used to describe a group within the church at Thyatira who are following an alternative teaching to that which John has taught. This characterization of the false teaching is designed to portray those who follow it as having been led astray by the deceptions of the evil one.[4]

Satan is not mentioned again until Chapter 12, where the story of his expulsion from heaven is told. He is identified as the Devil, the dragon, and the ancient serpent, thrown down to the earth (12.9; cf. 20.2).[5] The expulsion of Satan to the earth gives rise to great rejoicing on the part of those whose who live in heaven, as well as to a warning aimed at those on the earth who are about to experience the wrath of the Devil, whose deceptive activity is enhanced because he knows that he only has a short time to deceive the nations (12.12).

The identification of Satan, the Devil, the dragon and the serpent is repeated in 20.2 (cf. 12.9), where Satan is bound for a thousand years, and thrown into the bottomless pit that is locked and sealed over him.[6] Thus the statement that his time is short is seen to be fulfilled, as the faithful witness of the martyrs leads to the curtailing of Satan's power. He is then released from his imprisonment in the pit at the end of the thousand years (20.7), and once again deceives the nations, leading them in their final assault on God's people and surrounding the camp of the

saints and the beloved city, before being consumed by fire from heaven
(20.8–9). The Devil is then thrown into the lake of fire and sulphur, joining the beast and the false prophet, being tormented day and night for
ever and ever (20.10). Satan is therefore seen to be judged, imprisoned
and destroyed, resulting in humanity being finally freed from his deceptive wiles.

The great red dragon/The ancient serpent

The great red dragon is introduced in the story of the pregnant woman,
and is described in cosmological terms as an astrological constellation
(12.3). The background to this image in the Old Testament is to be found
in the Leviathan, a mythical sea-dwelling serpentine dragon that represents the primeval forces of evil arising from the deep in opposition to
the people and purposes of God.[7] The dragon as depicted by John in
Revelation has seven heads and seven diadems, indicative of its appearance of perfection,[8] and ten horns, indicative of its power (12.3).[9] Its
tail drags a third of the stars from heaven down to the earth (12.4),[10]
anticipating the result of the fight with Michael where the dragon and
his angels are cast from heaven to the earth (12.7–9).[11]

The dragon positions itself for an unsuccessful attack on the Christ-
child (12.4), recalling the attempt by Herod to take the life of the infant
Jesus (Matt. 2.1–12). Following the battle with Michael, the dragon
is cast to the earth together with his angels, and is identified as Satan
(12.7–9). This sets the context for the relationship between the evil one
and those in John's churches. The dragon pursues the woman, who symbolizes the people of God (12.13), and attempts to sweep her away with
a flood that issues from his mouth (12.15–16). He eventually becomes
angry that she keeps escaping, and sets off to make war on her other
children (12.17), taking a stand on the seashore (12.18). In this way, the
persecution facing the congregations to which John is writing is presented as the angry attacks of the dragon as he deceives the inhabitants
of the earth into opposition towards the people of God.

The strategy employed by the dragon as he seeks to attack the army
of the Lamb is made explicit in the following chapter, where the dragon
gives his power, throne and authority to the beast from the sea (13.2).
Significantly, the beast has the same number of heads and horns as the
dragon, emphasizing the closeness of the relationship between the two.
In this image, John portrays the dragon investing power in the political
and military might of Rome, in order to attract the idolatrous worship
of the nations of the world. This tactic is successful, as the whole earth
is seen worshipping the dragon (13.4).

The narrative moves away from the dragon at this point, following not the underlying force of evil, but rather its manifestation in the form of the beast. However the dragon comes back into view alongside the beast and the false prophet when three frogs issue from their mouths (16.13). These frogs represent demonic spirits, working in the world to deceive the nations still further into idolatrous worship of the beast (16.14), in contrast to the double-edged sword of God's word which issues from the mouth of Christ (1.16; 2.12, 16; 19.15, 21).

The dragon returns to view in Chapter 20, where he is once again identified as Satan, and is seized by the angel with the key, bound for a thousand years, locked and sealed in the pit, and prevented from deceiving the nations until the end of the thousand years (20.2–3). From this point onwards in Revelation, the dragon is no longer differentiated from Satan, and is therefore ultimately destroyed in the lake of fire (20.10).

The three horses with riders

As the Lamb opens the first four seals on the scroll, each of the four living creatures cries out in turn, 'Come!' and a rider on a coloured horse comes into view (6.1–7). The background to this imagery is found in the book of Zechariah. The post-exilic prophet's opening vision begins with the angel of the Lord riding a red horse, with further red, sorrel and white horses behind him (Zech. 1.8). Although the colours of the horses here have no obvious significance for Zechariah,[12] the importance of the vision is that these angelic horsemen have patrolled the earth and found it 'at peace' (Zech. 1.10–11). However, this is not a peace that comes from God, but from indifference on the part of the nations to the plight of the people of God (Zech. 1.14–15). Consequently, God promises to act in order to restore Israel and Zion following the Babylonian exile, bringing true *shalom* to the land in place of the apathetic inaction of Zechariah's time (Zech. 1.16–17). Coloured horses recur later in Zechariah's vision, when he sees four war-chariots pulled by horses coloured red, black, white, and dappled grey (Zech. 6.1–4). The four chariots represent the four winds of heaven, going out into the world to do battle on behalf of the people of God, replacing the false peace of indifference with the justice and *shalom* of God's universal sovereignty (Zech. 6.5–8). John adapts this imagery in his description of four horsemen riding coloured horses. He shares Zechariah's frustration that the world remains indifferent to the plight of the people of God, and he longs for the sovereignty of God to be recognized throughout the earth. The four horsemen he describes go forth into the world to execute judgement on the evil nations. While a case can be made that the first rider, on the white horse, represents Christ going forth with the gospel to do battle against evil,[13] the other three riders represent the unleashing of satanic forces on the earth, as the evil deeds of humanity attract their appropriate judgement. In each case, the riders are summoned by the living creatures within the divine throne room, emphasizing the fact that everything that follows in terms of judgement upon the earth has its origin with Christ himself.

The second rider to emerge is introduced with the phrase, καὶ ἐξῆλθεν ἄλλος ('and out came another' 6.4) in contrast to the phrase καὶ εἶδον, καὶ ἰδοὺ ('I looked, and there was' 6.2, 5, 8) used to introduce the other three riders. If the identification of the first rider with Jesus is correct, the use of the word 'another' here serves a significant rhetorical function: Jesus has just entered the world triumphantly, but then to the reader's surprise he is followed by 'another', indicating that the battle, far from being over, is merely just beginning.[14] This second rider arrives on a bright blood-red horse, a fitting colour for his role in the drama, which is to take peace from the earth and to cause great slaughter (6.4). Significantly, it is not the rider himself who kills people, rather it is the people of the earth who kill each other: the result of the nations of the earth involving themselves in the satanic empire is war and death on a grand scale. The 'great sword' given to the rider symbolizes the divine permission that results in humanity's experience of judgement through warfare, as God allows the effects of evil to work themselves out in the lives of those who have embraced the beast.

The third rider to be summoned is seen riding a black horse, and carrying in his hand a pair of scales (6.5). The scales in the hand of the rider are indicative of the need to distribute food according to strict rationing during a time of starvation.[15] The colour of the horse here is symbolic of the scorched earth and decaying bodies of famine and death, which is emphasized as the Lamb's voice is heard from among the four living creatures proclaiming: 'A quart of wheat for a day's pay, and three quarts of barley for a day's pay, but do not damage the olive oil and the wine!' (6.6). The cost given here for grain is exorbitant for a quantity amounting to only basic starvation rations,[16] and the implication is that those living under the empire of the beast will eventually face famine as its systems of exploitation set in place unsustainable levels of consumption. Howard-Brook and Gwyther note the Roman system of *latifundia*, where land was taken from smallholders and placed in the control of city-based landowners, making those who farmed the land become tenant-farmers. To cater for the spiralling demands of profitable luxury goods at the heart of the Empire, the landowners directed ever-increasing sections of land to be turned over to oil and wine production at the expense of grain, leading to a shortage of staple foods and a surplus of luxury items.[17] This provides a convincing explanation for the inflated prices of grain, coupled with a protected supply of oil and wine, as is reflected in the statement from the Lamb. On this understanding, the voice of the Lamb at this point can be understood as a cry of ironic judgement on the system which allows the poor majority to starve while the rich continue to enjoy their lavish lifestyles. The inequalities reflected in the system described here are at odds with the system of food distribution found in the Old Testament, where grain, oil and wine are seen as symbols of God's blessing and provision.[18]

The fourth rider appears on a pale green horse, and is the only rider to be positively identified by name: this rider is none other than Death, and he is followed by Hades (6.8). This personified duo have already been mentioned in Revelation, with the 'one like a son of man' holding the keys to Death and Hades (1.18), signifying that he has the power to release those held captive by them. This release is seen at the final judgement, where Death and Hades surrender those they have been holding before they themselves are cast into the lake of fire (20.13–14).[19] Such a personification of Death and Hades is not unique to John, but rather draws on both Greek and Jewish mythology.[20] They come into the world at the invitation of the fourth living creature (6.7), and are given authority over a quarter of the earth[21] to claim souls for their realm (6.8).[22] Death inevitably follows war and famine, sealing the hold of the satanic empire on the nations of the earth, a hold that is broken only at the final judgement.

The four angels who had been given power to damage earth and sea

Four otherwise unidentified angels come into view at the beginning of Chapter 7. They are initially seen standing at the four corners of the earth, holding back the four winds (7.1),[23] and are described as those who have been 'given power to damage earth and sea' (7.2). They are restrained from doing so by the angel from the sun until the servants of God have been sealed (7.3), before they are finally released to wreak their havoc on the world after the sealing of the 144,000 (cf. 8.7).[24] The background for destructive angels such as these is to be found in Jewish apocalyptic material, where they function to execute judgement on the wicked.[25] Within John's scheme, this image functions to reassure his audience that while they may have to live through the coming judgements on the earth, nonetheless such events are ultimately within the overall control of God, and that as the people of God they are secure against its eternally destructive effects.

Wormwood

The Jewish tradition of fallen angels lies behind John's image of a great star who falls from heaven to the earth at the blowing of the third trumpet

(8.10–11).[26] This is presumably one of the angels who serve Satan, whose expulsion from heaven is described in the story of the pregnant woman (12.9). The name given to this angel is Wormwood, a bitter-tasting plant commonly used in ancient times for treating intestinal worms. It is mentioned in the Old Testament to describe bitterness,[27] and John's use of the name to describe this angel is indicative of the poisonous effect that the angel has on the waters of the earth.[28] In contrast to Moses' sweetening of the bitter water at Marah (Ex. 15.23–5), Wormwood makes the waters of the earth fatally bitter, highlighting the way in which the satanic empire poisons the earth.

Abaddon/Apollyon/the angel of the bottomless pit

Following the sounding of the fifth trumpet, a further instance is recounted of a star which, like Wormwood, has fallen from heaven to the earth. As with Wormwood, this angelic being is best understood as one of Satan's angels (9.1; cf. 12.9).[29] He is given the key to the shaft of the bottomless pit, which he proceeds to open (9.1b–2). This is the first mention of the bottomless pit in Revelation, and it is seen to be the dwelling place of the locusts who emerge to torture those who are not sealed with the seal of God (9.2–10); it is also the place from where the beast emerges (11.7; 17.8), and the place where Satan is imprisoned for a thousand years (20.1, 3). The locusts have as their king a being named Abaddon (Apollyon in Greek),[30] who is described as the angel of the bottomless pit (9.11), although it is a matter of some disagreement among commentators as to whether the angel of the bottomless pit (9.11) should be identified with the angel holding the key to the bottomless pit (9.1).[31] If they are not the same, then Abaddon emerges from the pit with the locusts, whereas if they are the same, he takes control of the locusts after they have emerged. In either case, John depicts the locusts as being led by a satanic servant in their attack on the earth. It is significant that the key is passed to the fallen angel (9.1) as Jesus has already been seen to be in possession of the keys of Death and Hades (1.18); it is therefore presumably Jesus who passes the key to the fallen angel so that the bottomless pit can be opened.[32] This serves to reinforce to John's audience once again that the judgements on the earth originate within the throne room of heaven.

The locusts

The locusts that emerge from the bottomless pit following the fifth trumpet form a terrifying sight as they torture all those who are not sealed with the seal of God (9.3–10). Plagues of locusts were feared in the rural societies of the Mediterranean basin, as they have the ability to strip crops from the fields in a matter of hours, and John's use of the image draws on the plague of locusts visited by God upon the Egyptians (Ex. 10.4–19).[33] The description that John gives of the locusts involves layer upon layer of imagery, building up a picture of unearthly, horrifying creatures with stings like scorpions (9.5, 10), armoured like horses for battle with human faces, women's hair and lion's teeth (9.7–9). This description evokes the Parthian invaders, who were famously superb horsemen with their heavily armoured horses, the *cataphract*, and whose warriors wore their hair long.[34] Those living in the seven churches to which John was writing would remember the various battles fought between Rome and Parthia, in which the Romans frequently sustained heavy losses.[35] John plays on this fear of Parthian invasion to describe the incursion of the satanic forces upon the earth.

The four angels who are bound at the Euphrates

Following the sounding of the sixth trumpet, a voice from the horns of the altar in heaven[36] commands the release of four angels who are bound at the river Euphrates (9.14). John hears the number of their cavalry as two hundred million (9.16), and they ride forth at the appointed time to kill a third of humankind (9.15). Once again, just as with the image of the locusts, John has in mind here the invading Parthian hordes; the Euphrates marked the boundary between the eastern edge of the Roman Empire and the kingdom of Parthia.[37] The description John provides of the mounted army has strong similarities with his previous description of the locusts from the bottomless pit (9.17, 19; cf. 9.7–10).[38] The mounted forces of evil are pictured by John as sweeping over the earth like an innumerable army of Parthian horsemen invading the Roman Empire.

From the perspective of those in John's churches this image is both terrifying and comforting: its terror lies in the horror and severity of the damage that the evil empire attracts, yet the comfort is to be found in the assurance that the judgements John describes have their origin within the throne room of God. The destructive angels are released by a heavenly voice, at the appointed time, indicating that evil will not be allowed to rule the earth for ever, and that due judgement will in time come upon the satanic empire. The actions of humanity in its idolatrous worship of the beast are seen to be storing up judgement, with the agents of this judgement bound, awaiting the appropriate time for their unleashing. The pastoral message here is that evil will not be allowed to rule the earth unjudged for eternity; but rather the time will come when the consequences of humanity's idolatrous actions will be visited back upon the people of the earth. So it is that a third of humankind are killed (9.15, 18), but even despite this, those who survive fail to respond to the warning implicit in the judgement, and they continue in their idolatrous and wicked actions (9.20–1).

Three foul spirits like frogs

Following the pouring out of the sixth bowl, two things happen: first, the river Euphrates dries up, to prepare the way for the invasion from the east (16.12), and second, three 'foul spirits like frogs' are seen by John emerging from the mouths of the dragon, the beast, and the false prophet (16.13). This parallels two scenes from the Old Testament narrative of the exodus: the parting of the waters of the Red Sea (Ex. 14.21–2), and the plague of frogs in Egypt (Ex. 8.1–15). The three demonic frogs assemble the kings of the world for the battle at Harmagedon (16.14,16), indicating that the mobilization of earthly forces against the people of God has a satanic origin and motivation. Just as Pharaoh's heart was hardened and he refused to repent after the plague of frogs (Ex. 8.15), with his forces eventually meeting their doom in the waters of the Red Sea (Ex. 14.22–8; 15.4–5), so in Revelation the nations of the world set their hearts against the people of God, and meet their final judgement on the plain of Harmagedon.

Babylon

The name 'Babylon' appears six times in the book of Revelation (14.8; 16.19; 17.5; 18.2, 10, 21), and it represents for John the satanic empire which seeks to promote itself as an idolatrous alternative to the kingdom of the one who is seated on the throne in heaven. Within John's context, the current manifestation of Babylon is Rome and her all-conquering Empire.[39] However, John's use of the language of 'Babylon' to describe the Empire indicates that, in his view, Rome is simply the latest expression of the underlying tendency of humanity to offer worship and allegiance to institutionalized evil rather than to God himself.

The city of Babylon and the Babylonian Empire were ancient enemies of the people of God. The Babylonians had conquered Jerusalem in 587 BC, destroying the temple and taking many Jews into exile in Babylon. Even after the restoration of the exiles to their land in 537 BC, Babylon continued to function as a symbol of both oppression and God's judgement.[40] The similarities between Babylon of old and the Roman Empire of John's day were easy to draw, with both exhibiting characteristics of corruption and luxury (cf. Isa. 13.1–22; Dan. 4.30), and both actively oppressing the people of God. Smalley observes:

> Babylon, in John's visions, symbolizes the secular and unjust spirit of humanity which, in any age, forces others to compromise with the truth, to worship idols rather than the Creator (13:15; 14:7), and to behave as followers of the devil rather than of Christ (13:16–17).[41]

There are a number of images utilized within Revelation that refer to Babylon, and these will now be examined.

The great city

Each time Babylon is referred to in Revelation, it is in conjunction with the adjective 'great' (cf. Dan. 4.30).[42] In addition to this, there are also references to 'the great city' which function as a cipher for Babylon. The first occurrence of 'the great city' in Revelation is also the most contentious. The dead bodies of the two witnesses lie in the street of 'the great city that is prophetically called Sodom and Egypt, where also their Lord was crucified' (11.8). This description has led many commentators to identify 'the great city' in this instance as Jerusalem, rather than Babylon/Rome. Boxall's observations are particularly helpful here:

> It is not Jerusalem, nor is it Rome, though its citizens can be found in both locations. Revelation's great city can never be located on a terrestrial map, though its characteristics are those of Sodom and Egypt, both symbols of rebellion against God and, in the case of Egypt, oppression of God's people. The great city can manifest itself in any city in the world where God's sanctuary is attacked, where the Church is giving faithful witness: from Jerusalem to Rome, from Ephesus to Laodicea, from London to Beijing to New York.[43]

It is not without significance that Babylon is repeatedly referred to as 'great'; the city is seen by John as being 'great' in terms of power, influence, splendour, wealth, and might. In so many ways though, Babylon provides an idolatrous alternative to God himself, laying claim through its 'greatness' to the worship and adoration of the nations of the world. So it is fitting that the first reference to 'Babylon' in Revelation is to 'Babylon the great', who is proclaimed by an angel as 'fallen' (14.8).[44] Babylon is described as having 'made all nations drink of the wine of the wrath of her fornication' (14.8); like Satan himself, the satanic empire symbolized by Babylon is seen to be complicit in the deception of the nations of the world (12.9; 20.3, 8–10). John wants his audience to realize that Babylon, great and mighty though the city may be, is ultimately under the judgement of God, and will not endure eternally. For John's audience, living within the Roman Empire, this assurance that 'the eternal city'[45] was actually living on borrowed time was a matter of great importance to them as they sought to disassociate themselves from the ensnaring temptations of the Empire.

There are a number of passages that describe the downfall of the great city. Following the outpouring of the seventh bowl, the great city is seen to split into three parts (16.19). Just as Babylon has made the nations drink the wine of her fornication (14.8; cf. 18.3), so she in turn drinks the wine of God's wrath (16.19). The splitting-apart of the great city also destroys those other cities of the world that have built their success on that of Babylon (16.19). Further on, an angelic voice repeats the refrain that Babylon is 'fallen', saying that the city has become 'a dwelling place of demons' (18.2).[46] A picture is then painted of the relationship between Babylon and the nations of the world, who are depicted as having participated in Babylon's pleasures, becoming intoxicated with the city's success (18.3). The people of God are instructed to come out of the great city (18.4)[47] because of its great sinfulness (18.5–7). The kings and merchants of the earth, however, mourn the destruction of Babylon, because their wealth and power is built on the economic and political success of the great city (18.9–19). The description of the great city as 'clothed in fine linen, in purple and scarlet, adorned with gold, with jewels, and with pearls' (18.16), compares with the clothing of the great whore (17.4) and contrasts with that of the bride of the Lamb (19.8).[48] The seafarers lament when they see the great city burning, crying out in despair, 'what city was like the great city?' (18.8). The final destruction of the great city is symbolized when a mighty angel takes a great millstone and throws it into the sea, proclaiming: 'With such violence Babylon the great city will be thrown down, and will be found no more' (18.21).

The great whore

While the identification of 'the great city' with Babylon is clear, it is not so immediately obvious that a similar identification should be made for the great whore. However, as John's description progresses, it becomes clear that she is a dramatic and vivid representation of Rome.[49] In the background to John's presentation of the great whore is the goddess Roma, the deified personification of the city of Rome.[50] Roma had become particularly associated with the imperial family, to the extent that a number of temples were built in the first century AD dedicated jointly to both Roma and Augustus Caesar (63 BC–AD 14).[51] John, however, reinvents the goddess Roma as a temple prostitute.[52] The shocking effect that this would have had on John's audience should not be understated, with its invitation for them to re-imagine the Rome-dominated symbolic world that they had inherited. John's association of the sexual promiscuity normally expected of a prostitute with the goddess who personified Rome and the imperial family was a deeply subversive act.

John first encounters the great whore in his vision when he is invited by the bowl-angel to witness her judgement. He is told that she is seated on 'many waters' (17.1), which symbolize the peoples, multitudes, nations and languages of the world (17.15). The picture is thus created of Rome sitting astride the earth, dominating all of humanity. John is told that the whore has committed fornication with the kings of the earth, and that the inhabitants of the earth have become drunk with the wine of that fornication (17.2; cf. 14.8; 18.3). Having been introduced to the whore thus, John catches his first glimpse of her sitting on the scarlet beast (17.3).[53] She is herself clothed in imperial purple and scarlet, dripping with jewels (cf. 18.16), and holding a golden cup containing both abominations and the impurities of her fornication (17.4). The inhabitants of the earth are described as having become intoxicated by their consumption of the contents of this cup (17.2), thus creating the powerful image of the cup as a symbol of all the sinful yet seductive attractions of Babylon.[54]

Only at this point is the whore positively identified, when John sees written on her head, 'Babylon the great, mother of whores and of earth's abominations' (17.5). It becomes clear from this point that the 'great whore' is the 'great city', and that both of them together represent Babylon, the ancient enemy of the people of God, manifest in John's time as the city and Empire of Rome. The great whore is seen to be drunk with the blood of the saints (17.6), a reference to the bloody martyrdoms of Christians carried out by the Emperor Nero. While the nations have been drinking the wine of the great whore's fornication, the whore herself has been drinking the blood of the martyred people of God.

The identification of the great whore with Babylon/Rome then continues. The seven heads of the beast that she is riding are identified as seven mountains and seven kings (17.9–10); Rome was famously the city seated on seven hills, and the seven kings of whom 'five have fallen, one is living, and the other has not yet come' (17.10) almost certainly represent seven Roman emperors.[55] The great whore is once again explicitly named as the 'great city' (17.18), and then in the description of the fall of Babylon (18.2–19.3) the imagery of the great city is interspersed with descriptions appropriate to the great whore, as the following table illustrates.

The great whore	The great city
	18.2 [The angel] called out with a mighty voice, 'Fallen, fallen is Babylon the great! It has become a dwelling place of demons, a haunt of every foul spirit, a haunt of every foul bird, a haunt of every foul and hateful beast.
18.3a For all the nations have drunk of the wine of the wrath of her fornication, and the kings of the earth have committed fornication with her,	18.3b and the merchants of the earth have grown rich from the power of her luxury.'
18.4a Then I heard another voice from heaven saying, 'Come out of her, my people, so that you do not take part in her sins,	
	18.4b and so that you do not share in her plagues;
18.5 for her sins are heaped high as heaven, and God has remembered her iniquities.	
18.6–7 Render to her as she herself has rendered, and repay her double for her deeds; mix a double draught for her in the cup she mixed. As she glorified herself and lived luxuriously, so give her a like measure of torment and grief. Since in her heart she says, 'I rule as a queen; I am no widow, and I will never see grief,'	18.8 therefore her plagues will come in a single day – pestilence and mourning and famine – and she will be burned with fire; for mighty is the Lord God who judges her.'
18.9a And the kings of the earth, who committed fornication and lived in luxury with her,	18.9b–11 will weep and wail over her when they see the smoke of her burning; they will stand far off, in fear of her torment, and say, 'Alas, alas, the great city, Babylon, the mighty city! For in one hour your judgement has come.' And the merchants of the earth weep and mourn for her, since no one buys their cargo anymore,

	18.15–16a The merchants ... who gained wealth from her, will stand far off, in fear of her torment, weeping and mourning aloud, 'Alas, alas, the great city,
18.16b clothed in fine linen, in purple and scarlet, adorned with gold, with jewels, and with pearls!	18.17–18 For in one hour all this wealth has been laid waste!' And all shipmasters and seafarers, sailors and all whose trade is on the sea, stood far off and cried out as they saw the smoke of her burning, 'What city was like the great city?'
	18.21 Then a mighty angel took up a stone like a great millstone and threw it into the sea, saying, 'With such violence Babylon the great city will be thrown down, and will be found no more;
19.1–2 After this I heard what seemed to be the loud voice of a great multitude in heaven, saying, 'Hallelujah! Salvation and glory and power to our God, for his judgements are true and just; he has judged the great whore who corrupted the earth with her fornication, and he has avenged on her the blood of his servants.'	19.3 Once more they said, 'Hallelujah! The smoke goes up from her forever and ever.'

As is evident from the table above, John intertwines the imagery of the great whore and the great city to great dramatic effect as he describes the downfall of the satanic empire.[56] The call of the heavenly voice for the people of God to 'come out of her' (18.4) acquires a double meaning (or *double-entendre*); it is both a call for them to move their citizenship from the great city to the heavenly city, and also for them to cease and desist from participating in the seductive pleasures of the great whore. John's use of language here is vivid and compelling, designed to shock his audience into a realization of the nature of the symbolic world they inhabit, and to elicit an appropriate response in terms of their living-out of their membership of the army of the Lamb.

One specific image that John employs for the great whore deserves additional comment. Through Chapter 18, John uses the image of fire to describe the burning of the great city, evoking the picture of a city being put to the torch (18.8, 9, 18). However, he also describes the 'burning' of the great whore in the following terms: 'And the ten horns that you saw, they and the beast will hate the whore; they will make her desolate and naked; they will devour her flesh and burn her up with fire' (17.16). This description of the stripping, rape, cannibalistic consumption and burning of the body of the great whore is as deeply shocking to modern readers as it would have been to John's first audience. It is worth noting that John is consciously employing such powerful imagery to deconstruct the worldview of those living in the seven churches of Asia Minor under the Roman Empire. He is not seeking to describe an actual physical and sexual assault; rather he is using the language of such a violation as an image to describe the downfall of the idolatrous satanic empire.[57] It is to this end that the heavenly multitude praise God for the justice of his judgement of the great whore, and for avenging on her the blood of his servants. They rejoice at her burning (19.2–3), because the evil empire finally receives judgement for all the wrong done against the people of God.

There is a very real question here as to the effect such imagery has on modern readers, and also of the effect that it has had down through the centuries since it was first written. John's association of the alluring female form, laid vulnerable and violated, with God's fitting judgement on evil in the world, has doubtless played its part in promoting a negative and exploitative view of women. Artistic representations of this scene have fed the male desire to see women dominated and abused, even lending divine authorization to such imagery.[58] While this may not have been John's original intent in constructing this image, nonetheless it must be recognized that this is part of the effect that it has had and continues to have. Although Tina Pippin's comments may be seen as a little naïve in their imposition of modern genre categories onto an ancient text, they nonetheless provide a useful introduction to the way in which this imagery may be interpreted by some:

> The Apocalypse is less like the shower scene in *Psycho* than the all-out killing in the *Texas Chain Saw Massacre*, but there are elements of both these forms of subtle and big-screen gross-out horrors in the text ... [A]t the murder scene of the great whore in 17:16 is grotesque horror ... The Apocalypse has similarities to the genre of horror literature in the splattering of blood and gore on the reader and in the intensity in which it draws the reader to gaze on the ripped flesh ... The Whore of Babylon is a siren calling to men ... Is the Apocalypse pornographic? Are apocalypses the pornography of the end time? Pornography, like horror and utopian literature, goes beyond societal boundaries. Like horror, pornography is iterative; the act of violence repeats itself in

our re-readings, in the violence done on the psyche of the victim. Does the Apocalypse do psychological damage? The wrathful, judging God is alongside the joy (*jouissance*) of the believer. The deadly desire of godly utopia targets the unbeliever – and wayward women.[59]

The beast from the bottomless pit

The first occurrence of τὸ θηρίον ('the beast') in Revelation is found in 11.7, where 'the beast' ascends from the bottomless pit to make war on and kill the two witnesses.[60] It is not specified whether this is the beast from the sea (cf. 13.1), or the beast from the earth (cf. 13.11), and it is probably best to identify it as neither. Rather, the beast from the bottomless pit serves to demonstrate that the forces behind the satanic empire, which oppose and persecute the Church, find their origin in the pits of hell itself. In John's descriptions of the various beasts, he draws on Daniel's vision of four beasts that come from the sea (Dan. 7.1–8). The closest parallel within this Old Testament passage to the beast from the bottomless pit of Revelation 11 is found in the 'little horn' of Daniel's fourth beast, which makes war on the 'holy ones', and is seen 'prevailing over them' (Dan. 7.21).

The scarlet beast from the sea

A further image that John utilizes for Babylon is that of the scarlet beast which arises from the sea (13.1) after the dragon has taken its stand on the seashore (12.8). Having failed to overcome the woman, the dragon sets about making war on the woman's other children (12.17), and calls forth the beast from the depths with this intent. It is therefore clear from its first appearance that the scarlet beast exists at the bidding of the dragon, with the goal of doing the dragon's will in terms of opposing those who hold the testimony of Jesus. This association between the dragon and the beast is reinforced by the physical similarity between them: like the dragon, the beast also has seven heads and ten horns. The background to this image lies in the Leviathan of Jewish mythology, who ascends from the chaos of the deep seas to wreak havoc on the land.[61] However, John is also drawing on the four beasts that ascend from the sea in Daniel's vision (Dan. 7.2–7). The beasts that Daniel sees are described as a winged lion, a three-tusked bear, a winged four-headed leopard, and a strong beast with ten horns. John amalgamates these images to make his beast with seven heads, ten horns, a leopard's body, a bear's feet, and a lion's mouth (13.2). Whereas Daniel's four beasts represented four kingdoms (Dan. 7.17, 23),[62] John's scarlet beast represents just one: Rome.

The seven heads with the blasphemous names (13.1; cf. 17.9) symbolize the idolatrous claims made by the city on the seven hills, as it positions itself as an alternative to the one on the throne in heaven.

The beast is then duly invested with the power of the dragon (13.2), and sets about deceiving the earth into following it (13.3). Crucial to its success in gaining the support and allegiance of the nations is a specific characteristic exhibited by one of the seven heads of the beast: this head looks as if it has been slaughtered (ἐσφαγμένην) but has been miraculously healed. At one level this image functions as a satanic imitation of the Lamb who was slaughtered (ἐσφαγμένον) but is still alive (5.6), drawing the nations to worship the beast instead of the Lamb. However, there is a specific contextual background to John's imagery here. The Emperor Nero, the archetypal dictator and persecutor of Christians, had reportedly committed suicide with a sword in AD 68, some years before the most likely date for the writing of the book of Revelation.[63] In that intervening period, a myth had emerged that Nero would either come back to life, or come out of hiding, and lead a Parthian invasion of the Roman Empire.[64] John, it seems, knows of this myth, and finds the imagery of Nero's rebirth too compelling to ignore. While returning to Nero more fully in his image of the beast from the earth, he utilizes this *Nero Redivivus* myth in his picture of the scarlet beast. From John's perspective, although Nero may be dead and gone, his mythology is alive and well, providing powerful propaganda for the Roman Empire. The great persecutor may have gone, but his spirit is still active in the satanic empire, leading the nations of the world in idolatrous opposition to the Lamb.

So successful is the beast in attracting the allegiance of the inhabitants of the earth, that John sees the whole earth worshipping not just the beast of Rome, but also the underlying force of evil that sustains it. There is an expression of hopelessness in the cry uttered by the nations when they say: 'Who is like the beast, and who can fight against it?' (13.4) They are both seduced by the might of the beast, and also discouraged from thoughts of resistance by their sense of futility in the face of such overwhelming power. This cry would surely have been echoed by those in the seven churches, as they pondered their own insignificance and powerlessness in the face of the might of the imperial machine. This sense of frustration becomes more palpable as the beast acquires the ability to speak blasphemous words (13.5). However, a note of hope is then sounded, as a time-limit of 42 months is placed on the beast's authority.[65] During this period of persecution, the beast utters blasphemies both against God himself and against those who dwell in heaven (13.5), and makes war on the saints and conquers them, taking authority over the nations of the earth (13.7). The result is that all the nations of the earth worship the beast, excepting only those whose names are written in the Lamb's book of life (13.8). The picture here is of the beast's total domination of the earth. The Church is a beleaguered minority, but nonetheless only the faithful can see the satanic empire for what it is because only they recognize the idolatrous and blasphemous nature of the claims made by the beast.

However, in all of this, John's language is *passive*: he says that the beast *was given* a mouth to utter blasphemies and that it *was allowed* to exercise authority (13.5); it *was allowed* to make war on the saints and it *was given* authority over the nations (13.7). In this way, the idolatrous claims of the beast are relativized, because its power is seen as existing only by divine permission, and even then only for a little while. Once again, John is addressing the question of the extent to which God is in control even during times of judgement and suffering on the earth. Once again his answer is that, however much it might appear that the beast is in control, true authority resides solely with the one on the throne in heaven, and that therefore any blasphemous pretension to that authority, however convincing it may appear to be, is ultimately doomed to failure.

The beast from the sea is next seen following the pouring out of the sixth bowl-plague onto the waters of the river Euphrates, which causes them to dry up in preparation for the invasion of the kings from the east (16.12). At this point, John sees three foul spirits like frogs emerging from the mouths of the dragon, the scarlet beast, and the false prophet. These foul spirits mobilize the armies of the world for battle against the army of the Lamb, something that is depicted as having a threefold satanic origin.

The scarlet beast reappears in the narrative in Chapter 17, where the great whore is seen riding the beast full of blasphemous names with seven heads and ten horns (17.3). This close association between the great whore and the beast indicates that they are to be understood as two different presentations of the same underlying signifier. Both, in their own way, function as images for Rome as an expression of Babylon, and Bauckham suggests that the beast is a representation of the military and political might of the satanic empire, while the great whore represents the economic corruption that supports and bankrolls the beast.[66]

The *Nero Redivivus* myth explored above also lies behind the next appearance of the scarlet beast, where it is described as that which 'was and is not and is to come' (17.8; cf. 17.11). Once again, John presents the myth of Nero's return from the grave as a satanic and idolatrous parody of the one in heaven 'who was and is and is to come' (4.8; cf. 1.4, 8). So successful is this alternative claim on the worship and allegiance of the people of the earth, that the inhabitants of the earth whose names are not written in the book of life are 'amazed'.

The scarlet beast from the sea makes its final appearance at the great battle of Harmagedon, when it joins its army with that of the kings of the earth to make war against the rider on the white horse and his army (19.19). This final conflict between the nations of the world and the people of God ends with the scarlet beast being captured and thrown into the lake of fire (19.20). There is no place for Babylon in any guise within the new Jerusalem, and so the powerful and mighty satanic empire is cast into the flames for destruction.

There are two beasts in Revelation that have seven heads and ten horns: the dragon (12.3) and the scarlet beast from the sea (13.1; 17.3, 7, 9–12). The presence of these heads and horns on the scarlet beast is clearly indicative of its familial relationship to the dragon, the underlying source of evil that calls the beast to life and gives it its power. However, they also pose something of an interpretative puzzle that will now be briefly explored.

The seven heads of the scarlet beast

The number seven is the Jewish number of perfection, and at one level the presence of seven heads on the beast is indicative of Babylon's idolatrous claim to perfection. However, John provides two further levels of interpretation: 'This calls for a mind that has wisdom: the seven heads are seven mountains on which the woman is seated; also, they are seven kings, of whom five have fallen, one is living, and the other has not yet come; and when he comes, he must remain only a little while. As for the beast that was and is not, it is an eighth but it belongs to the seven, and it goes to destruction' (17.9–11). The seven mountains almost certainly represent the fabled seven hills of Rome, indicating once again the link between the scarlet beast and the seat of the Empire.[67]

The seven kings, however, are harder to identify. It is most likely that the seven kings are intended to signify Roman emperors, given their identification with the seven hills of Rome; but the difficulty lies in deciding which are the specific emperors that John has in mind. John states that five have already passed, one is current, and one is yet to come, with the beast making an eighth that belongs to the seven (17.11). A historical-correlation approach has significant implications for the dating of the work, and the picture is further complicated by the fact that John may be setting a fictional date for his text earlier than the time of his actual writing. The following table illustrates three of the major suggestions for tying together John's list and the date of composition.[68]

		mid–60s	early 70s	early 90s
Julius Caesar	d. 44 BC	1		
Augustus	d. AD 14	2	1	
Tiberius	14–37	3	2	
Caligula	37–41	4	3	1

		mid–60s	early 70s	early 90s
Claudius	41–54	5	4	2
Nero	54–68	6	5	3
Galba	68–9			
Otho	69		Ignore	Ignore
Vitellus	69			
Vespasian	69–79		6	4
Titus	79–81			5
Domitian	81–96			6
'the other'	Rev. 17.10	7	7	7
'an eighth'	Rev. 17.11	8	8	8

It will be seen that two of these suggestions ignore the three short-lived emperors of Galba, Otho and Vitellus. This is not as arbitrary as it may appear, as these three were never universally recognized across the Empire even during their own brief reigns.

Rather than adopting a strictly historical approach, an alternative way of understanding John's imagery here is to treat his list as figurative. According to this understanding, while John may or may not have specific emperors in mind, his overall intent in employing these images is to convey that wherever and whenever human power seeks to usurp God's kingly rule, it is to be understood as a manifestation of the beast.[69]

John's description of a seventh 'other' head which will 'remain only a little while' (17.10), followed by an eighth head described as 'the beast that was and is not' (17.11; cf. 17.8), is often understood as a further reference to the *Nero Redivivus* myth in which the next emperor (whoever it may be) will shortly give way to a resurrected Nero returning from the grave to resume his reign of terror over the Empire. The significance of this for John's audience was that they were living in a time when the beast seemed all-powerful, to the extent that it even posed a challenge to the lordship of the resurrected Christ among the congregations of the faithful, in its seemingly all-encompassing claim on the hearts and minds of the nations of the earth. It is therefore to those seeking to resist the idolatrous assertions of the beast that John affirms the ultimate destruction of the beast (17.11).

The ten horns of the scarlet beast

The interpreting angel, who has explained the mystery of the seven heads, then continues to tell John that the ten horns of the beast symbolize ten kings who have not yet received a kingdom (17.12; cf. Dan. 7.7–8, 20, 24). Rather than emperors, the ten horns symbolize Roman client kings,[70] possibly the same kings of the earth who commit fornication with the whore.[71] The ten kings receive power to rule the earth in league with the beast, but this reign is short-lived (17.12) as they cede their authority and power to the beast (17.13). Within John's scheme, those human rulers who give their allegiance to the beast in exchange for earthly power will find that their reward is merely temporary. Those who join with the beast in making war against the Lamb will ultimately be unsuccessful, as John assures his audience once again that the Lamb will be victorious against all the forces of evil (17.14).[72]

The ten horns/kings have one final role to play in the drama of the judgement of Babylon. John says that they, together with the beast, will turn on the great whore and destroy her (17.16). John returns here to his theme of evil bringing upon itself its own self-destructive judgement.[73] The final annihilation of the great whore, who has so successfully seduced the kings and nations of the world, is ironically seen to be completed by the hands of those who have previously been her lovers (cf. 17.2). Utilizing imagery from the Old Testament, John paints a shocking picture of the demise of the great whore, as the ten horns and the beast turn on her and desolate her,[74] devouring her flesh,[75] and burning her with fire.[76]

The ten horns attack the great whore in conjunction with a beast (17.16), which may be a further reference to the *Nero Redivivus* myth. If the beast working in league with the ten kings here is the eighth head, 'the beast that was and is not' (17.11; cf. 17.8), then this may be an allusion to the myth of a returning Nero in league with the kings of the east (cf. 16.12), coming to destroy and burn his former capital city. John's clear message for his audience here is that the actions of the ten kings and the beast in destroying the great whore form part of God's overall purpose for the final destruction of evil and the fulfilment of his words of judgement (17.17).

The beast from the earth

It has already been seen how the spectre of Nero looms large over John's portrayal of Babylon, particularly as he utilizes the *Nero Redivivus* myth in his descriptions of the scarlet beast from the sea.[77] However, if Nero is implicit as an aspect of the beast from the sea, he is explicitly personified as the beast from the earth. Whereas the beast from the sea symbolizes the ancient enemy of God's people, Babylon currently incarnated in the Empire of Rome, the beast from the earth depicts Nero as the blasphemous mythology of Rome personified. The Old Testament background for these two beasts, one from the sea and one from the earth, is found in the Leviathan and the Behemoth. The Leviathan is the mythical evil serpent from the deep,[78] while the Behemoth is the unconquerable land-dwelling monster.[79]

The image being presented here for John's audience is of Rome as the latest and greatest manifestation of the long-running satanic project to draw humans away from the worship of God, while opposing and destroying all those who might attempt to resist this idolatrous call. Rome, symbolized by the beast from the sea, therefore draws its might and power from none other than Satan himself, symbolized by the great dragon. However, Rome does not function alone; and this is the role of Nero. During his lifetime he was not only the despotic head of the Roman Empire, and the object of the worship and adoration of all those who looked to Rome, but also a persecutor of Christians. However, since his suicide, a mythology had developed about him which made him in some senses more powerful in death than he had been in life, at least as far as John's understanding of him as a symbolic personification of the scarlet beast's idolatrous impersonation of God. The idea that Nero might come back from the grave, in a blasphemous parallel to the resurrection and parousia of Jesus, gave him an apparent power over death that rivalled that of the Lamb who had been slaughtered and yet who lived. So John presents Nero as the beast from the earth, exercising the authority of the scarlet beast from the sea, and causing the inhabitants of the earth to worship the scarlet beast (13.12). The parallel between the beast from the earth and the Lamb that was slaughtered is apparent in the fact that he has two horns like the Lamb, while his satanic allegiance is evident from the fact that he speaks like the dragon (13.11).

Just as the beast from the sea has multiple layers of interpretation, being simultaneously Rome, Babylon, or indeed any satanically inspired attempt to draw worship away from God on the throne in heaven, so also the beast from the earth has multiple layers of meaning. While Nero is clearly foremost in John's mind, the beast from the earth nonetheless represents all those individuals or powers which operate in a 'Neronic' manner, calling the nations of the world to engage in blasphemous worship of the beast. This would include, for example, the priests of the Roman imperial cult, as they exercised social control on the populace by calling worshippers in every city of the Empire to give allegiance and devotion to the one on the throne in Rome.[80] The beast from the earth in effect functions as the propaganda machine of the satanic empire.[81] To this end, it performs great signs on behalf of the first beast (13.13),[82] deceiving the inhabitants of the earth into making an idolatrous statue of the scarlet beast from the sea (13.14), a reference to the many statues of the Emperor which would have formed the main focus of the worship offered in the temples of the imperial cult. Just as Nero put to death those who refused to engage in emperor-worship, so the beast from the earth kills those who refuse to engage in idolatrous worship (13.15).

One of John's categories for the inhabitants of the earth is those who are marked with the mark of the beast from the earth.[83] In its quest to secure the idolatrous allegiance of all peoples, the beast causes them to be marked either on the right hand or on the forehead (13.16). This is a symbol of ownership, and it serves to demarcate those who belong to the beast from those marked with the seal of God.[84] The mystery of the meaning of the mark of the beast is one of the interpretative riddles of Revelation that has occupied more than its fair share of commentators' time.[85] John simply says that the mark is the name of the beast, or the number of its name (13.17). He then issues a challenge to his audience: 'This calls for wisdom: let anyone with understanding calculate the number of the beast, for it is the number of a person. Its number is six hundred sixty-six' (13.18). The practice of translating the letters of a name to their numerical equivalents and then adding those numbers together was not uncommon in first century Judaism, and was known as *gematria*.[86] The most compelling explanation of John's riddle is that it represents the Greek form of 'Nero Caesar', transliterated into Hebrew to give the numerical equivalent of 666. This interpretation is further strengthened by the fact that if the Latin *Nero* rather than the Greek *Νέρων* is used, the numerical equivalent becomes 616, which is reflected in a variant reading of this passage. The following table summarizes this suggestion.[87]

Latin	N	e	r	o			C	a	e	s	a	r
Greek	N	ν	ρ	ω	ν		K	α	ι	σ	α	ρ
Hebrew	נ		ר	ו	ן		ק			ס		ר
Number	50		200	6	50		100			60		200

Bauckham also notes that if the same gematria is performed on the Greek for 'beast', the number 666 also results, demonstrating that the *number* of the beast is indeed the *name* of Nero.[88]

Greek	θ	$\acute{\epsilon}$	ρ	ι	o	ν
Hebrew	ת		ר	י	ו	ן
Number	400		200	10	6	50

It is also possible that in addition to the gematria-based identification of Nero with the beast from the earth, John is also here seeking to make a theological point. The number 7 represented totality, or perfection, within Jewish understanding. The fact that the number of the name of the beast is three consecutive instances of the number 6 serves to demonstrate that the beast is satanically short of perfection. Picture John here as a first-century equivalent to the modern fan of the cryptic crossword, delighting in this complex and meticulous process through which he can reinforce his thesis that Nero is a manifestation of the satanic beast.

The false prophet

After setting the riddle of the number of the beast (13.18), John then changes his language, and henceforth refers to the beast from the earth as 'the false prophet'. The first use of this designation occurs following the pouring out of the sixth bowl, when John witnesses three foul spirits like frogs emerging from the mouths of the dragon, the beast from the sea, and the false prophet (16.13). The role that the three foul spirits adopt is to mobilize the kings of the earth for the final great battle against the people of God, and John is here ascribing the origin of this to Satan (the dragon), aided by Rome (the beast from the sea) and Nero (the beast from the earth, now described as the false prophet). The image of a reborn Nero riding at the head of a Parthian army is once again in the background to John's image here.[89]

The description of Nero as a 'prophet' is telling: the role of prophets was to ensure that their god was worshipped appropriately. In this way, the prophets of the imperial cult ensured that the emperor was ascribed due worship across the Empire. To depict Nero as the false prophet of the Empire is to confirm once again that the worship he elicits for the beast from the sea is blasphemous and idolatrous (13.14). It is therefore fitting that the false prophet, together with the beast from the sea, is thrown into the lake of fire (19.20; cf. 20.10).

This chapter has provided an overview of John's characterization of the forces of evil. The overriding theme that emerges is that within John's scheme, all those forces that oppose the lordship of the one on the heavenly throne are ultimately destined for destruction. The satanic empire, symbolized by Babylon, is presented as an idolatrous alternative to the kingdom of God, drawing the nations of the earth away from their true eternal home. To this end, the burning of Babylon represents the release of the nations from the tyranny of imperial slavery, freeing them to begin the journey towards the new Jerusalem.

Draw your own conclusions

- In your experience, how is 'Satan' typically understood within contemporary culture?
- How would you summarize John's understanding of 'evil'?

- What are the implications of regarding *deception* as Satan's greatest power?
- How do you react to John's characterization of empire as a satanic puppet?
- Do you agree that evil is a 'self-destructive' entity? Why?
- What view of God and the Church emerges from John's imagery of violent judgement on Babylon delivered in response to the prayers of the saints?

Notes

1 See the discussion of Satan in the Old Testament on p. 202.

2 Some have suggested that they are the local Jewish synagogue, flexing their civic muscle to instigate persecution of the Christians. Others suggest that they are a Jewish-Christian group who, in John's eyes, have compromised with the satanic kingdom. See Ian Boxall, 2003, *Revelation: An Introduction to the Apocalypse*, London: SPCK, pp. 53–5.

3 There is considerable discussion as to which aspect of the city of Pergamum should be identified as 'Satan's throne'. Suggestions include: the temple to Zeus; the temple to Augustus; the shrine of Asklepius; and the Roman acropolis. See Boxall, *Revelation*, p. 58.

4 The 'deep things of Satan' can be contrasted with 'the deep things of God' (Job 11.7; cf. Dan. 2.22; 1 Cor. 2.10), probably indicating an over-attendance to the acquisition of hidden teachings at the expense of the gospel of Christ.

5 For a more detailed discussion of this image see pp. 150–1.

6 J. Webb Mealy comments: 'Equipped with the context supplied by the previous visions of Satan's expulsion from heaven, the indication that he had but a "little time", and the apparent identification of that time with the career of the beast, the reader would know enough to expect to encounter some kind of definite judgement and defeat of Satan at the end of the beast's career.' J. Webb Mealy, 1992, *After the Thousand Years*, Journal for the Study of the New Testament Supplement Series, Sheffield: JSOT Press, p. 118.

7 Cf. Job 3.8; 7.12; 41.1; Ps. 74.14; 104.26; Isa. 27.1; 51.9; 4 Esdras 6.49–52.

8 In Jewish understanding the number seven denoted perfection. John subverts this in his image of the dragon and the beast which it spawns, by linking the seven heads of the beast from the sea (13.1) with the seven hills of Rome (17.9), indicating that however perfect the dragon may appear, it is actually a personification of evil. Compare the seven diadems of the dragon with the 'many diadems' worn by the rider on the white horse (19.12; cf. 13.1).

9 Cf. Dan. 7.7, 24; Rev. 5.6.

10 Cf. Dan. 8.10; Rev. 6.13.

11 This story of the casting down of Satan and his angels has its origins in the Old Testament story of the Nephilim (Gen. 6.4), which is expanded in the story of the fall of the angels in 1 Enoch 6—11, 'In those days, when the children of man had multiplied, it happened that there were born unto them

handsome and beautiful daughters. And the angels, the children of heaven, saw them and desired them; and they said to one another, "Come, let us choose wives for ourselves from among the daughters of man and beget us children." ... And they were altogether two hundred; and they descended into 'Ardos, which is the summit of Hermon' (1 Enoch 6.1-2, 6). Translated by E. Isaac in James H. Charlesworth (ed.), 1983, *The Old Testament Pseudepigrapha Vol. 1*, New York: Doubleday, p. 15. On stars representing angelic beings, see Isa. 24.2-23. Cf. Edward Adams, 2007, *The Stars Will Fall from Heaven: Cosmic Catastrophe in the New Testament and its World*, London: T&T Clark, pp. 242-3.

12 Elizabeth Achtemeier, 1986, *Nahum-Malachi*, Interpretation, Atlanta: John Knox Press. p. 113

13 See pp. 76-7 for a discussion on whether this rider should be identified as an image for Christ or as a satanic parody of Christ.

14 Smalley disagrees, and suggests that the word 'another' here is, 'merely a synonym for "second"'. Stephen S. Smalley, 2005, *The Revelation to John: A Commentary on the Greek Text of the Apocalypse*, London: SPCK, p. 151.

15 Cf. Lev. 26.26; 2 Kings 7.1; Ezek. 4.10, 16. Smalley, *Revelation*, p. 153.

16 Aune comments that the prices given here are 'about eight times the normal price for wheat and five-and-one-third times the normal price for barley'. David E. Aune, 1998a, *Revelation 6—16*, Nashville: Thomas Nelson, p. 397. Cf. also Smalley, *Revelation*, p. 153.

17 Wes Howard-Brook and Anthony Gwyther, 2001, *Unveiling Empire: Reading Revelation Then and Now*, New York: Orbis Books, p. 98.

18 Cf. Deut. 7.13; 2 Kings 18.32; Jer. 31.12; Hos. 2.8; Joel 2.19. See Howard-Brook and Gwyther, *Unveiling Empire*, p. 142.

19 Cf. 1 Cor. 15.26.

20 Greek mythology features Thanatos, a personification of death, while the Jewish scriptures speak of death in personified terms (Job 18.23; 28.22; Ps. 49.14; Isa. 25.8; Jer. 9.21; Hos. 13.14; Hab. 2.5). Hades is the Greek term for both the underworld and the god of the dead, and has similarities with the Jewish underworld of Sheol, with the Greek translation of the Old Testament, the Septuagint (LXX), substituting Hades for Sheol. Sheol is sometimes personified in the Old Testament (Prov. 30.15-20; Isa. 5.14). Cf. Boxall, *Revelation*, pp. 111-12.

21 Note the increasing severity of the judgements on the earth: one quarter (6.8); one third (8.7-12; 9.15, 18); every living thing (16.3). These are indicative of the growing cycle of judgement and destruction that human allegiance to the beast attracts.

22 Cf. Ezek. 5.16-17.

23 Cf. Jer. 49.36; Dan. 7.2; 11.4.

24 See the discussion of the first trumpet judgement on p. 124.

25 For example 1 Enoch 66.1-2, 'After this he showed me the angels of punishment who are prepared to come and release all the powers of the waters which are underground to become judgement and destruction unto all who live and dwell upon the earth. But the Lord of the Spirits gave an order to the angels who were on duty that they should not.' Translated by E. Isaac in Charlesworth (ed.), *Pseudepigrapha Vol. 1*, pp. 45-6. See also Ezekiel 9.1-11 for a further

image of a destructive angel. Some have suggested that these four angels are synonymous with the four riders of 6.1–8; see G. K. Beale, 1999, *The Book of Revelation*, Carlisle: The Paternoster Press, pp. 407–8. However it is more likely that John has a different group of angelic beings in mind here, as argued in Smalley, *Revelation*, pp. 179–80.

26 1 Enoch 86.1–3, 'as I looked, behold, a star fell down from heaven ... and I saw many stars descending and casting themselves down from the sky upon that first star.' Translated by E. Isaac in Charlesworth (ed.), *Pseudepigrapha Vol. 1*, p. 63.

27 Cf. Prov. 5.4; Lam. 3.15; Amos 5.7.

28 Although wormwood itself is not a poisonous plant, there is a tradition within the Old Testament of associating it with poisonous water (Jer. 9.15; 23.15; cf. Amos 6.12).

29 See the discussion of Wormwood above for the Jewish background to fallen angels. Smalley notes that: 'It was an accepted element of Judaic cosmology that stars were living beings, who possessed a conscious personal nature.' Smalley, *Revelation*, p. 225.

30 Abaddon derives his name from the Hebrew word for *destruction*, which is fitting for his role in Revelation as the leader of the destructive army of the locusts. Although Prov. 30.27 says that 'the locusts have no king', within John's scheme the locusts are led by Abaddon, who points the way to the underworld (cf. Job 28.22; 31.12; Ps. 88.11; Prov. 15.11; 27.20). Apollyon, the Greek version of the name, would have evoked in John's readers a connection with the Hellenistic god Apollo, with whom Nero sought to identify. Cf. Boxall, *Revelation*, p. 145.

31 See the discussion in Beale, *Revelation*, p. 492, who argues in favour of such an identification. Smalley, on the other hand, argues that the fallen star is an agent of God sent to earth to unlock the bottomless pit. See Smalley, *Revelation*, p. 226.

32 The key is back in the possession of Jesus following the final judgement, as an angel comes from heaven with the key to seal Satan in the pit for a thousand years (20.1–2).

33 Cf. 2 Chr. 7.13; Joel 1.4–7; Amos 4.9.

34 Boxall, *Revelation*, p. 145. An alternative interpretation of John's description of the locusts is provided by Hal Lindsey, who suggests that John is actually seeking to describe a vision of advanced attack helicopters, with the crowns of gold representing the helmets of the pilots, and the sound of their wings the noise of the engines. See Hal Lindsey, 1997, *Apocalypse Code*, California: West Front, p. 42. In making this identification, Lindsey is taking an approach to Revelation whereby John's imagery represents a time-slip vision of the end of the world. By this reading, John's imagery is accessible only to those who have sufficient knowledge of, for example, attack helicopters to decode the visions. See pp. 24–5.

35 For example, the Battle of Carrhae (53 BC) was one of the worst defeats ever sustained by the imperial army. Threat of renewed hostilities between Parthia and Rome had heightened in the AD 60s, to the extent that some believed Nero had fled to Parthia with the intention of returning to Rome with an invasion force. Cf. Boxall, *Revelation*, p. 145.

36 See the discussion of the voice from the horns of the altar on p. 129.

37 It is also worth noting that both the Assyrian and Baylonian invaders of Israel came from beyond the Euphrates. See Boxall, *Revelation*, p. 147.

38 The Parthian cavalry would bind the tails of their horses, giving them a snake-like appearance. Cf. Smalley, *Revelation*, p. 241.

39 Although the majority of modern commentators are agreed that John primarily has Rome in view when constructing the imagery of Babylon, Barker makes a forceful argument on the basis of the Old Testament language of Zion as an unfaithful woman (cf. Lam. 2.1; Ezek. 23.30) that actually John's image of the 'harlot city' was originally intended as a critique of Jerusalem, the city rebuilt with Babylonian money after the end of the Jewish exile (Isa. 1.21). She suggests that it was only in later interpretation of the Apocalypse that Babylon came to symbolize Rome for its readers. See Margaret Barker, 2000, *The Revelation of Jesus Christ*, Edinburgh: T&T Clark, pp. 279–85.

40 This is demonstrated by the early second century AD Jewish apocalypse 2 Baruch, which uses Babylon as an image for Rome. The following passage refers to the sacking of Jerusalem by the Romans in AD 70, and compares the Roman Empire to the Babylonians: 'Now this I, Baruch, say to you, O Babylon: If you had lived in happiness and Zion in its glory, it would have been a great sorrow to us that you had been equal to Zion. But now, behold, the grief is infinite and the lamentation is unmeasurable, because, behold, you are happy and Zion has been destroyed' (2 Baruch 11.1–2). Translated by A. F. J. Klijn in Charlesworth (ed.), *Pseudepigrapha Vol. 1*, p. 625. It is also significant that when the author of the book of Daniel, writing in *c.*165 BC, wanted to construct a narrative which would express his theological resistance to the Seleucid ruler, Antiochus IV (175–163 BC), he turned to stories of the Babylonian exile from the sixth century BC. Cf. D. S. Russell, 1989, *Daniel: An Active Volcano*, Edinburgh: The Saint Andrew Press, pp. 11–12.

41 Smalley, *Revelation*, p. 364.

42 Cf. Smalley, *Revelation*, p. 362.

43 Boxall, *Revelation*, pp. 165–6.

44 Cf. Isa. 21.9; Rev. 18.2.

45 Pratt observes that the concept of Rome as the *Urbs aeterna* (the 'eternal city') dates from the fourth century BC. See Kenneth J. Pratt, 1965, 'Rome as Eternal', *Journal of the History of Ideas*, vol. 26, no. 1 (Jan–Mar): 25–44, pp. 25–8.

46 Cf. Isa. 13.20–2; Rev. 14.8.

47 Cf. Jer. 51.45.

48 For a more detailed exploration of the similarities and differences between Babylon and the new Jerusalem see pp. 111–13.

49 The Old Testament background for John's use of this image is found in Isa. 23.15–18, where the city of Tyre is condemned through comparison with a prostitute.

50 Cf. Richard Bauckham, 1993, *The Theology of the Book of Revelation*, Cambridge: Cambridge University Press, pp. 17–18.

51 Cf. Pratt, 'Rome as Eternal', pp. 27–8.

52 Cf. Bauckham, *Theology*, pp. 17–18.

53 For further analysis of the beast, see pp. 163–6.

54 Cf. Jer. 51.7.

55 The debates over the identification of these kings are extensive, and contribute to the discussions around the dating of the book of Revelation. For more on the seven kings, see pp. 166–7.

56 For an exploration of the Old Testament background to Chapter 18, see Iain Provan, 1996, 'Foul Spirits, Fornication and Finance: Revelation 18 from an Old Testament Perspective', *Journal for the Study of the New Testament*, vol. 64: 81–100.

57 See the discussion of the ten horns of the scarlet beast on pp. 167–8.

58 In a fascinating article, Rowland discusses various portrayals of the Apocalypse in art down the centuries. His article contains a number of images which are unavailable elsewhere. However, many of the images he discusses are freely available via online image-search at http://images.google.com/. See Christopher Rowland, 2005, 'Imagining the Apocalypse', *New Testament Studies*, vol. 51: 303–27, pp. 307–8, 318, 323. Also Kovacs and Rowland, *Revelation*, pp. 177–89. The following website is a useful repository of images relating to the book of Revelation, and includes some interesting portrayals of the great whore which are illustrative of the points made above, including Albrecht Dürer's late fifteenth-century woodcut, and the illustration taken from Luther's 1522 New Testament: http://www.payer.de/christentum/apokalypse. htm.

59 Tina Pippin, 1999, *Apocalyptic Bodies: The Biblical End of the World in Text and Image*, London: Routledge, pp. 83, 92, 93–4. Cf. also Jean K. Kim, 1999, '"Uncovering Her Wickedness": An Inter(Con)Textual Reading of Revelation 17 from a Postcolonial Feminist Perspective', *Journal for the Study of the New Testament*, vol. 73: 61–81.

60 See the discussion of the two witnesses on pp. 102–4.

61 For references regarding the Leviathan, see pp. 150–1. Compare the Behemoth, on whom the beast from the earth is modelled, pp. 168–9.

62 Possibly the kingdoms of Babylonia, Media, Persia and Greece, with the 'little horn' of Dan. 7.8 representing Antiochus IV Epiphanes (175–164 BC), the ruler of the Hellenistic Seleucid empire, who sacked Jerusalem and desecrated the temple, triggering the Maccabean uprising. See Boxall, *Revelation*, p. 187.

63 See the discussion on dating on pp. 15–16.

64 J. Nelson Kraybill, 1996, *Imperial Cult and Commerce in John's Apocalypse*, Sheffield: Sheffield Academic Press, pp. 162–3. This myth may also lie behind the images of Parthian invasion found elsewhere in Revelation (cf. 9.7–9; 14–16; 16.12; 19.11). Cf. Richard Bauckham, 1993, *The Climax of Prophecy: Studies in the Book of Revelation*, Edinburgh: T&T Clark, pp. 407–31.

65 Cf. Rev. 11.2–3; 12.6, 14. For more on the period of 42 months experienced by the Church as a time of persecution, see p. 131.

66 Bauckham, *Theology*, pp. 35–6. This imagery is explored in more detail below, pp. 212–13.

67 Although, in defence of her thesis that Babylon is Jerusalem, Barker suggests that Jerusalem was also mythically understood to be a city of seven hills. See Margaret Barker, 2000, *The Revelation of Jesus Christ*, Edinburgh: T&T Clark, p. 285.

68 This table is a simplification of the many complex theories which have emerged to attempt to account for John's language here. For more detailed analyses of this problem, see David E. Aune, 1998b, *Revelation 17–22*, Nashville: Thomas Nelson, pp. 946–7; Beale, *Revelation*, pp. 872–5.

69 This is the approach favoured by Smalley, who comments: 'Just as "Babylon" (17.1) represents the idolatrous forces of the state in any period of world history, so the satanic beast symbolizes *any* incarnation of the worldly misuse of power.' Smalley, *Revelation*, p. 437.

70 The 'client kings' of Rome were local rulers who chose to ally themselves with the Empire to avoid an otherwise inevitable invasion. They paid tribute to Rome in return for continuing to rule their own territories and having access to the imperial armies in defence against other tribes.

71 Cf. Rev. 17.2, 18. See also the discussion of the kings of the earth on pp. 139–40.

72 Cf. Rev. 16.14, 16; 19.17–21.

73 As Boxall comments: 'Evil and injustice bear within themselves the seeds of their own destruction, and ultimately the whole edifice will come tumbling down.' Boxall, *Revelation*, p. 249.

74 Cf. Ezek. 23.26–30.

75 Cf. 1 Kings 21.23–4; 2 Kings 9.10, 36–7.

76 Cf. Ezek. 23.25. For comment on the contemporary and historical impact of the description of the desolation of the whore see pp. 161–3. It is possible that John also has in mind here the burning of Rome at the hands of Nero.

77 Cf. Rev. 13.12, 14; 17.8, 11, 16.

78 See the discussion of the Leviathan on p. 150.

79 Cf. Job 40.15–24. 1 Enoch describes both the Behemoth and the Leviathan, portraying them as male and female respectively: 'On that day, two monsters will be parted – one monster, a female named Leviathan, in order to dwell in the abyss of the ocean over the fountains of water; and (the other), a male called Behemoth' (1 Enoch 60.7–8). Translated by E. Isaac in Charlesworth (ed.), *Pseudepigrapha Vol. 1*, p. 40.

80 Bauckham, *Theology*, p. 38.

81 Bauckham, *Theology*, p. 91.

82 Cf. 1 Kings 18.38.

83 See the discussion of 'those marked' on pp. 136–7.

84 See the discussion of the 144,000 on pp. 96–8.

85 The range of solutions which have been proposed to this puzzle is immense and occasionally bewildering, with the 'number of the beast' being used to identify the Pope, all Roman Catholics, those French kings named Louis, Hitler, the contemporary global political system, the period of Saracen rule (AD 635–1300), the year of the beginning of Muslim political expansionism (AD 666), the period between the execution of Charles I of England and the expected overthrow of Parliament, a tattoo on the forehead, and barcodes. Cf. Judith L. Kovacs and Christopher Rowland, *Revelation*, 2004, Oxford: Blackwell, pp. 157–8; Hal Lindsey and C. C. Carlson, 1970, *The Late, Great Planet Earth*, Grand Rapids: Zondervan, p. 101.

86 For example, Bauckham cites graffiti from Pompeii which reads, 'I love the girl whose number is 545'. Bauckham, *Climax*, p. 385.

87 For a comprehensive and widely accepted defence of this interpretation see Bauckham, *Climax*, pp. 387f.

88 Bauckham comments: 'Thus John is saying that the number of the *word* beast is also the number of a man. The gematria does not merely assert that Nero is the beast: it demonstrates that he is.' Bauckham, *Climax*, p. 389.

89 See the discussion of the *Nero Redivivus* myth on pp. 164–5.

Part 3

Engaging the Imagery

8

The Church, the Empire and Prayer

So far in this Core Text, we have encountered the various characters who inhabit the narrative of Revelation. This next section will engage with the imagery of the text, particularly with a view to seeing how it relates to the pastoral context of the seven churches of Asia Minor. Attention will also be given to various ways in which the imagery has been interpreted during the course of Christian history, and to how it might resonate with readers from the contemporary world.

Heaven's perspective on the Church
Revelation 1.1—4.11

Where does true power reside?

The seven letters to the churches (2.1—3.22) form the heart of the opening section of Revelation, sandwiched as they are between two accounts of John's visionary experiences (1.12–20; 4.1–11). This coupling of the real-world scenarios of John's congregations, and the other-worldly imagery of his visions of heaven, provides an important key for the interpretation of the book: everything that John sees in his visions has a pastoral intention. This is something that is true not just of the visions of Chapters 1 and 4, but of the entire work.

The key questions that John addresses in these opening chapters of the Apocalypse revolve around issues of power and worship, as he invites his audience to consider who is *really* sitting on the throne. This is neither an idle nor speculative question, because the one on the throne holds not just power, but also attracts worship from those who give their allegiance to the throne. From the perspective of those living in the seven cities of Asia Minor, the answer was clear: the emperor in Rome occupies the position of ultimate power and worship (cf. 2.13).[1] However, John wants those in the seven churches of the seven cities to come to realize that supreme power actually resides with the one seated on the throne in heaven, and that he alone is worthy of worship (1.4; 3.2; 4.2–8).

Those in the seven congregations therefore find themselves caught between two competing ideologies, and are faced with the choice as to which power they will recognize, and before which throne they will bow. To help them in this choice, John wants them to learn to see the earth from heaven's perspective, and so he carefully structures the opening four chapters to draw his audience rhetorically into his vision.[2] He begins with an explanation of the 'revelation' that he is passing on to them through the text of the Apocalypse (1.1). This 'revelation' is seen to begin with God himself, the supreme being who will shortly be seen enthroned in heaven. It then passes downward through the heavenly realm from God to Jesus, then to an angel, and finally it touches the earth as the angel gives the revelation to John whose task is then to pass it on to the seven congregations. In this way, John clearly demonstrates that the origin of his visions is with none other than God in heaven.

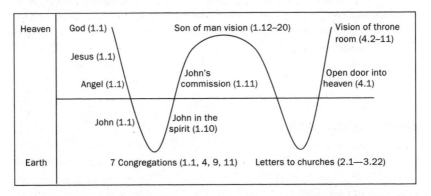

John then describes the beginning of his own visionary experience, as he moves from earth-bound Patmos into the heavenly realm, receiving from the divine voice his commission to write down what he sees and send it to the seven churches (1.9–11). This is then followed by his vision of the 'one like a son of man', in which he sees and worships the ascended Jesus (1.12–20). The dramatic nature of this opening vision, coupled with John's worshipful response (1.17), serves to draw his audience into the vision as they share his sense of awe and wonder at the sight of their glorified Lord. The 'son of man' figure reiterates John's commission to write what he sees, once again bringing the narrative from heaven down to earth, and preparing the way for the seven letters to the seven congregations that follow (1.19). After the letters, with their content thoroughly grounded in the contexts of the recipients (2.1–3.22), John draws his audience back to heaven, describing an open door through which both he and they must pass as they enter the throne room of heaven (4.1).

If the vision of the 'son of man' figure was spectacular and terrifying, the vision of the enthroned one in heaven is overwhelming in its complexity and magnificence. The sequence of images that John constructs of the worship in heaven offers direct competition to the extravagant worship on offer in the temples of the imperial cult. However, the heavenly throne room is not depicted as an alien environment for John's audience. Rather he portrays the Church, through the image of the twenty-four elders, as present within heaven, joining with the various angelic and heavenly beings in offering worship to the one on the throne (4.9–11).[3] Those in John's churches are thereby invited to realize something profound about the nature of the congregations of which they are a part. Although, from an earthly perspective, these congregations may appear to be isolated, earth-bound and feeble representations of the body of Christ, from heaven's perspective they form part of the heavenly court, and have a role to play in the proclamation of judgement on the forces of evil. It is significant that the twenty-four elders are seen offering worship to the one seated on the throne in heaven, as this once again challenges John's audience to consider where their own offerings of adoration will be directed. The twenty-four elders give voice to a hymn of praise to God the creator (4.11), which becomes both a political and religious statement when it is heard in the context of an empire that demands absolute allegiance of all its citizens.

The Church here in John's vision is both radical and subversive; it is threatening to authority in its challenge of what John perceives to be the idolatrous claims of empire. John would have those in his congregations worship only the one who is truly worthy of adoration. This call to disassociate from worshipping the gods of Rome, and the emperor in particular, meant that for John's congregations, as for generations of followers of Jesus down the centuries since, worship became a political act,[4] placing them in opposition to the dominant authorities of state-embedded religion.

In this way, the opening four chapters of Revelation can be seen as a carefully constructed rhetorical and pastoral composition, that seeks to engage those living in the seven churches, inviting them to begin to re-imagine their world and to learn to see its dominant images differently. Through its pattern of heaven–earth–heaven–earth–heaven, it draws its audience into the visionary world that John is seeking to convey. The pastoral intent of this is to enable those in the churches to see the earth from heaven's perspective, and to start acting accordingly.

The context of the seven churches

The order in which John lists the seven churches: 'Ephesus, Smyrna, Pergamum, Thyatira, Sardis, Philadelphia, Laodicea' (1.11; cf. 2.1, 8, 12, 18; 3.1, 7, 14), transcribes a clockwise circular route, beginning with the church that is closest to the island of Patmos where John is imprisoned (1.9). This provides a clue as to how the book of Revelation would have been initially distributed. There is often a tendency when dealing with a book with as complex an interpretative history as Revelation, to forget that it started with real people, in real circumstances, and addressed real pastoral needs. The map below of the locations of Patmos and the seven churches serves to ground the text in its original context, as a piece of pastoral writing, originating with John on Patmos, and then being circulated round each of the seven churches in turn, probably with a copy being made in each city before the original manuscript from John continued its journey to the next location.

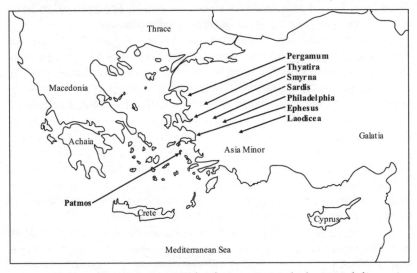

In a culture where literacy was far from universal, the initial dissemination of Revelation was through public readings, either in the context of worship or through smaller mid-week meetings (1.3; 22.18).[5] It needs to be remembered that first-century churches bore little resemblance to the form of church that has dominated Western Christianity in the millennia since. There were no basilicas, no cathedrals, no parish churches, no chapels. Instead, most churches were based in and around a private home. Those who were Jewish converts may have continued attending synagogue worship, at least for a time, but meetings for the breaking of bread in memory of the death and resurrection of Jesus occurred in people's houses,[6] and if a congregation grew beyond the point where it could be accommodated in one room, an additional meeting would be started elsewhere. There is evidence from the third century that some of the more wealthy church hosts were knocking rooms together to form permanent, larger, places of worship,[7] and this is certainly a step towards the basilica-based worship that emerged in the fourth century. However, in the first-century context of John's Apocalypse, the churches in each of the seven cities of Asia Minor would have consisted of a loose affiliation of house-based congregations.

This context makes sense of the problems with false teaching that are identified in the seven letters.[8] Rather than one large meeting, with everyone present and one authorized person presenting a sermon, what existed were a number of smaller congregations, each with its own leadership. The congregation hosts had control over who entered their home, and would have therefore exercised a considerable degree of control over the congregation. It is entirely feasible therefore to reconstruct a situation where one or more congregations within the network of congregations in any given city might have become a breeding ground for alternative teaching such as that about which John is so concerned.

In this way, a picture starts to emerge of small, often beleaguered congregations, struggling to live out their faith in the midst of an environment that is forever pulling them away from their call to discipleship. To this end, the seven letters refer to congregations facing difficulty (2.2), with some who had once attended having fallen away or lost their faith.[9] John even envisages the possibility of persecution (2.10; 3.19). He therefore repeatedly calls those who remain in the congregations to faithful endurance in the face of adversity and discouragement.[10] However, there is another side to John's engagement of his congregations in the seven letters, and this is the often-repeated tone of rebuke and call to repentance. While on the one hand John wants to encourage his audience to endure through difficulty, on the other hand he also wants to ensure that they take seriously the effects of any compromise. To this end, on several occasions he issues a call to repentance,[11] and the description of the churches is often bleak, especially so with Laodicea (3.14–22) where there is no praise at all for the congregation, but merely a description of how far they have fallen followed by an unambiguous call for repentance.

It is from this earthly context that John invites his audience to pass through the door into heaven (4.1), to see with him the throne of God, and to gain heaven's perspective on the earthly situation. The visions that follow are therefore bound into the context of the seven letters, providing an alternative worldview, that John wants those in his churches to learn to inhabit. Instead of living as citizens of the satanic empire, they are invited to live as citizens of the new Jerusalem (2.7; cf. 22.2).

Heaven's perspective on empire
Revelation 5.1—8.1

John has carefully constructed Chapters 1—4 to draw those in the seven churches of Asia Minor into his visionary world. In the following three chapters, he continues his task of leading them into his critique of their world, wanting them to learn to see things from heaven's perspective.

John has already shown them the heavenly alternative to the idolatrous power claims of the Roman Empire, and in the images surrounding the opening of the seven seals he seeks to deconstruct still further the images of empire with which his audience are surrounded.

The scroll

At the beginning of Chapter 5, John sees a scroll in the right hand of the one seated on the throne. It is described as having writing on both sides, and as being sealed with seven seals (5.1). There is considerable debate among commentators as to whether the scroll of Chapter 5 should be regarded as the same as that found in Chapter 10, where a 'little scroll' is passed to John for him to eat (10.2, 8–10). The difficulty resides in the fact that John uses two different words; in Chapter 5 he speaks of the βιβλίον ('scroll' cf. 5.1), whereas in Chapter 10 he speaks of the βιβλαρίδιον ('little scroll' cf. 10.2). However, Bauckham argues convincingly that the diminutive form found in Chapter 10 need not indicate two separate scrolls.[12] If it is accepted that the same scroll is present in both chapters, then a striking parallel becomes apparent. The path taken by the scroll as it descends from God is exactly the same as that taken by the 'revelation' of Chapter 1.[13] The following chart illustrates this similarity.

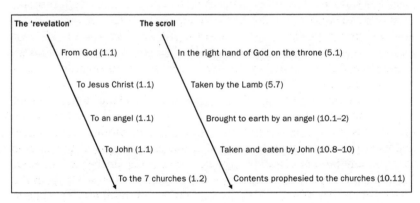

The 'revelation'	The scroll
From God (1.1)	In the right hand of God on the throne (5.1)
To Jesus Christ (1.1)	Taken by the Lamb (5.7)
To an angel (1.1)	Brought to earth by an angel (10.1–2)
To John (1.1)	Taken and eaten by John (10.8–10)
To the 7 churches (1.2)	Contents prophesied to the churches (10.11)

This parallel may provide a solution to one of the more intractable problems that has faced commentators seeking to understand John's image of the scroll, namely the question of the scroll's contents. Bauckham, building on his suggestion that there is only one scroll, suggests that the content of the scroll is revealed in summary form in the story of the two witnesses which immediately follows John's consumption of the scroll (11.1–13).[14] By this account, the story of the Church's faithful witness leading to the conversion of the nations, in the face of opposition, persecution and martyrdom, is understood as the content of the scroll.[15] The similarity with the 'revelation' from 1.1, however, suggests that the contents of the scroll, while summarized in the narrative of the two witnesses, may also function as an image for the entire content of the Apocalypse itself. This suggestion is strengthened by John's repeated use of the word βιβλίον ('scroll') to describe the book he has written (22.7, 9, 10, 18, 19).

The Old Testament background to John's image of the scroll is found in the books of Jeremiah and Ezekiel. The prophet Jeremiah receives an instruction from the Lord to take a scroll and write on it the judgements the Lord has declared against Israel and Judah (Jer. 36.2).[16] The Lord says to Jeremiah: 'It may be that when the house of Judah hears of all the disasters that I intend to do to them, all of them may turn from their evil ways, so that I may forgive their iniquity and their sin' (Jer. 36.3), and it appears that there is a similar intention in John's use of the image of a scroll of judgements against evil; the purpose of the judgements contained within the scroll is to provoke repentance and turning towards God.

However, this is not the only scroll that Jeremiah writes, and his scroll of judgements against Babylon (Jer. 51.60) is also in view in John's image of the scroll with the seven seals.[17] Jeremiah's Babylon-scroll is read aloud in Babylon, but is then tied to a stone and thrown into the water of the river Euphrates as a prophetic and dramatic enactment of its prophecies against Babylon: 'Thus shall Babylon sink, to rise no more, because of the disasters that I am bringing on her' (Jer. 51.64). John envisages a similar prophetic act against the Babylon-like Rome of his own day when the great angel throws a millstone into the sea, proclaiming: 'With such violence Babylon the great city will be thrown down, and will be found no more' (18.21).

These two scrolls of Jeremiah, the Judah-scroll and the Babylon-scroll, point to two key aspects of the scroll seen by John: on the one hand, the judgements it unleashes are warnings designed to produce repentance, while on the other hand they are also judgements against the satanic forces of empire that cannot be allowed to continue unchecked for ever. In this, John is seeking to help his audience distance themselves from the dominant culture in which they live, and to begin to share his prophetic perspective of the inevitability of judgement on all who persist in allying themselves with the satanic empire.

Ezekiel's experience with a scroll closely parallels that of John: he receives his scroll from the divine hand (Ezek. 2.9), and sees writing on both sides of it proclaiming 'words of lamentation and mourning and woe' (Ezek. 2.10). He is instructed to eat the scroll, and to proclaim the contents to Israel, finding the scroll as sweet as honey in his mouth (Ezek. 3.1–4). Unlike John of Patmos,[18] Ezekiel is not described as finding the

scroll bitter in his stomach. However, the difficulty that he faces in com-
municating his message (Ezek. 3.7–9), may indicate something of what
John is seeking to convey about the message of the scroll being unpalatable. Those hearing the message of the scroll, revealed through the text
of the Apocalypse, are thereby warned that the glory of the gospel is
inextricably coupled with suffering and persecution. Those whom John
is leading into heaven will face bitterness on the earth as the inevitable
counterpart to partaking of the sweetness of his vision.

There is a further possible Old Testament allusion to John's use of
the image of the scroll. In the time of Josiah king of Judah (seventh
century BC), the high priest Hilkiah rediscovered the 'scroll' of the law
(βιβλίον τοῦ νόμου LXX 2 Kings 22.8),[19] triggering the repentance of
Josiah and the consequent religious reforms in which idolatrous practices were purged from the land, with the paraphernalia of idol worship being burned (2 Kings 23.3–4, 6, 11, 15), and the priests of the
high places executed and burned (2 Kings 23.20). This cleansing of
the earth from idolatry may inform John's imagery of the burning of
Babylon and the destruction of all associated systems and structures,
with the scroll received from the one on the throne finding its parallel
in the scroll which elicited Josiah's act of repentance. In this way, the
gospel scroll which John sees, consumes and reports becomes the fitting
conclusion to the entire sweep of salvation history from the gift of Torah
onwards, calling the nations of the world to repentance from idolatry
through the faithful witness of those who follow the path of the Lamb
that was slain.

The worship of the Lamb

When John first encounters the scroll (5.1), he is immediately curious
as to its contents, and when it appears that no one can be found who
is worthy to break open its seals, he begins to weep bitterly (5.2–4).
However, it soon becomes clear that Jesus is able to open the seals, his
qualification being his sacrificial death and resurrection (5.5–10).

There are then three hymns of praise offered to the Lamb after he
takes the scroll from the right hand of the one seated on the throne,
and each hymn is offered by an increasing number of singers. The three
hymns function together to denote the enthronement of the Lamb, who
from this point forward is seen to be located on the heavenly throne.

Hymn 1 (5.8–10)	The four living creatures and the twenty-four elders
Hymn 2 (5.11–12)	Thousands and thousands of angels
Hymn 3 (5.13)	Every creature

The expanding panoply of worship apparent in the three hymns serves to draw those in John's churches further into the visionary world. The singing is seen to originate with the people of God before the throne, before expanding through the heavenly realm ultimately to encompass every creature in the heavens, on the earth, and in the underworld. From an earthly perspective, the worship of Jesus by the faithful saints in the churches may appear a futile exercise; to direct worship anywhere other than the gods of empire may appear akin to whistling into the wind. However, from heaven's perspective, the worship offered by the saints resounds throughout creation, drawing all beings, even those already in the underworld, into worship of the risen Christ. In this way, not only is the worship offered by those in the seven churches seen as an act of resistance to the idolatrous ideology of empire, but it is also presented as being instrumental in the drawing of every created being into a united hymn of praise. The hymns of worship that John records are therefore not about making Jesus feel good about himself, but are rather about reversing the human tendency to direct worship elsewhere. As Christ is proclaimed worthy, so power is drawn away from the earthly throne at the centre of the satanic empire, and the very act of worship itself once again becomes a politically subversive act.

The song offered by the twenty-four elders and the four living creatures in 5.9–10 introduces a theme that is recurrent throughout the Apocalypse. The Lamb is praised for ransoming people from 'every tribe and language and people and nation' (5.9), and for making them 'a kingdom and priests serving our God' (5.10). This directly parallels the promise God made through Moses after he led the people of Israel out from slavery in Egypt: '[Y]ou shall be for me a priestly kingdom and a holy nation' (Ex. 19.6). John takes the Old Testament narrative of the exodus, and reworks it to depict the exodus of the redeemed from slavery in Babylon. The following table illustrates the main points of comparison between the Old Testament account and John's application of it within the Apocalypse.

This image of new exodus helps those in John's churches to gain a theological understanding of their role within the overall scheme of salvation history. Just as the people of Israel journeyed from slavery to the promised land, so the people of the Lamb are depicted as being on a journey from slavery to a new land. However, this image does not simply function to show how the saints escape the current evil age and flee to a place where they can live happily ever after. Rather, just as the purpose of the gift of the promised land to Israel was to bring the blessing of God to all nations,[20] so the promise of the new creation is also given with the intent of drawing all nations into the blessing.[21]

In a sense, the whole eschatological scheme of Revelation is complete by the end of Chapter 5, with the worship of every creature being offered

	First Exodus	New Exodus
Who is the slave master?	Pharaoh in Egypt (Ex. 6.11)	Satan in Babylon (Rev. 13.2)
Who is rescued?	Israel (Ex. 12.31)	People from every tribe, language, people and nation (Rev. 5.9)
Who is the agent of delivery?	Moses (Ex. 7.1–2)	The Lamb (Rev. 5.9)
How are the redeemed saved from death?	The Passover lamb (Ex. 12.21)	The Lamb that was slaughtered (Rev. 5.9)
What are the signs of release?	10 Plagues (Ex. 7.14—10.29)	Seal- Bowl- & Trumpet-plagues (Rev. 6, 8–9, 16)
What water do they pass through?	Waters of the Red Sea (Ex. 14.21–2)	Waters of Baptism (Rev. 15.2)
What do people sing?	The song by the sea (Ex. 15.1f)	The song by the sea (Rev. 15.3–4)
Where is the wilderness?	Desert of Sinai (Ex. 16.1f)	The world inhabited by the Church (Rev. 12.14)
What do they eat in the wilderness?	Manna (Ex. 16.35)	Divine (Eucharistic) nourishment (Rev. 12.14)
What do they drink?	Water from the springs at Mara and Elim (Ex. 15.23–7)	Water from the spring of the water of life (Rev. 21.6)
What happens to the forces of the oppressor?	They meet their doom in the Red Sea (Ex. 14.23–8)	They meet their judgement at Harmagedon (Rev. 19.19–21)
Where does the exodus lead?	Land of Canaan (Josh. 1.2–4) Jerusalem (2 Sam. 5.5–7)	New creation (Rev. 21.1) new Jerusalem (Rev. 21.2–26)

to the Lamb. John then revisits the process whereby the Church's faithful witness to, and worship of, their risen Lord results in this universal declaration of praise (cf. 5.13). This he begins to do in the sequence of seal-openings which follow, as he explores the theme of the spiritual battle between the followers of the Lamb and the forces of evil.

The seven seals

The sequence of the seven seal-openings recapitulates once again the overall theological scheme of the Apocalypse.[22] The following table provides a summary of the narrative development which John constructs as the seven seals are opened by the Lamb. In all that follows, the action of the Lamb in initiating the events is significant, reinforcing the fact that everything which happens on the earth is ultimately within the control of the one seated on the throne in heaven.

6.1–2	First seal	The rider on the white horse (Jesus) • Conquering
6.3–4	Second seal	The rider on the red horse (War) • Takes peace from the earth
6.5–6	Third seal	The rider on the black horse (Famine) • Perpetuates injustice and inequality
6.7–8	Fourth seal	The rider on the pale green horse (Death) • Followed by Hades
6.9–11	Fifth seal	The souls of the martyrs • Crying for justice
6.12–17	Sixth seal	Cosmic catastrophe
7.1–17	Interlude	Naming the servants of God
8.1–2	Seventh seal	Silence in heaven

It begins with Jesus, sent into the world to conquer evil and death.[23] The second, third and fourth riders then present the state of the earth under the satanic empire, with war and injustice paving the way for the progression of death and despair through the world. In this context are heard the forlorn cries of the martyrs, who articulate the cry of the Church, 'how long?' (6.10).[24] The judgement of the Lamb on the evil in the world then becomes apparent in the scenes of cosmic catastrophe that follow the opening of the sixth seal, with the sky being rolled back to expose the earth to the heavenly gaze (6.14–16).[25] The message to those in John's churches here is clear: the reign of war, injustice and death is not eternal, and when viewed from heaven's perspective, the pretensions of the satanic empire are seen to be fragile and vulnerable. Assurance is therefore given that the prayers of the martyrs will not remain unanswered, and that evil will not be allowed to endure into eternity.

There is then an interlude during which the faithful people of God are sealed on the forehead and numbered. The Church is thus seen, from heaven's perspective, as the 144,000 secure before the throne of God.[26] For those in John's churches facing famine, war and death (6.4–8), the assurance that from heaven's viewpoint they are safe before the throne

(7.15–17) provides a strong message of comfort. The seventh seal, when it is opened, takes the reader back to the praise of 5.13–14, except that rather than every creature crying out in praise, every creature is instead silenced (8.1). This half-hour of silence in heaven prepares the way for the noise of the seven trumpet blasts that follow, as they once again rehearse the sequences of judgement on evil.

Heaven's perspective on prayer
Revelation 8.2—11.18

Following the silence in heaven at the opening of the seventh seal, John sees an angel burning incense on the heavenly altar (8.3–4). Earlier in the Apocalypse, before the opening of the seals, John has already seen the four living creatures and the twenty-four elders each holding a harp and a bowl; the bowls containing the incense of 'the prayers of the saints' (5.8). It is this incense that is once again in view after the opening of the seventh seal, when it is presented as a burnt offering on the altar before God. The fire of the burning incense is then thrown to the earth in preparation for the sounding of the seven trumpets (8.5). The Old Testament background for this image is found in Ezek. 9.4—10.2, where a heavenly being throws burning coals from heaven to the earth, after marking the faithful on their foreheads.[27] There is a further parallel between this story and that of Elijah and the prophets of Baal at Mount Carmel (1 Kings 18.20–40). Elijah asks God for a sign to demonstrate to the people of Israel that the Lord is the true god, and the Lord accordingly sends fire from heaven.[28] This demonstration of divine power then triggers the judgement on the idolatrous prophets of Baal.

John reworks these images of divine judgement on evil to help those in his churches understand the importance of their steadfast witness in the midst of difficulty and tribulation. The fire from heaven that John sees in Revelation is sent as a result of the prayers of the faithful, and it reveals the reality of God's rule. The effect of this for John's audience is to motivate and encourage them in their praying. The heavenly perspective is that it is the prayer and worship of the saints that precedes the breaking of the seals, triggering the judgements on evil symbolized by the events of the sounding of the seven trumpets.

The seven trumpets

The seven trumpets and the events that they trigger are images designed to demonstrate the effectiveness of the prayers of the faithful, especially in terms of divine judgement on evil. The smoke of the prayers rises

8.7	First trumpet	• Hail and fire mixed with blood are thrown to earth • 1/3 of earth and trees burned up • All grass burned up
8.8–9	Second trumpet	• A burning mountain is thrown into the sea • 1/3 of sea becomes blood • 1/3 of sea creatures die • 1/3 of ships destroyed
8.10–11	Third trumpet	• A star (Wormwood) falls from heaven onto the rivers and streams • 1/3 of the waters become bitter • Many die from the water
8.12	Fourth trumpet	• 1/3 of all light is darkened (sun, moon, stars, daylight)
8.13	Interlude	• Eagle crying three woes
9.1–12	Fifth trumpet (first woe)	• The bottomless pit is opened • The locusts emerge • They torture all those not marked with the seal of God • People seek death but do not find it
9.13–21	Sixth trumpet (second woe)	• The four angels and 200,000,000 cavalry are released • 1/3 of humankind is killed • The rest of humankind do not repent
10.1–11 11.1–14	Interlude	• The descent and consumption of the scroll • The two witnesses
11.15–19	Seventh trumpet (third woe)	• Heavenly worship • The temple in heaven is opened

before the throne (8.4) and is then hurled back to the earth with dramatic effect (8.5, 7). The horrific events described in this series are problematic to many readers. How can it be, one might ask, that the result of prayer should be the destruction of one third of the world? What view of God is implied in such acts of vengeance and ruination? In his poetical commentary on the book of Revelation, D. H. Lawrence articulates a characteristically negative reaction:

What we realize when we have read the precious book a few times is that John the Divine had on the face of it a grandiose scheme for wiping out and annihilating everybody who wasn't of the elect, the chosen people, in short, and of climbing up himself right on to the throne of God.[29]

Revelation, be it said once and for all, is the revelation of the undying will-to-power in man, and its sanctification, its final triumph. If you have to suffer martyrdom, and if all the universe has to be destroyed in the process, still, still, still, O Christian, you shall reign as a king and set your foot on the necks of the old bosses! This is the message of Revelation.[30]

Interpreted thus, Revelation becomes an imperialist text. It reflects a desire to conquer the earth, to subjugate enemies, to dominate the cosmic order. The apocalyptic hope, by this reading, becomes a yearning for power. The kingdom of heaven becomes victor over the kingdoms of the earth. Babylon gives way to the new Jerusalem, and the saints rule for a thousand years. Revelation becomes, in short, a manifesto for Christendom.[31] For Lawrence, writing at the height of the British Empire, the Nietzschean 'will to power'[32] that he ascribes to Revelation would have provided a compelling analogy for all that he found distasteful in the materialistic 'Christian' imperialism of his day. In the same way, it supports a similarly attractive reading for many in the contemporary world who identify Christianity with a drive for control or a desire for vindication. The journalist Will Self, in his 1998 introduction to Revelation, expresses similar feelings:

I read *The Book of Revelation* once – I never wanted to read it again. I found it a sick text ... The riot of violent, imagistic occurrences; the cabalistic emphasis on number; the visceral repulsion expressed towards the bodily, the sensual and the sexual. It deranges in and of itself ... In its vile obscurantism is its baneful effect ... the text is a guignol of tedium, a portentuous horror film ... In this century the star called Wormwood *has* fallen, and the sea has become as black as sackcloth of hair, and the moon has become as blood. We have heard the silence – about the space of half an hour – that accompanied the opening of the seventh seal, yet still we are here ... If *Revelation* conjures up one single feeling in me, as we stand on the cusp of a new millennium ... it is one of superstitious awe, 'Look on my works, ye Mighty, and despair'.[33]

Given the divine mandate frequently cited by those who wield earthly imperial power, including many in the twentieth and twenty-first centuries,[34] it is understandable that those who find the way in which that power is exercised questionable should also find the apparent religious justification similarly unpalatable.

However, this is not the only way of reading John's imagery here. It has been argued above that the starting point for any interpretation of Revelation needs to be the meaning it would have had for its original recipients. Although the Apocalypse clearly has its origins in a context of empire, it is far from certain that the vision it presents is one where a Christian empire simply replaces the satanic one. This is not a vision of revolution, although such a claim has been made countless times in the intervening millennia. Rather, John pictures two kingdoms existing alongside each other, with the kingdom of heaven offering an alternative vision of humanity, a different way of living in relation to the world and the divine. To this end, he exhorts his audience to transfer their citizenship from Babylon to the new Jerusalem (cf. 18.4), and it is in this context that the series of trumpet-judgements on the satanic empire need to be heard.

The reason the saints are praying for an end to the influence of the Roman Empire on the earth is not so they can assume control in its place; it is so that humanity can be freed from the idolatrous deception which leads to oppression by, and enslavement to, the beast. The images of judgement therefore need to be heard not from a perspective of imperial conquest, with one empire overthrowing another and torturing the subjugated citizens in the process. Rather, they need to be seen from the perspective of the oppressed and the enslaved. Like Moses and the Israelites living in slavery in Egypt, desperate to see release from the oppressive power that held them captive, John wants to lead the people of God from slavery into freedom. The judgements on the evil empire therefore ultimately concern release, both for the people of God and for humanity as a whole, and they are unleashed in response to the prayerful appeals of the faithful that freedom and justice might come upon the earth.

With regard to the imagery of destruction as it is visited on humans and the creative order, this becomes particularly problematic ethically if the book is read as an attempt to describe actual events that are occurring or will occur on the earth.[35] However, if this imagery is read as a metaphor for the destructive effects of human idolatry, for the events which follow the allying of people with the beast, then it becomes instead a fitting image for the way in which evil sows the seeds of its own destruction and ultimately reaps the harvest (cf. 14.18–20). The harsh reality of human allegiance to the satanic empire is war, death and destruction, and John's imagery vividly portrays these effects. What is significant in John's scheme is that this destruction is not all-encompassing. There is still hope that people will turn and repent in response to the judgements (9.20–1). Thus the prayers of the people of God for an end to the evil empire assume a tenor, not of vengeance, but deliverance.

The first four trumpets function together as a set, much as the first four seal-openings form a group (6.1–8). The events that follow the first four trumpets echo events from the exodus story, as the following table illustrates.

Exodus Event	Trumpet Plague
Hail (7th plague; Ex. 9.13–35)	1) Hail
Nile becomes blood & fish die (1st plague; Ex. 7.14–24)	2) Sea becomes blood Sea creatures die
Bitter water is sweetened (Ex. 15.22–6)	3) Water becomes bitter
Darkness (9th plague; Ex. 10.21–9)	4) Darkness

These echoes of the exodus reinforce the point made above regarding the interpretation of the plagues as triggers of freedom. Egypt, Babylon and Rome become synonymous with each other as earthly manifestations of the satanic empire that draws worship away from God, and which oppresses and enslaves humanity. John's concern is that those in his churches should identify with the Israelites as fellow travellers on the path to freedom, and that they should not be overwhelmed by the power of the Roman Empire because the destruction of its oppressive regime is ultimately assured. The emperor who rules over Rome is as doomed as the Pharaoh who ruled over Egypt, and if the people of God doubt this, they are identifying themselves with the grumbling people of Israel in the desert, who doubted that God would provide them with clean water.

The descriptions of the events that follow the fifth and sixth trumpets are greatly extended in comparison to the four that precede them. In the fifth trumpet, John introduces the satanic agent Apollyon, the king of the locusts (9.11).[36] Beasley-Murray notes that: 'Not only did the cult of Apollo use the symbol of the locust ... but more importantly both Caligula and Nero aped the deity of Apollo.'[37] This has the effect of identifying Apollyon with the ruler of the Roman Empire. The emperor may appear to be the king of a great and noble Empire, but when John sees him from heaven's perspective he becomes the king of a swarm of locusts devouring the earth in their own greed. The sounding of the sixth trumpet triggers a vision of invasion from the east, as the four angels bound at the Euphrates are released and, together with two hundred million cavalry troops,[38] ride forth to decimate the earth (9.13–19). This is John's depiction of the tragic and terrible result of humanity's alliance with the beast.

At this point there follows an interlude during which John eats the scroll, and narrates the vision of the two witnesses. In this story, John explores the content of the scroll he has just eaten,[39] showing how the faithful witness of the Church is inevitably accompanied by suffering and martyrdom. The scroll that John consumes has a double effect on

him: it is sweet in his mouth, yet bitter in his stomach (10.10). The meaning of this sweetness coupled with bitterness becomes clear with John's
realization that faithful witness can only be achieved at the expense of
suffering. The two witnesses represent the people of God,[40] who follow
the path of Jesus through suffering and death (11.7–10) to resurrection
after three days (11.11). In many ways the story of the two witnesses
presents the theology of Revelation in microcosm, as John repeatedly
revisits these themes of witnessing and suffering.

Following this interlude, the seventh trumpet sounds (11.15). Just as at
the end of the vision of the throne room (5.11–14), and after the opening
of the seventh seal (8.1), there is a heavenly response to the preceding
events. Heaven's perspective on the earthly judgements is heard as loud
voices proclaim that: 'The kingdom of the world has become the kingdom of our Lord and of his Messiah' (11.15). Christ is seen enthroned as
Lord of all (cf. Ps. 2.1–8), seated on the heavenly throne as the eternal
ruler. From the perspective of the earth, the Emperor may still occupy the
throne in Rome, but from the perspective of heaven, Christ is enthroned
and the satanic empire is already destroyed. Once more John's narrative
has reached a point of closure (cf. 5.11–14). The time of final judgement
is at hand, the prayers of the saints for freedom have been answered, and
those in the churches are drawn into the heavenly worship through the
thanksgiving hymn of the twenty-four elders (11.16–18).

This chapter has shown how John presents the heavenly perspective
on the people of God. It has looked at how the Church exists in relation
both to the one on the throne in Rome, and to the one on the throne in
heaven. The people of God are those called to desist from idolatry in all
its forms, resisting the allure of the satanic empire and holding firm to
the truth of the 'revelation' that John receives and communicates. The
followers of the Lamb thus become those who, when seen from heaven's
perspective, prayerfully participate in the downfall of Babylon as they
lead the nations of the world from slavery under empire to freedom in
Christ.

Draw your own conclusions

- What are the effects of John leading his audience through the open
  door into the throne room of heaven?
- How would you summarize the 'bitter-sweet' nature of John's
  message?
- Why does John combine images of comfort with a repeated call to
  repentance?
- Why does John present worship as a political activity?
- How does John envisage the coming kingdom of God?

Notes

1 There were sacred precincts in both Ephesus and Pergamum dedicated to the worship of the Emperor from about 29 BC. See Ittai Gradel, 2002, *Emperor Worship and Roman Religion*, Oxford Classical Monographs, Oxford: Clarendon Press, pp. 73–4; Simon Price, 1986, *Rituals and Power: The Roman Imperial Cult in Asia Minor*, Cambridge: Cambridge University Press, pp. 28, 65. Cf. also Steven J. Friesen, 2005, 'Satan's Throne, Imperial Cults and the Social Settings of Revelation', *Journal for the Study of the New Testament*, vol. 27.3: 351–73; J. Nelson Kraybill, 1996, *Imperial Cult and Commerce in John's Apocalypse*, Sheffield: Sheffield Academic Press, pp. 26–9.

2 Cf. David A. deSilva, 1999, 'Honor Discourse and the Rhetorical Strategy of the Apocalypse of John', *Journal for the Study of the New Testament*, vol. 71: 79–110.

3 For the twenty-four elders as a representation of the people of God see p. 95.

4 For example, the seventeenth-century Baptists in England experienced considerable persecution at the hands of the state church for their refusal to participate in Anglican services, baptism and communion. See the chapter 'The Era of the Great Persecution 1660–1688', in B. R. White, 1996, *The English Baptists of the Seventeenth Century*, A History of the English Baptists, vol. 1, Didcot: The Baptist Historical Society, pp. 95–133.

5 The blessings of 1.3 on the one who reads the prophecy aloud, and on those who hear and keep it, reflect a context where public reading of longer texts in worship was not uncommon. There are a number of places within the Apocalypse which seem rhetorically to require a response from the listening congregation (1.5–6; 2.7, 17, 26, 19.7, 9; 22.17, 20). Ian Boxall, 2006, *The Revelation of St John*, London: Continuum, p. 26.

6 Cf. Acts 2.46; 20.7–8; Rom. 16.3–5; 1 Cor. 16.19; Col. 4.15; Philemon 2; Heb. 10.24–5.

7 The Dura Europos house church in Syria is the only house church of this kind so far discovered, but nonetheless it indicates that this practice was not unknown. See Peter G. Cobb, 1992, 'The Architectural Setting of the Liturgy', in Cheslyn Jones et al. (eds), *The Study of Liturgy*, London: SPCK, pp. 529–31.

8 Cf. Rev. 2.2, 6, 9, 14, 15, 20–3; 3.9.

9 Cf. Rev. 2.4, 13; 3.1, 15–16.

10 Cf. Rev. 2.2, 3, 10, 13, 19, 25; 3.4, 5, 8, 10, 11, 12.

11 Cf. Rev. 2.5, 16, 21–2; 3.3, 19.

12 It should be noted that βιβλίον is itself a diminutive of βίβλος. Richard Bauckham, 1993, *The Theology of the Book of Revelation*, Cambridge: Cambridge University Press, p. 81. Cf. Richard Bauckham, 1993, *The Climax of Prophecy: Studies on the Book of Revelation*, Edinburgh: T&T Clark, pp. 243–57. Boxall agrees on this count, noting that the βιβλαρίδιον of 10.2 reverts to βιβλίον in 10.8. Boxall, *Revelation*, p. 153. cf. also Frederick David Mazzaferri, 1989, *The Genre of the Book of Revelation from a Source-Critical Perspective*, Berlin: Walter de Gruyter, pp. 267–9; Stephen S. Smalley, 2005, *The Revelation to John: A Commentary on the Greek Text of the Apocalypse*, London: SPCK, pp. 258–9. For an argument against identifying them as the

same scroll, see A. J. P. Garrow, 1997, *Revelation*, New Testament Readings, London: Routledge, pp. 25–32.

13 Bauckham, *Theology*, p. 81.

14 Bauckham, *Theology*, p. 83–84.

15 For an exploration of the image of the two witnesses, see pp. 102–4. Other suggestions for understanding the significance of the scroll include interpreting it as: the Lamb's book of life, the marriage contract of the bride and the Lamb; the deeds of the kingdom being handed to God's people; the last will and testament of the Lamb; and the canon of Old Testament scriptures. See Boxall, *Revelation*, pp. 94–5.

16 Cf. Walter Brueggemann, 1991, *To Build, to Plant: A Commentary on Jeremiah 26–52*, International Theological Commentary, Grand Rapids: Wm. B. Eerdmans, pp. 128–30.

17 Cf. Brueggemann, *To Build, to Plant*, p. 281.

18 Cf. Rev. 10.10.

19 Brueggemann notes: 'Since definitive research in 1805, scholars have assumed that the scroll found in the temple is some form of the book of Deuteronomy, and that hypothesis is still widely accepted.' Walter Brueggemann, 2000, *1 & 2 Kings*, Smyth & Helwys Bible Commentary, Macon, Georgia: Smyth & Helwys Publishing, p. 545.

20 Cf. Gen. 26.4.

21 Cf. Rev. 15.4; 21.24, 26; 22.2.

22 The similarity between the events of the first six seals and the first six calamities of the second-century AD Jewish apocalypse of 2 Baruch is striking. Although there is no need to posit a direct literary dependence between them, the presence of such material in both documents indicates the apocalyptic milieu within which John was writing. 'In the first part: the beginning of commotions. In the second part: the slaughtering of the great. In the third part: the fall of many to death. In the fourth part: the drawing of the sword. In the fifth part: famine and the withholding of rain. In the sixth part: earthquakes and terrors' (2 Baruch 27.2–7). Translated by A. F. J. Klijn in Charlesworth (ed.), *Pseudepigrapha Vol. 1*, p. 630.

23 For a discussion on the identification of the first rider with Jesus see pp. 76–8.

24 Cf. Isa. 6.11; Rev. 22.20.

25 Cf. Isa. 34.4. Also Adams, *The Stars Will Fall from Heaven*, p. 246.

26 See pp. 96–8 for a discussion of the 144,000.

27 Cf. Rev. 7.3.

28 Cf. 1 Kings 18.37–8.

29 D. H. Lawrence, 1931, *Apocalypse*, Harmondsworth: Penguin Books, p. 9. Lawrence was not a fan of Revelation, particularly in terms of the negative effects he believed it to have had throughout its history of interpretation: 'The Apocalypse of John is, as it stands, the work of a second-rate mind. It appeals intensely to second-rate minds in every country and every century.' Lawrence, *Apocalypse*, p. 14.

30 Lawrence, *Apocalypse*, pp. 14–15.

31 Stuart Murray describes Christendom thus: 'Although the term "Christendom" was coined in ninth-century England, the story begins in fourth-

century Rome ... [Constantine's] adoption of Christianity as the imperially favoured religion was a turning point in Christian and European history ... The church's journey from illegality and susceptibility to persecution, via toleration and preferential treatment, to official status as the imperial religion had taken only eighty years. Christendom had arrived.' Stuart Murray, 2004, *Post-Christendom*, Carlisle: Paternoster, pp. 23, 37, 40.

32 The 'will to power' was one of the tenets posited by the German philosopher Friedrich Nietzsche (1844–1900).

33 Will Self, 1998, *Revelation*, Edinburgh: Canongate Books, pp. xxii, xxiii, xiv. Self's final reference here is to the sonnet 'Ozymandias' by Percy Shelley (1792–1822), which is itself about false pretensions to imperial greatness.

34 The following from 2005 is illustrative: 'President George W Bush told Palestinian ministers that God had told him to invade Afghanistan and Iraq – and create a Palestinian State, a new BBC series reveals ... Nabil Shaath says: President Bush said to all of us: 'I'm driven with a mission from God. God would tell me, "George, go and fight those terrorists in Afghanistan." And I did, and then God would tell me, "George, go and end the tyranny in Iraq ..." And I did. And now, again, I feel God's words coming to me, "Go get the Palestinians their state and get the Israelis their security, and get peace in the Middle East." And by God I'm gonna do it."' http://www.bbc.co.uk/pressoffice/pressreleases/stories/2005/10_october/06/bush.shtml. Accessed 24.10.07. It was also reported that President George Bush and British Prime Minister Tony Blair prayed together in 2002 at the meeting which agreed the invasion of Iraq in principle. http://www.guardian.co.uk/usa/story/0,12271,1586978,00.html. Accessed 24.10.07. In a similar vein, again regarding the Iraq war, Tony Blair commented in 2006, 'In the end, there is a judgement that, I think if you have faith about these things, you realize that judgement is made by other people ... and if you believe in God, it's made by God as well.' http://news.bbc.co.uk/1/hi/uk_politics/4772142.stm. Accessed 25.10.07.

35 There have been numerous attempts to identify the events depicted in the trumpet sequence with events which have happened or are about to happen on the earth. For a fascinating list of examples both ancient and modern, see Kovacs and Rowland, *Revelation*, pp. 109–12.

36 For a discussion of Apollyon, see p. 154.

37 G. R. Beasley-Murray, 1974, *The Book of Revelation*, London: Oliphants, p. 162. Cf. also Robert H. Mounce, 1997, *The Book of Revelation*, revised edn, The New International Commentary on the New Testament, Grand Rapids: Wm. B. Eerdmans, p. 191.

38 For the identification of these angels as the feared Parthian invasion see pp. 155–6.

39 See the discussion of the scroll on pp. 186–8.

40 See the discussion of the two witnesses on pp. 102–4.

9

History, Mercy, Judgement and Economics

Heaven's perspective on history
Revelation 11.19—13.18

Having reached a point of climax following the sounding of the seventh
trumpet, John once again shows his audience a vision of heaven opened
(11.19; cf. 4.1). This time it is the heavenly temple that is opened, and
the ark of the covenant is seen. The ark was the box containing the tab-
lets of the Mosaic Law that travelled with the people of Israel through
their wilderness journey before finding its resting place in the Holy of
Holies in Solomon's temple in Jerusalem.[1] Generally believed to have
been destroyed or lost at the time of the Babylonian sack of Jerusalem
(586 BC), the ark had passed into the realm of Jewish legend. One strand
of Jewish tradition held that the ark would be revealed on earth at the
end times,[2] however in John's vision the ark is revealed in heaven. Whereas for the Jews the ark was the symbol of their covenant with God, in
John's vision it is now seen to be available to the followers of the Lamb
as they make their own exodus journey towards the new Jerusalem. In
this way, the exclusivity of the direct equation of the people of Israel
with the people of God is challenged. No longer is the fulfilment of the
Abrahamic covenant restricted to those who keep the Mosaic Law,[3] but
rather the presence of God is seen by John to be with all those who journey from Babylon to the new Jerusalem. This vision of heaven opened
prepares the way for the sequence of visions that follow.

The next two chapters contain some of the most vivid and compelling
images in the book of Revelation. John introduces his audience to the
woman dressed in sunlight, standing on the moon and crowned with
twelve stars (12.1);[4] he then brings into view her son, the child who shep-
herds the nations and ends up in heaven (12.5).[5] There is also the unholy
trinity of the dragon (12.3)[6], the scarlet beast from the sea (13.1),[7] and
the beast from the earth (13.11),[8] not to mention the mark of the beast
(13.16–17)[9] and the mysterious number 666 (13.18).[10] If ever there were
chapters guaranteed to cause confusion and misunderstanding, these are
good candidates. The key to making sense of them is to try and discern
the motivations behind John's writing.

The story of the pregnant woman, her child, and the dragon serves as a reminder of the events so far. Today's readers might find this technique similar to the way in which one may watch a television programme and discover that it is in fact the second part of a series, beginning with a compressed version of the previous episode. In Revelation 12, at the half-way point in the book, John undertakes a recapitulation of history in order to remind his audience of what has gone before. He does this using the three characters of the woman, her child, and the wicked dragon, as he presents a potted spiritual history of the world. The woman represents the faithful people of God down the ages, with the twelve tribes of Israel reflected in her crown of twelve stars (12.1), and she gives birth to a child who is proclaimed to be the ruler of the nations (12.5). In this John is painting a picture of the Messiah, Jesus Christ, coming into the world through the nation of Israel, being born from within the people of God.

John then introduces the dragon, the Devil thrown out of heaven for bad behaviour to roam the earth wreaking havoc (12.7–9, 13). This account of the expulsion of Satan is unique to the Apocalypse, although it has its origins in a number of Jewish traditions. Genesis provides the mythological account of 'sons of God' coming to the earth to take human wives, resulting in the giant-like Nephilim (Gen. 6.1–4), a tradition that is reworked as the story of the Watchers in the second-century BC Jewish apocalypse of 1 Enoch 6–19. Isaiah refers to the Ugaritic myth of the casting down of Helel (Venus, the morning star) from the heavens by the great god Elyon (the sun, in whose rays the light of the morning star dims), and reworks it as a taunt of the Assyrian king whose glory will similarly fade before the light of the Lord (Isa. 14.10–15).[11] These traditions of angelic beings descending from heaven to the earth thus provide the background to John's image of the dragon being cast to the earth. The name 'Satan' only occurs in three places within the Old Testament, all of them exilic or post-exilic.[12] The Hebrew word שָׂטָן 'satan' simply means 'adversary', and although the later traditions of Satan as an evil spiritual opponent are clearly derivative of the Jewish material, the Old Testament references must be allowed to stand in their own right without being overlaid with later developments. A being described as 'a satan' prompts David to count the people of Israel (1 Chr. 21.1), but this may be no more than a reference to a human who gives David bad advice;[13] in the book of Job, Satan appears as one of the heavenly beings who has been walking about on the earth (Job 1.6–7);[14] and in the prophecy of Zechariah 'Satan' appears as a prosecuting counsel in the heavenly courtroom (Zech. 3.1–2). This final notion of 'Satan' as a designation of 'one who opposes' lies behind Jesus' description of Peter as 'Satan' (Matt. 16.23). However, there are other places within the New Testament where Satan appears as a personified adversary (cf. Matt.

4.10; Mark 4.15). It is worth noting, however, that Satan in Scripture is always only ever the enemy of humanity, and not the enemy of God. The notion of Satan as one who is fallen is referred to by Jesus who says: 'I watched Satan fall from heaven like a flash of lightning' (Luke 10.18). However, this is a reference to the effects of his own ministry, not to an ancient time when Satan was cast from heaven. Fallen angels are mentioned in the book of Jude,[15] but this is a passage derivative of the Watchers myth from 1 Enoch, and does not convey any concept of evil angels being expelled from heaven before the fall of Adam.[16] It is against the background of all these different images that John's own imagery needs to be read.

The dragon, known as the Devil and Satan, tries to lead the world astray (12.9), to kill the Messiah-child (12.4) and to devour the people of God (12.13). But God is seen protecting his people, leading them into the desert for a wilderness experience that parallels that of the people of Israel in Old Testament times (12.6, 14). God snatches his son from the jaws of the dragon, taking him from death to eternity (12.5) and leaving the dragon to roam the earth making war on the other children of the woman (12.13, 17). This is where John locates his own audience within the story: they are those who keep God's command and hold firm to the witness of Jesus in the face of the onslaught from the dragon (12.17).

The people of God, according to John's scheme here, are therefore to be seen in the wilderness with the dragon still poised to make war on all those who owe their allegiance to the Messiah, Jesus Christ. This imagery would have made perfect sense to John's first audience. They only had to look around them to see ample evidence that the dragon was poised to strike! The Roman Empire towered over the congregations of the faithful like a mighty beast set on their destruction, and the people of God in John's churches were living out their lives in the shadow of the imperial dragon.

Having thus reminded them of their history, by giving them another glimpse of the throne room in heaven where all his visions began and showing them the Messiah-child in his place before God's throne, John turns his attention once more to the difficult and dangerous situation facing the people of God as they live out their lives under the authority of Rome. Again John presents them with an alternative way of viewing their lived reality, and confronts them with the heavenly perspective on their earthly situation. In this way he seeks to prepare his audience for their difficult task of holding firm to the truth of the gospel, and of over-coming evil as they endure as faithful witnesses to the end.

John gives his audience this heavenly perspective by introducing them to the dragon and the two beasts. Bauckham identifies the dragon as the underlying source of all opposition to God, the beast from the sea as the military and political power of Rome, and the beast from the earth as the propaganda machine that promotes the Empire and all it stands for.[17] However, the beast from the earth also has a face that can be recognized as the focus of the propaganda of Roman imperialism, namely the Emperor Nero, both in terms of his claims to divinity and his post-mortem mythology of rebirth.[18] Through this imagery, John is seeking to give his audience a new level of understanding about both their current situation and the events that have led up to where they find themselves. From their perspective they see the Roman Empire in all its terrible glory, endlessly promoting itself as the bringer of peace through its military strength: the temptation they faced was to believe the Roman propaganda. However, the way John presents it, Rome is simply the latest and greatest manifestation of the ancient force of evil that has been roaming the world seeking to destroy the faithful children of God since time began. Rome, from John's perspective, is not the bringer of peace through the *Pax Romana*,[19] but is rather a purveyor of violence.[20] Only in Christ, John wants to say, can peace be found. So when Rome claims to be the one who brings peace by violence, she is blaspheming God and making herself an idol for her people to worship. In this way, John places his audience right in the centre of what he perceives as a great cosmic battle between the dragon and the faithful people of God that has been raging for millennia. It is, therefore, wherever the forces of evil are manifested through idolatrous, powerful and corrupt institutions, that the children of God, the army of the Lamb, are called by John to battle.

In this way, John challenges the received view of history, which presented the Empire as a glorious and beneficent institution. In place of this, he shows that from heaven's perspective, the Empire is an idolatrous system that has deceived the 'whole earth' (13.3–4) into worshipping it through participation in its ideology. Also in view here is the imperial cult that provided a direct religious focus for the claims of the Empire over the hearts, minds and bodies of its citizens. The place of the faithful Church is therefore one of wilderness journeying, protected by God, resistant to empire, and on the way from slavery to freedom.

Heaven's perspective on mercy and judgement
Revelation 14.1—16.21

John seeks to address two related issues in this section of the Apocalypse, and they can be expressed as two questions: first the question of whether the reign of evil on the earth will ever end, and second that of whether a life of suffering and faithful witness is ultimately worthwhile. In these two problems are reflected two desires: the desire for the overthrow of evil, and the desire for mercy towards sinners. On the face of it, these two desires can seem to be mutually contradictory. After all, if

God is to be merciful to those who have sinned, how can he simultaneously punish them for their sinfulness?[21] The temptation for those in the congregations of Asia Minor, perhaps becoming convinced by John's imagery that Rome is actually a satanic empire drawing idolatrous worship from the one true God, would have been to desire nothing less than the total destruction of the Roman Empire and all who continued to be associated with it. However, this attitude of total divorce between Church and world can too easily lead to an isolationist perspective, where the Church's task becomes that of remaining pure while the rest of the world 'justifiably' goes to hell. It is in order to avoid reaching this conclusion, that John is concerned that those in his congregations come to understand the importance not only of maintaining their own purity, but also of their role as a light to all nations. By John's understanding, witnessing is the central task of the faithful Church,[22] even if it means persecution and martyrdom,[23] and this core task cannot be set aside in the interests of isolationist purity. Thus it is that before describing the final judgement of the satanic empire, John addresses the issue of God's mercy towards sinners.

John begins with an image of the Church, depicted in both its heavenly and earthly manifestations: the twenty-four elders are seen in heaven (14.3), and the 144,000 are in view once again as those who have been redeemed from the earth (14.1, 4).[24] There is then heard a new song from heaven, that only the 144,000 are able to learn (14.2–3). John is here emphasizing the inherent difference between those in the Church, and those who are still embroiled in Babylon. The vital function of the Church is that it alone of all the inhabitants of the earth can learn the song of heaven and sing it to the earth. This is a picture of the witnessing Church, and the message is clear: if the Church fails to sing the new song, then the song will remain in heaven. However, if the Church picks up the heavenly refrain, the glory of heaven is brought to the earth. Once again, therefore, worship is seen as both a spiritual and a political activity, proclaiming the kingdom of Christ on the earth in place of the idolatrous claims of empire; drawing the nations of the earth from Babylon to the new Jerusalem. An angelic messenger then confirms this perspective, echoing the witness of the Church by proclaiming an 'eternal gospel' to 'every nation and tribe and language and people' (14.6), calling all people to repent and give God glory (14.7).[25]

These visions of the witnessing Church are then juxtaposed with proclamations from two further angelic messengers, who declare the coming judgement of both Babylon and those who still inhabit the satanic empire (14.8–11). The fulfilment of these pronouncements will be depicted in Chapters 17—19 with the visions of the judgement of Babylon and the armies of the beast. However, it is interesting to note that the angelic declaration denotes the past tense: 'Fallen, fallen is Babylon the great!'

(14.8).[26] From heaven's perspective, Babylon is already destroyed, even though the earthly presence of the Empire is still strong and vibrant. John is here once again making his point that the seeds of the Empire's destruction are already latent within it, even if their fruit is yet to be seen from an earthly perspective.[27] The violence and horror of the imagery here need not be read as the actions of a violent and vengeful God, nor as the violent and vengeful aspirations of those who follow the Lamb, but rather as the inevitable consequence of human actions committed out of allegiance to the satanic empire. Babylon thus begets the violence that eventually destroys the Empire itself. It is in this context that John calls those in his churches to endurance, instructing them to 'keep the commandments of God and hold fast to the faith of Jesus' (14.12).

John then sets before his audience two harvest images, the harvest of grain (14.14–16) and the harvest of grapes (14.17–20).[28] The Old Testament background for these images is found in the two harvests referred to in the book of Joel: 'Put in the sickle, for the harvest is ripe. Go in, tread, for the wine press is full.' (Joel 3.13). This verse also lies behind other New Testament images of harvesting as eschatological fulfilment.[29]

The grain harvest, as John presents it, is a positive image, representing the ingathering of the entire earth (14.16).[30] In this image is found the end goal of the faithful witnessing of the people of God, as all peoples are harvested by Jesus himself (14.14).[31] Just as in Chapter 7 the 144,000 becomes the great multitude (7.4, 9), so here in Chapter 14 they become the great harvest. John describes the 144,000 as 'first fruits' (14.4), evoking the Jewish practice of offering the first fruits of a harvest to symbolize that the whole harvest belongs to God.[32] In this way, the faithful witness of the Church is seen once again to result in the salvation of all the nations of the earth, as the Abrahamic covenant is fulfilled. So, to return to one of John's key questions: is it worth persevering in witnessing even through difficulty and persecution? Yes, says John, it is! As Bauckham summarizes:

> [The people of God] are to participate in Christ's victory by bearing witness, as he did, as far as death in a great conflict with the idolatrous power of the Roman Empire. In this way, they will witness to all the nations and bring them to repentance and faith in the true God.[33]

However, this positive harvest image is then followed immediately by a more negative counterpart, in the form of the image of the grape harvest. In this image, John addresses his other question, that concerning the desire for judgement on evil in the world. The grapes are harvested by an angel (14.19), placed in the winepress, and trampled by Jesus (cf. 19.15). The wine that flows from the press is identified as blood, and it flows 'as high as a horse's bridle, for a distance of about two hundred miles' (14.20). This image forms a parallel to the outcome of the great battle of Harmagedon, where the armies of the beast are put to the sword by the one who treads 'the press of the fury of the wrath of God' (19.15, 21). The grape harvest represents the uncompromising judgement of God on the beast and all his powers and structures, and it offers assurance to John's audience that the satanic empire will eventually face the consequences of its actions. As with the violent imagery of 14.9–11, the blood that flows from the winepress represents the very real and bloody human consequences of humanity's infatuation with the beast.

John then moves from harvest to exodus imagery, once more depicting the people of God as those who are on a journey from slavery to freedom, from Egypt to the promised land, from Babylon to the new Jerusalem. The new exodus image is signalled by the 'song of Moses' sung by those who conquer, as they stand beside the sea (15.3; cf. Deut. 32.1–43), and in this song John returns to the image of universal salvation as the people of God proclaim: 'All nations will come and worship before you' (15.4). As with the other images in this section, mercy is juxtaposed with judgement, as John goes on to describe the seven bowl-plagues. As with the trumpet-plagues, the bowl-plagues approximate to events narrated in the exodus story, as the following table demonstrates.

Bowl Plague	Exodus Event
1) Sores	Sores (6th plague; Ex. 9.8–12)
2) Sea becomes blood Sea creatures die	Nile becomes blood & fish die (1st plague; Ex. 7.14–24)
3) Water becomes blood	Nile becomes blood (1st plague; Ex. 7.14–24)
4) Sun scorches with fire	Inversion of plague of darkness (9th plague; Ex. 10.21–9)
5) Darkness	Darkness (9th plague; Ex. 10.21–9)
6) Three frog-like spirits	Frogs (2nd plague; Ex. 8.1–15)
7) Thunder, earthquake and hail	Thunder and hail (7th plague Ex. 9.18–35)

The bowl-plagues mark the end of the three sequences of judgements, the first two of which focused on the opening of the seals and the sounding of the trumpets (15.1). What is presented in these plagues is an intensification of the earlier plague cycles, with no limitation of 'a third' being placed on the extent of the damage,[34] as the damage inflicted on the planet by the satanic empire continues to increase. The destructive tendency inherent within the empire continues to bring ever-increasing levels of suffering to those living within its territory, and are seen through the next three chapters to result in the total destruction of Babylon itself. Bauckham perceptively notes: 'The judgements of chapters 16—19 are primarily aimed at destroying the *systems* – political, economic and religious – which oppose God and his righteousness and which are symbolized by the beast, the false prophet, Babylon, and the kings of the earth.'[35]

In the bowl-plagues John presents the agony experienced by those who have wedded themselves to the satanic empire when that empire finally experiences the judgement it has brought upon itself through its evil deeds.[36] Those individuals caught up within the systems of empire experience in their lives the consequences of the systemic (self-)destruction. However, the purpose of the judgements is ultimately seen to be the removal of the structures of the beast, to allow the whole of humanity to follow the path blazed by the people of God through the wilderness on their journey towards freedom from satanic tyranny.

Through the series of images utilized in Chapters 14—16, John holds his answers to the two key concerns of a longing for judgement on evil coupled side-by-side with a desire for mercy towards sinners. His imagery alternates between mercy and judgement, as the following table illustrates:

Mercy		Judgement	
14.1–7	The 144,000 sing a new song, and an angel proclaims an eternal gospel for all people	14.8–11	Two angels proclaim Babylon is fallen, and those who worship the beast are judged
14.14–16	Grain harvest of the whole earth	14.17–20	Grape harvest with judgement in the winepress
15.2–4	The song of Moses proclaims universal salvation	15.1, 5–8; 16.1–21	The seven bowl-plagues

An insight from the world of liberation theology is of value here: namely that the images of judgement in Revelation are only truly problematic when they are read from the perspective of the wealthy oppressor.[37] Within John's symbolic world, it is powerful Babylon and those who buy into the ideology of empire who are on the receiving end of judgement understood as God's righteous wrath against evil, oppression and injustice. Thus it is that, when read from a perspective of collaboration with empire, the judgements of Revelation might be heard as the vindictive vengeance of a wrathful God. However, when viewed from the perspective of the poor and oppressed, the victims of the satanic empire, the situation is totally reversed. No longer are the judgements threatening, rather they are liberating. From this perspective, the prayer 'your kingdom come' becomes the 'how long' cry of the martyrs (6.10), and is heard as a prayer for release and justice and judgement. As McLaren comments: 'God's wrath is God's justice in action ... [and] only the oppressors fear God's justice.'[38]

Heaven's perspective on the environment

An issue that arises out of a consideration of the bowl-plagues is that of what, if anything, the book of Revelation has anything to say about the relationship between humanity and the created environment. There are some key themes that emerge from both the text and its interpretation which begin to open this topic up for further reflection.[39]

The Apocalypse, with its horrific images of judgement being meted out on the earth, readily lends itself to interpretations that focus around the destruction of the planet. During the twentieth century the looming nuclear weapons crisis was seen by some as predicted in John's visions of the earth's destruction.[40] A possible future 'nuclear apocalypse' was interpreted as the righteous judgement of God on a corrupt society, and thus as something to be welcomed by those who consider themselves part of the elect, awaiting the rapture and the second coming of Christ.[41] By this understanding, it is only after Christ returns to the earth that the scorched creation will be re-created, with the vindicated Church taking centre stage.[42] A related perspective sees the injunction to have 'dominion' over the earth (Gen. 1.26–31) as giving permission for divinely sanctioned exploitation of creation, on the expectation that God will re-make the earth at the time of the parousia. What these interpretations overlook, however, is an understanding of the judgement sequences of Revelation as warnings designed to produce repentance (cf. 9.20–1; 16.9–11). Too often, the repentance required by John in Revelation has been reduced to spiritual penitence, where some of those from among the nations 'repent' to join the élite band of the saints. However, the 'repentance' John speaks of is more properly understood as a 'turning' on the part of 'the nations', as they heed and respond to the warning judgements (cf. 11.13), and start to act in ways which reject rather than capitulate to the idolatrous claims of the satanic empire.

It is an enduring feature of empires throughout human history that they perpetrate ecological, as well as social and economic violence. For example, the Levitical perspective on the Babylonian exile was that it allowed the land the overdue 'Sabbath' denied it by the pre-exilic Jewish empire (Lev. 26.34–5, 42).[43] Within John's scheme, such violence against creation *cannot* be allowed to endure eternally. Indeed, John depicts these exploitative practices as actually carrying within themselves the seeds of their own destruction.[44] On this understanding, the environmental judgements of Revelation are not personally targeted punishments aimed at those who deny the lordship of Christ, but are rather images evoking the inevitable end-results of the human capacity for empire and exploitation.

It is interesting to note that the first trumpet only destroys a third of the created order (8.7), and that the locusts from the abyss bring judgement only on people, while being specifically prohibited from harming 'the grass of the earth or any green growth or any tree' (9.4). Although the effects of human imperial aspiration are seen to have a severe effect on the earth, these judgements on empire are in fact limited in the extent to which they harm the totality of the created realm. In a manner which finds echoes in the contemporary warning that: 'There is still time to avoid the worst impacts of climate change if we act now',[45] Revelation's trumpet sequence depicts the death of only a *third* of life on earth (8.7–12; 9.15–18). Thus it is that within John's scheme, creation is depicted as suffering the consequences of humanity's alliance with the beast. Following the seventh trumpet, the twenty-four elders sing that the time has come 'for destroying those who destroy the earth' (11.18). The destructive demonic forces led by Apollyon the destroyer are not to be allowed to roam the earth for ever. As Boxall comments: 'The apocalyptic imagery of destruction and cosmic collapse is shown ... as a challenge to all that would itself destroy the creation, all that keeps it out of kilter and removed from its divinely ordained destiny.'[46]

Thus, the vision that John presents is not without hope. Inherent in John's scheme is the message that judgement and destruction are not the end of the story, either for the nations or for the ravaged earth which bears on its skin the wounds of imperial exploitation. The opening vision of the one seated on the throne includes the description of a rainbow around the throne (4.3; cf. Ezek. 1.28), recalling the Noachic covenant that God would never again destroy the earth (Gen. 9.13–16).[47] All the images of judgement that follow this initial vision need therefore to be heard in the context of God's faithfulness to this promise towards creation.

Just as the purified nations reappear outside the new Jerusalem (21.24–6),[48] bringing their 'glory' into it (21.24, 26), so the new Jerusalem is itself set within a new earth and a new heaven (21.1–5).[49] In a scene which parallels the creation account of Genesis, God's new creation is also centred around a tree. The leaves of the tree in the centre of the new Jerusalem are said to be 'for the healing of the nations' (22.2), indicating that creation itself has a role in the restoration of the fractured human condition. In a dramatic reversal, just as the tree in the garden of Eden was implicated in the human attempt to usurp God (Gen. 3.2–7), so ultimately it is the faithfulness of creation to its creator which points humanity back to its rightful place within the created order. In accord with this positive view of creation, the earth takes an active role in re-creation and restoration, playing its part in the protection of the faithful people of God by swallowing the river sent by the dragon to destroy them (12.18).[50] It is in the context of renewed creation, with its overt echoes of Eden, that the divine presence is once again found among humans, at ease within a restored creation (21.22–3; cf. Gen. 3.8).

The image of the new Jerusalem offers a vision of creation once again comfortable with God, with all those living on the earth finally recognizing the rightful place of God within creation.[51] The praise that is offered in the renewed creation comes from every *creature* in heaven and earth (5.13),[52] with all of creation participating in the praise of God (cf. Phil. 2.10). Bauckham suggests that the four living creatures (4.6f.)[53] represent the created order offering a united song of worship before the throne.[54] In this way, the worship offered by those in the churches is contextualized as one aspect of the total worship that creation directs back to its creator.[55] Once the satanic empire is judged, and the deceptive tendency to idolatry is removed, humanity and the natural order join their voices in recognizing the dominion of the one seated on the throne. Caird helpfully comments:

> The pastoral relevance of the new Jerusalem to the needs of the seven churches becomes still clearer … [T]his voice from the ultimate future has something urgent to say about the critical present: '**I am making all things new**'. This is not an activity of God within the new creation, after the old has been cast as rubbish into the void; it is the process of re-creation by which the old is transformed into the new. In Smyrna and Thyatira, in Sardis and Laodicea, in all places of his dominion, God is for ever making all things new, and on this depends the hope of the world.[56]

All is not, it seems, hopelessly lost. The effects of empire on the created order are, within John's vision, not irreversible. But the source of hope for creation-under-empire is seen to lie in the prophetic witness of the Church that the one on the true throne is God rather than the satanically idolatrous emperor (4.2). It is the Church's faithful witness to the divine antidote to idolatry that points the way for the redemption of creation. The theological point that John is making is that whenever the human quest for power attempts to usurp the place of God, that way lies the path of judgement and destruction. But when God is worshipped once again as the Lord of creation (3.14; 10.6; 11.4; 14.7), that way lies the heavenly hope of restoration and re-creation.

Within John's vision it is the resurrected Messiah who has conquered death, it is the slain-yet-living Lamb who offers the hope of new life from death, the hope of renewal and re-creation.[57] Those who enlist in the army of the Lamb are therefore not called to sit tight and wait for cosmic obliteration and divine rescue, but rather to bear witness to the lordship of Christ over creation, because this is the path to life in a world otherwise destined to destruction. It is the persistent challenge that the Church poses to the values and ideologies of empire, through faithful witness and fervent worship, which forms the way in which John envisages the world journeying away from evil towards restoration. It is only through the prophetic activity of the Church that John's glimpse of a renewed creation is brought into being on the earth.

The environmental call of Revelation is therefore for the Church to discover its vocation as witness to an alternative, non-exploitative expression of humanity, focused around the lordship of the one on the heavenly throne. However, any such activity will always be perceived as a direct challenge to the idolatrous claims exercised by the satanic empire of Babylon in all its forms, something that inevitably places the Church at odds with the dominant powers of the creation-destroying empires of the earth. It is for this reason that John's vision of the Church is a combination of glory and suffering. The bitter-sweet message of the eternal gospel (10.9–10; 14.6) is one of salvation only through suffering and death, because it is only after death that resurrection can be experienced.

Heaven's perspective on economics
Revelation 17.1—18.24

John's critique of empire, inherent in so much of the imagery used throughout the Apocalypse, becomes more focused through Chapters 17 and 18. Whereas elsewhere his deconstruction of empire centres around the idolatrous pretensions of the one occupying the Roman throne, he turns in these chapters to address the satanic economics that sustain the imperial machine.[58] He does this through an extended description of the judgement of the great whore.

Bauckham suggests that the great whore is John's symbolic reworking of the goddess Roma as a temple prostitute, and that as such she represents heaven's perspective on the Roman Empire.[59] He then goes on to identify the great whore as a symbol of the corrupt economic systems of Rome, predicated on the military and political strength of Rome, as symbolized by the scarlet beast that the great whore rides.[60] This vision of Rome as a combination of corrupt and corrupting economics coupled with a brutal military regime provides a damning critique of the Empire.

As Bauckham says: 'The harlot rides on the beast (17.3), because the prosperity of the city of Rome at the Empire's expense and her corrupting influence over the Empire rest on the power achieved and maintained by the imperial armies.'[61] John's vision of the destruction of the great whore therefore represents divine judgement on the economic systems of Rome. What is significant, though, is the manner of her devastation since the whore is ultimately destroyed not by direct divine action, but by the feeding frenzy of the kings of the earth who had previously been her lovers (17.16–17; 18.3).[62] This is in accord with John's overall presentation of the satanic empire as a self-destructive entity that brings upon itself the fitting judgement for its idolatrous activities.[63]

The temptation before John's congregations was to buy into the seductive luxuries of the great whore without questioning the cost; to participate in the economic miracle of Rome without seeing the corruption behind the bewitching exterior. John's concern is to help those in his churches learn to see Rome as heaven sees it, to realize their need to exercise restraint, and to avoid capitulating to the temptation to compromise themselves. It is to this end that he records the voice from heaven issuing the summons: 'Come out of her, my people, so that you do not take part in her sins, and so that you do not share in her plagues' (18.4). John has already spoken earlier in the Apocalypse of the financial implications faced by those who defy the satanic empire, reporting that those who refuse to accept the mark of the beast are prevented from buying and selling (13.7).[64] This picture of an empire that rewards those who participate and punishes those who resist is compelling,[65] and it is to those who are facing financial hardship for their non-compliance that John writes his economic critique of Rome.

Having described the destruction of the great whore-city of Babylon in Chapter 17, John then records the mourning and grief of those who have lost their investment in the satanic empire. So it is that the kings who lived in luxury with the whore (18.9),[66] the merchants who profitably sold her their cargo (18.11, 15), and the seafarers who plied her with international trade (18.17)[67] all mourn the passing of the Empire. John's mention of these three groups makes his economic critique of empire highly specific: those who have sought to profit from the corrupt excesses of Babylon will in the end be seen to have squandered their investment.[68]

The list of goods in which Rome traded is indicative of the excessive luxury enjoyed by those at the centre of its Empire.[69] Such goods include: gold, silver, jewels, pearls, fine linen, purple silk, scarlet, scented wood, carved ivory, carved expensive woods, bronze, iron, marble, cinnamon, spice, incense, myrrh, frankincense, wine, and olive oil (18.11–13).[70] The Roman system of *latifundia* has already been noted,[71] whereby agricultural practices throughout the Empire resulted in the sacrifice of local staple-food production in order to maintain the supply of luxury goods to those living in the imperial heartlands.[72] The picture here is once again that of the unsustainable nature of the Empire that directs money towards luxuries while exploiting those living in poverty at the fringes.[73]

In addition to these luxury items, Rome is also depicted as a consumer of staple foods taken from throughout the Empire, importing flour, wheat, cattle and sheep (18.13), often leading to near-starvation in the provinces. As Bauckham notes: 'A city of a million people – the largest city in the western world before eighteenth-century London – could not have grown and survived without the resources of the whole empire to support it.'[74] The maintenance of the vast supply chain flowing into Ostia, the nearest port to Rome, relied not just on merchants and seafarers, but also on the imperial navy to protect supply ships from attack. This co-operation between the military strength of Rome and the city's economic supply systems ably demonstrates the force inherent in John's image of the great whore riding the scarlet beast.

The final items in the list represent a further aspect of John's deconstruction of Roman economics. The import of horses and chariots portrays the Roman addiction to convenience and entertainment, providing both domestic transport and arena-based sport.[75] It is telling that following the horses and chariots, John then mentions slaves and human lives (18.13), also commodities that functioned for both convenience and entertainment. Not only was the Roman economic system founded on slavery, requiring a regular supply of fresh blood, but slaves also played an important function in the entertainment industry as they fought to the death in the amphitheatres of Rome.[76] John's placement of the human commodities at the end of the list has a rhetorical function, and serves to convey his horror at the depths to which the Roman economic system had sunk in its idolatrous opposition to divine rule.

In terms of the way in which John's economic critique of empire is read in the contemporary world, care needs to be taken not to draw overly-simplistic direct parallels between John's engagement with ancient Rome and present-day critique of any specific nation or institution. There have been many down through the centuries who have sought to equate John's description of the judgement of the great whore with imperial power in their own time, and Kovacs and Rowland provide a fascinating and extensive list of such attempts at identification. Examples they cite include the Roman Catholic Church, Turkish Islam, Mary Queen of Scots, The Anglican Church, London, and America.[77]

Nonetheless, this is not to say that the critique of empire offered by John has no relevance beyond the first century. Bauckham provocatively suggests:

In view of the prominence of the economic theme in Revelation 18, it is hard to avoid seeing a modern parallel in the economic relations between the so-called First and Third Worlds. It is easy, from our cultural distance, to recognize the decadence of a culture in which party guests were served with pearls dissolved in wine – thousands of pounds consumed in a few mouthfuls. But the affluent West of today has equally absurd forms of extravagant consumption.[78]

It is to this end that Howard-Brook and Gwyther identify the ideology of global capitalism as a contemporary expression of the economic empire about which John is so scathing. They comment:

When empire was embodied in clearly defined entities like nation-states, it was relatively easy to trace the contours of imperial power. Global capital, however, is a more elusive reality. Nonetheless, it may be startling to see how precisely the reality of global capital matches both that of the Roman Empire in particular and Revelation's wider critique of empire generally.[79]

They then embark on a detailed analysis of contemporary market forces, globalization, multi- and trans-national corporations, and international trade and financial institutions. The compelling picture that they draw is one in which the merchants of the contemporary world grow rich from participation in the system of global capital, with those at the centre of the first world benefitting from generally high standards of living while those on the margins in the third world are held in economic slavery and poverty to service the demand for luxury, convenience and entertainment at the heart of the Empire.[80]

This is not to suggest that they believe Revelation was written as a critique of twenty-first century global economics; in fact quite the opposite. Within Howard-Brook and Gwyther's methodology John's critique of Rome's satanic economic systems is in the initial instance targeted specifically within the first century, but also becomes applicable whenever a system arises within human history that perpetrates the corrupt economic ideals of ancient Rome. So as John uses imagery of Babylon to convey his critique of Rome, Howard-Brook and Gwyther use imagery of Rome to convey their critique of the contemporary economic system of global capital. In this way, they point to unsustainable levels of growth and consumption, and echo for the twenty-first century John's first-century proclamation that empire *is* fallen (cf. 14.8; 18.2). To this end they quote the American billionaire financier George Soros: 'I cannot see the global system surviving ... we have entered a period of global disintegration only we are not yet aware of it.'[81] According to Howard-Brook and Gwyther, the contemporary system of global capital has already sown the seeds of its own destruction through its oppressive, exploitative and unsustainable levels of consumption. Just as within John's vision the great whore receives her due judgement at the hands of her former lovers (17.16–17), so a comparable judgement is due wherever the satanic empire is re-invented within human history.

Draw your own conclusions

- In what ways does John's deconstruction of the propaganda of empire affect the way he wants his audience to view their lives?
- What are the implications of John's image of the Church being at the centre of a cosmic battle?
- What hope does John offer to those facing suffering and persecution?
- How do you react to John's juxtaposition of mercy and judgement?
- In what ways can the book of Revelation be considered 'good news' for the environment?
- What are the economic implications of John's critique of empire?
- What might it mean to 'come out' of Babylon today?

Notes

1 Cf. Ex. 25.16; 1 Kings 8.5–6; 2 Chr. 5.1–10.

2 The following two quotations illustrate the belief that the ark would remain hidden until the end times: 'Jeremiah came and found a cave-dwelling, and he brought there the tent and the ark and the altar of incense; then he sealed up the entrance. Some of those who followed him came up intending to mark the way, but could not find it. When Jeremiah learned of it, he rebuked them and declared: "The place shall remain unknown until God gathers his people together again and shows his mercy. Then the Lord will disclose these things' (2 Macc. 2.5–8). 'I saw that [the angel] descended in the Holy of Holies and that he took from there the veil, the holy ephod, the mercy seat, the two tables, the holy raiment of the priests, the altar of incense, the forty-eight precious stones with which the priests were clothed, and all the holy vessels of the tabernacle. And he said to the earth with a loud voice: Earth, earth, earth, hear the word of the mighty God, and receive the things which I commit to you and guard them until the last times' (2 Baruch 6.7–8) Translated by A. F. J. Klijn in James H. Charlesworth (ed.), 1983, *The Old Testament Pseudepigrapha Vol. 1*, New York: Doubleday, p. 623.

3 Cf. Gen. 22.17–18.

4 See the discussion of the pregnant woman on pp. 105–6.

5 See the discussion of the 'child who rules the nations with a rod of iron' on pp. 75–6.

6 See the discussion of the dragon on pp. 150–1.

7 See the discussion of the scarlet beast on pp. 163–6.

8 See the discussion of the beast from the earth on pp. 168–71.

9 See the discussion of those who are 'marked' on pp. 136–7.

10 See the discussion of the mark of the beast on p. 170.

11 Brevard S. Childs, 2001, *Isaiah*, Old Testament Library, Louisville, Kentucky: Westminster John Knox Press, pp. 126–7. The identification of this 'morning star' (Heb: *Hēlēl*) as Lucifer, the fallen angel otherwise known as Satan, only occurs much later in the post-canonical Christian tradition, having been adopted from the Latin for *'light-bearer'* as used in the Vulgate of Isa. 14.12. Jesus is described as the 'bright morning star' in Revelation (2.28; 22.16; cf. 2 Peter 1.19), probably a reference to messianically interpreted prophecy uttered by Balaam that 'a star shall come out of Jacob' (Num. 24.17).

12 For a further discussion of John's characterization of 'Satan' see pp. 148–50.

13 John Jarick, 2002, *1 Chronicles*, Readings: A New Biblical Commentary, London: Sheffield Academic Press, p. 125.

14 Cf. Job 38.7 where these beings are identified with the 'morning stars'. Cf. also David J. A. Clines, 1989, *Job 1–20*, Word Biblical Commentary, vol. 17, Dallas: Word Books, pp. 19–20.

15 Cf. Jude 6.

16 Richard Bauckham, 1983, *Jude, 2 Peter*, Word Biblical Commentary, vol. 50, Waco, Texas: Word Books, pp. 50–2.

17 Richard Bauckham, 1993, *The Theology of the Book of Revelation*, Cambridge: Cambridge University Press, p. 89.

18 See pp. 168–71 for a discussion of Nero as the beast from the earth.

19 The *Pax Romana*, or 'peace of Rome', is the term coined to describe the period of relative political and military stability achieved through Roman dominance, spanning approximately the first two centuries AD. Pliny the Elder spoke of 'the immeasurable majesty of the Roman peace'. See Colin Wells, 1992, *The Roman Empire*, 2nd edn, London: Fontana Press, p. 223.

20 A comparable act of empire-deconstruction is that offered by Martin Luther King, Jr. who famously commented in 1967, 'the greatest purveyor of violence on earth is my own government'.

21 This contradiction is explored within the Jewish tradition in the book of Jonah, with Jonah's frustration evident at the mercy shown to the sinful inhabitants of Nineveh (Jonah 4.1–3, 11). Cf. Douglas Stuart, 1987, *Hosea-Jonah*, Word Biblical Commentary, vol. 31, Waco, Texas: Word Books, pp. 508–10.

22 Cf. Rev. 11.3.

23 Cf. Rev. 11.7–10; 17.6.

24 Cf. Ex. 15.13.

25 Bauckham identifies the 'eternal gospel' as an allusion to Ps. 96.2b, which he summarizes as 'the call to all nations to worship the one true God who is coming to judge the world and to establish his universal rule.' Richard Bauckham, 1993, *The Climax of Prophecy: Studies in the Book of Revelation*, Edinburgh: T&T Clark, p. 288.

26 Cf. Rev. 16.19; 17.16; 18.2–3.

27 An analogy which may help explain John's use of language here is the American prison-guard tradition of proclaiming: 'Dead man walking, dead man walking here!' as a new prisoner is brought on to death row. The point of

this is that the man may be alive and walking, but yet he is also already 'dead' because as a condemned man he cannot escape his fate. The eschatological truth is thus proclaimed in the midst of the present.

28 For detailed and insightful analysis of these passages see Bauckham, *Theology*, pp. 94–8; Bauckham, *Climax*, pp. 290–6.

29 E.g. Matt. 9.37–8; 13.24–30, 36–43; Mark 4.29; Luke 10.2; John 4.35–8. Cf. John Nolland, 2005, *The Gospel of Matthew*, The New International Greek Testament Commentary, Bletchley: Paternoster, p. 408.

30 Although there is a superficial similarity to the Matthean parable of the wheat and the weeds (Matt. 13.24–30, 36–43), there is no indication that John has in mind a separation of wheat from weeds with only the righteous being harvested.

31 For a discussion of this Christological image, see pp. 66–8.

32 Cf. Ex. 23.16, 19; Lev. 23.10, 17. The image of 'first fruits' is present elsewhere in the New Testament (cf. Rom. 8.23; 11.16; 1 Cor. 15.20, 23; 2 Thess. 2.13; James 1.18), always conveying the hope of a larger, greater harvest to follow. Cf. Ian Boxall, 2006, *The Revelation of St John*, London: Continuum, p. 203.

33 Bauckham, *Theology*, p. 104.

34 Cf. Rev. 8.7–12; 9.15, 18.

35 Bauckham, *Theology*, p. 102.

36 Cf. Rev. 18.9–10, 16–19.

37 See the discussion of liberationist readings on p. 34.

38 Brian D. McLaren, 2005, *The Last Word and the Word after That*, San Francisco: Jossey-Bass, p. 70. For a helpful survey of differing approaches taken by scholars to the issue of the violent imagery of Revelation, see Rebecca Skaggs and Thomas Doyle, 2007, 'Violence in the Apocalypse of John', *Currents in Biblical Research*, vol. 5.2: 220–34.

39 For a fascinating introduction to this topic, see Sarah Hobson and Jane Lubchenco (eds), 1997, *Revelation and the Environment AD 95–1995*, Singapore: World Scientific Publishing Co.

40 For a summary of such interpretations, see Judith L. Kovacs and Christopher Rowland, 2004, *Revelation*, Oxford: Blackwell, p. 175.

41 See the discussion on premillennialism on pp. 30–2.

42 Harry Maier comments: 'If premillennialism continues to fascinate and enthral the consumers of Western popular culture and their leaders, then it is a matter of great urgency to return that reading with a critical evaluation that seconds Earth's voices of resistance to its inevitable destruction. This is all the more urgent if ... one place where that voice of resistance is loudest is in the Apocalypse itself ... The need to second Earth's voices of resistance becomes all the more pressing once it is recognized that premillennialist dispensationalim arises out of and expresses the economics and politics that makes the majority of the Earth's inhabitants slaves to greed and Earth-destroying ambition.' Harry O. Maier, 2002, 'There's a New World Coming! Reading the Apocalypse in the Shadow of the Canadian Rockies', in Norman C. Habel and Balabanski (eds), *The Earth Story in the New Testament*, London: Sheffield Academic Press, pp. 171–2.

43 Further examples include: Abimelech's victory over Shechem being

followed by him sowing the ground with salt to ensure nothing could grow there in the future (Judg. 9.45); the Roman system of agriculture ensuring the land was overworked for the production of luxury goods in place of food staples, see Howard-Brook and Gwyther, *Unveiling Empire*, p. 248; and the Roman demand for ivory leading to the near-extinction of the Syrian elephant in the first century, see Richard Bauckham, 2005, 'The New Testament Teaching on the Environment: A Response', in R. C. J. Carling and M. A. Carling (eds), *A Christian Approach to the Environment*, London: The John Ray Initiative, p. 99.

44 Northcott notes that 'the writer of the Book of Revelation [speaks] of a time when the whole cosmos will be brought into a relationship with the supreme justice of the Lord who is God in Christ. Christians have often proclaimed this justice to people of their own race and gender and class. They have more rarely proclaimed it among people different from themselves. Far more rarely has it been proclaimed to those orders of life which are not human flesh and blood. But the connections between human justice, and the good of the land and its non-human inhabitants, remain as clear today in environmental disasters which destroy the land of greedy land-owners who have burnt the tree and leaf, as they did in the time of Isaiah and Amos.' Michael S. Northcott, 1996, *The Environment & Christian Ethics*, New Studies in Christian Ethics, Cambridge: Cambridge University Press, p. 326.

45 Sir Nicholas Stern, author of the Stern Report into climate change. http://www.timesonline.co.uk/tol/news/uk/article619828.ece. Accessed 31.10.07.

46 Boxall, *Revelation*, p. 171.

47 Cf. Boxall, *Revelation*, p. 84.

48 E. Lucas notes that: 'It may be significant that this picture of the culmination of God's purpose is not a simple return to the garden of Eden, but a City of Eden. In Genesis 4 the city is a human artefact, with the first one being built by Cain. This might imply that in the new Jerusalem that has come from heaven to earth God has incorporated the best of human endeavours in the working out of his purposes.' Ernest Lucas, 2005, 'The New Testament Teaching on the Environment', in R. C. J. Carling and M. A. Carling (eds), *A Christian Approach to the Environment*, London: The John Ray Initiative, p. 83. Reichenbach and Anderson make a related point, commenting, 'the garden has become the city, but the city is reminiscent of the garden.' Bruce R. Reichenbach and V. Elving Anderson, 2006, 'Tensions in a Stewardship Paradigm', in R. J. Berry (ed.), *Environmental Stewardship: Critical Perspectives – Past and Present*, London: T&T Clark International, p. 124.

49 Cf. Isa. 65.17–25. Rasmussen understands the new creation as 'a radical transformation *of* the created order and not its utter obliteration in favor of realms literally out of this world'. Larry L. Rasmussen, 1996, *Earth Community, Earth Ethics*, Geneva: WCC Publications, p. 256. Lucas agrees, commenting that the divine statement, 'See, I am making all things new' (21.5) indicates, 'a renewing of the old by a radical transformation, not the abolishing of it to start again *de novo*'. Lucas, 'New Testament Teaching on the Environment', p. 83. Cf. Celia Deane-Drummond, 1996, *A Handbook in Theology and Ecology*, London: SCM Press, pp. 24–5; Bauckham, *Theology*, p. 49; D. M. Russell, 1996, *The 'New Heavens and New Earth': Hope for the Creation in Jewish Apocalyptic and the New Testament*, Philadelphia: Visionary Press, p. 6.

50 See pp. 105–6 for the identification of the woman with the people of God. For a discussion on the 'heroic action' of the earth in Revelation 12 see Barbara R. Rossing, 2002, 'Alas for Earth! Lament and Resistance in Revelation 12', in Norman C. Habel and Balabanski (eds), *The Earth Story in the New Testament*, London: Sheffield Academic Press. Rossing suggests that: 'In the lament of Rev. 12.12 God gives voice to the Earth ... lamenting Rome's unjust domination over the whole Earth as a manifestation of Satan's presence ... Earth's heroic swallowing of the dragon's river in Rev. 12.16 is an action that models ... the principle of resistance' (p. 181). The swallowing of the river by the earth is thus interpreted as an act of, 'resistance against Roman conquest' (p. 190).

51 Cf. Steven Bouma-Prediger, 2001, *For the Beauty of the Earth: A Christian Vision for Creation Care*, Grand Rapids, Michigan: Baker Academic, p. 115.

52 Due to the telescopic nature of Revelation, 5.13 is actually a proleptic vision of the worship offered in the new Jerusalem. Cf. Ruth Page, 2006, 'The Fellowship of All Creation', in R. J. Berry (ed.), *Environmental Stewardship: Critical Perspectives – Past and Present*, London: T&T Clark International, p. 99.

53 See the discussion of the four living creatures on pp. 128–9.

54 Bauckham comments: 'If creation needs priests, here they are in heaven, the central worshippers in creation, worshipping continuously in the immediate presence of God and doing so representatively, offering all creation's worship until the time when all creation will perfectly and fully follow them in their worship.' Bauckham, 'New Testament Teaching on the Environment', pp. 101–2.

55 Only one of the four living creatures has a human face (4.7).

56 G. B. Caird, 1984, *The Revelation of St. John the Divine*, London: A&C Black, pp. 265–6. Bold his.

57 Elsdon comments: 'The promise of the renewal of creation still lies in the future, but what the New Testament adds to the Old is the way that the kingdom of God has already broken into the present world order through the Incarnation, death and Resurrection of Jesus Christ.' Ron Elsdon, 1992, *Greenhouse Theology*, Tunbridge Wells: Monarch, p. 161.

58 Bauckham suggests that: '[John's] condemnation of Rome's economic exploitation of her empire is the most unusual aspect of the opposition to Rome in Revelation, by comparison with other Jewish and Christian apocalyptic attacks on Rome.' Richard Bauckham, 1991, 'The Economic Critique of Rome in Revelation 18', in Loveday Alexander (ed.), *Images of Empire*, JSOT Supp: 122, Sheffield: JSOT Press, p. 47. This chapter is reproduced in Bauckham, *Climax*, pp. 338–83. Cf. also the chapter 'The Fallen City: Revelation 18' in Richard Bauckham, 1990, *The Bible in Politics: How to Read the Bible Politically*, Louisville: Westminster John Knox Press, pp. 85–102.

59 See the discussion of the great whore on pp. 158–63.

60 Bauckham, *Theology*, pp. 35–6. For a detailed discussion of the image of the scarlet beast see above, pp. 163–6.

61 Bauckham, *Theology*, p. 36.

62 For a discussion of the feminist implications of this image, see pp. 162–3. See also the discussion of the ten horns of the scarlet beast on pp. 167–8.

63 The words of Paul could equally be applied to John's understanding of

Rome and the Church: 'Do not be deceived; God is not mocked, for you reap whatever you sow. If you sow to your own flesh, you will reap corruption from the flesh; but if you sow to the Spirit, you will reap eternal life from the Spirit' (Gal. 6.7–8).

64 See the discussion of those who bear the mark of the beast on pp. 136–7.

65 There are resonances here with the view of empire implicit in Luke's account of the parable of the pounds (Luke 19.11–28), in which Jesus is the servant who refuses to do business with his satanic master's money, ultimately paying with his life the price of his non-compliance. Cf. C. S. Song, 1980, *Third Eye Theology: Theology in Formation in Asian Settings*, Guildford: Lutterworth Press, pp. 223–6.

66 See the discussion of the kings of the earth on pp. 139–40.

67 See the discussion of the merchants and seafarers on pp. 140–1.

68 This critique of those who invest in empire has resonances with similar teaching by Jesus (cf. Matt. 6.19–21; 19.21; Mark 10.21; Luke 12.16–21, 33–4; 18.22).

69 Cf. Peter S. Perry, 2007, 'Critiquing the Excess of Empire: A Synkrisis of John of Patmos and Dio of Prusa', *Journal for the Study of the New Testament*, vol. 29: 473–96, pp. 488–9.

70 This list is derivative of Ezekiel's similar list of goods traded in the city of Tyre (cf. Ezek. 27.12–24). For a detailed examination of the items listed, showing how they relate to the specific context of Rome, see Bauckham, *Climax*, pp. 352–66.

71 See pp. 152–3, where latifundia is seen as the backdrop to the image of the rider on the black horse (cf. 6.5).

72 Pliny the Elder (AD 23–79) commented on these large-scale farms: '[W]e must confess the truth, it is the wide-spread domains [*latifundia*] that have been the ruin of Italy, and soon will be that of the provinces as well. Six proprietors were in possession of one half of Africa, at the period when the Emperor Nero had them put to death.' Natural History 18.7.35. J. Bostock and H. T. Riley, 1856, *The Natural History of Pliny*, vol. IV, London: Henry G. Bohn, pp. 14–15.

73 In a contemporary parallel, consider the following by George Monbiot: 'It doesn't get madder than this. Swaziland is in the grip of a famine and receiving emergency food aid. Forty per cent of its people are facing acute food shortages. So what has the government decided to export? Biofuel made from one of its staple crops, cassava. The government has allocated several thousand hectares of farmland to ethanol production in the county of Lavumisa, which happens to be the place worst hit by drought. It would surely be quicker and more humane to refine the Swazi people and put them in our [fuel] tanks.' Published in the *Guardian*, 6 November 2007. Retrieved from http://www.monbiot.com/archives/2007/11/06/an-agricultural-crime-against-humanity/. Accessed 6.12.07.

74 Bauckham, *Climax*, p. 363.

75 The Circus Maximus in central Rome provided regular horse and chariot races for approximately 300,000 spectators.

76 Construction of the 50,000 seat Colosseum commenced in *c*. AD 70 under Vespasian's reign. This may correspond closely to the date of composition for Revelation; cf. the discussion on pp. 15–16.

77 Kovacs and Rowland, *Revelation*, pp. 178–88.

78 Bauckham, *The Bible in Politics*, p. 101.

79 Howard-Brook and Gwyther, *Unveiling Empire*, pp. 237–8. cf. John M. Court, 1997, 'Reading the Book 6. The Book of Revelation', *The Expository Times*: 164–6.

80 Howard-Brook and Gwyther, *Unveiling Empire*, pp. 236–67.

81 George Soros quoted in Howard-Brook and Gwyther, *Unveiling Empire*, p. 260.

10

Martyrdom and a Tale of Two Cities

Heaven's perspective on martyrdom
Revelation 19.1—20.15

The destruction of the great whore of Babylon triggers a sequence of heavenly worship, with the great multitude praising God (19.1–3).[1] This vision is of the rejoicing expressed by humanity at its release from the seductive temptations of Babylon, and it represents the heavenly perspective on the end of empire. In place of the satanic kingdom the great multitude proclaims the reign of 'the Lord our God the Almighty' (19.6). The people of the earth rejoice because the prayer of the Church, that the kingdom of God should come, is being answered.[2] The time of union between Jesus and the Church is at hand (19.7), and all creation is to be freed from the tyranny of the beast. The twenty-four elders representing the Church, and the four living creatures representing the created order, together cry 'Amen. Hallelujah!' in response to the worship offered by the great multitude.[3] In this way, John provides heaven's perspective on the human suffering entailed in the destruction of empire. Even those who suffered and mourned empire's passing are seen to join the great multitude in thanking God for their release from slavery when viewed with heaven's eyes.

The next scene in John's vision is of the rider on the white horse (19.11–16)[4] and the great battle of Harmagedon (19.17–21; cf. 16.16). The sword that comes from the mouth of the rider defeats the armies of the kings of the earth, as the word of God is seen to be victorious over the satanic deceptions of the beast (19.21). The same armies that destroyed the great whore are thus themselves subject to the judgement of God, as the purificatory task continues and evil is progressively banished. In an echo of the judgement on the great whore, the beast and the false prophet are thrown into the lake of fire, deceiving the nations no longer (19.20).[5]

Following the millennium passage, the visions of final judgement on the forces of evil continue. Satan, the dragon, the scarlet beast and the false prophet have all found their eternal destiny in the lake of fire, and John moves on to address the fate of humanity itself. The universal nature of the final judgement means that all of humanity, living and dead, are present before the divine throne (20.12–13).[6] The final satanic hold on humanity is broken, as death itself is consigned to the lake of fire (20.14), and creation is readied for the vision of the new heaven and the new earth that follows.

The millennium
Revelation 20.1–10

In the image of the millennium, John revisits the theme of martyrdom.[7] It is worth noting at this point that it can often seem as though there are as many suggestions as to how the millennium should be interpreted as there are interpreters to suggest them.[8] The approach adopted here is that John's image of the millennium functions as a *metaphor*, in other words as a non-literal symbol.[9] Against this, however, there are many interpreters who espouse some form of literal interpretation.[10] There are several aspects of John's image of the millennium that have been especially problematic for interpreters, and these will now be looked at in more detail.

What are the 'thousand years'?

It will be helpful at this stage to outline how the 'thousand years' function within the passage. An angel comes from heaven and binds the dragon, throwing him into the pit and locking it over him. Satan is therefore unable to deceive the nations for a thousand years. John then describes a judgement scene, with those seated on the thrones being given authority to judge, and, without elaborating this any further, moves on to depict those who have been beheaded for their testimony to Jesus. They are raised to life and reign with Christ for 'a thousand years'. At the end of this millennium Satan is released, rampages on the earth, and tries unsuccessfully to overpower the faithful saints. Those who have followed Satan are then consumed by fire from heaven, and the Devil is thrown into the lake of fire for ever. The second resurrection and the final judgement then occur.[11]

A key question that needs to be asked is, why a *thousand* years? Is there any clue in the choice of this particular number that can aid the interpretation of the passage? The two main biblical texts that provide the background to the thousand years are Ps. 90.4: 'For a thousand years in your sight are like yesterday when it is past, or like a watch in the night', and 2 Peter 3.8, 'with the Lord one day is like a thousand years, and a thousand years are like one day.' The passage from 2 Peter, which is in essence a midrash[12] on Ps. 90.4,[13] represents a strand of thought present

224

within Second Temple Judaism whereby some believed that the course of the world's history could be found paralleled in the seven days of creation.[14] By this understanding history would continue for either six or seven thousand years from its creation, and then would be followed by a sabbath age.[15] Thus there was a Jewish tradition of a period of time, associated with the end time, which was expected to last for a thousand years.[16] John adopts and adapts this accepted Jewish concept in order to convey his own theological message.[17]

Why is the last judgement split by the millennium?

The millennium passage separates the beginning of the last judgement (20.4) from its conclusion (20.11–15),[18] and an examination of why this is highlights the difference between a metaphorical approach, and some form of literal interpretation. Three representative examples, those of G. B. Caird, G. K. Beale and R. Bauckham, will now be examined in order to demonstrate this crucial difference.

Caird advocates a 'follow the clues' approach to interpreting the millennium.[19] By this, he means paying attention to the detail and the background, in the hope that the larger picture will emerge out of the detail. To this end, he notes that Satan is confined 'so that he would deceive the nations no more' (20.3). From this, Caird concludes that there must be a considerable world population throughout the thousand years, and that therefore it is these people that the martyrs rule over with Christ. In this way, for Caird the millennium occurs in the course of human history, as a 'golden age' when Satan is bound and the righteous are vindicated.

Having started down this path of interpreting the millennium in a historical sense, even if the number 1,000 is not to be taken literally, Caird finds himself having to ask and answer increasingly complex questions in order to tie all the details of the passage into the historical time-frame he is constructing. In this way, he concludes that the battle of Chapter 19 cannot represent the end of history, but must instead signify the destruction of political power prior to the binding of Satan. Similarly, the judgement in 20.4 cannot, he contends, be understood as referring to the last judgement, but rather must refer to a judgement that occurs in the course of history as the martyrs assume the empire of the defeated beast. The millennium, for Caird, therefore comes after this, and represents the ongoing presence of the Church preaching the gospel to each successive generation, while the resurrected martyrs function with Christ as spiritual priests and rulers. It is only after this historical and indeterminate period that the final judgement occurs, death is banished, and Satan is defeated permanently prior to the establishment of the heavenly kingdom.

By way of contrast, Beale contends that the millennium is to be understood non-literally in the first instance. He pays close attention to John's
use of the Old Testament, relating the structure of the book to the structure of the relevant parallel passages in the Old Testament.[20] His careful attention to the structure of the text, both in terms of its internal
structure and also how it relates to other passages, leads him to identify the 'key' to the abyss (20.1), with other references to keys earlier in
the Apocalypse (cf. 3.7; 9.1). He notices that these earlier references are
all concerned with what he calls 'inter-advent realities',[21] and this leads
him to conclude that the reference to the key in Chapter 20 needs to be
similarly understood as denoting an event that occurs before the second
coming of Jesus. Thus the binding of Satan and the millennial reign are,
he contends, 'best understood as Christ's authority restraining the Devil
in some manner during the church age.'[22] He then goes on to define this
binding as the cessation of Satan's authority over the realm of the dead,
following the resurrection of Jesus.

In this way, Beale envisages the millennium as a period of human
history, stretching from the resurrection of Jesus to the second coming.
During this time Satan is bound, having no more authority over the
realm of the soul after death, and the deceased saints reign with Christ
after their earthly deaths as priests and kings over spiritual death.[23] It
can be seen, therefore, that in spite of Beale's assertion that the millennium is to be taken figuratively, he nonetheless sees it as being worked
out in a historical sense. This leads him to hypothesize answers to questions such as: What is the timing and nature of the first and second
resurrections? How is it that the saints rule during the millennium? And
how can the saints inherit eschatological promises in advance of the
parousia?[24]

Bauckham, like Beale, pays close attention to John's use of Old Testament allusions.[25] He draws attention to four key parallels between John's
narrative and Dan. 7.9–14:[26] Both contain descriptions of thrones (Rev.
20.4; Dan. 7.9),[27] open books (Rev. 20.10; Dan. 7.10), a beast that is
destroyed (Rev. 19.11–21; Dan. 7.11–12), and a kingdom handed over
to the 'son of man' (Rev. 20.4–6; Dan. 7.13–14). Bauckham suggests
that John, while drawing his imagery from Daniel, alters the ordering to
make a theological point.[28] A diagram may help here:

Rev.	19.11–21	20.4	20.4–6	20.10
	Destruction of beast	Thrones	Transfer of kingdom	Opening of books
Dan.		7.9		7.10
	7.11–12		7.13–14	

Bauckham suggests that what John achieves by altering Daniel's ordering is, in effect, a commentary on the final judgement. There is a negative aspect to it, the destruction of the beast, and then a positive counterpart. He comments: 'The negative aspect of the final judgement (19:11–21), in which the beast was condemned, requires as its positive counterpart that judgement be given in favour of the martyrs, who must be vindicated and rewarded.'[29]

Thus John's separation of the initial stages of the final judgement from its conclusion, by the insertion of the millennium, allows him to use the millennium as a metaphor for the vindication of the martyrs, which Bauckham sees as necessary (on the basis of Daniel 7) as the positive counterpart to the destruction of the beast. This suggestion does not require that the millennium be worked out in history at all, rather it is freed to function theologically as a metaphor.[30]

It is clear that martyrdom forms a significant part of the backdrop to the book of Revelation.[31] John was writing to those who may have seen friends and family martyred, and who may have feared that they would face the possibility of martyrdom themselves. Understood from an earthly perspective, the killing of a believer represents the ultimate triumph of evil over good, but what John achieves in this passage is to convey the message that from a heavenly perspective, at the very instant the beast creates martyrs by putting believers to death, the destruction of the beast and the vindication of the martyrs is assured.[32] The situation facing the recipients of Revelation is therefore utterly reversed. If they go to their deaths for their faith, they do so not demonstrating the victory of the beast, but as those whose witness through martyrdom will assure the destruction of the beast, and as those who will themselves be vindicated. Bauckham comments:

> This shows that the theological point of the millennium is solely to demonstrate the triumph of the martyrs: that those whom the beast put to death are those who will truly live – eschatologically, and that those who contested his right to rule and suffered for it are those who will in the end rule as universally as he – and for much longer: a thousand years![33]

In this way, the millennium functions in an almost hyperbolical manner. Within John's visionary framework, it represents the period of time during which the beast is bound and the martyrs rule with Christ. However, this is not to suggest that John intends it as predictive prophecy for the distant future, or as being worked out in a temporal sense during the course of human history. Rather, it is best understood as a metaphor for the scale and magnitude of the vindication of those who suffer and die for the kingdom of God.[34]

Who are those who reign with Christ in the millennium?

The preceding interpretation has been offered on the basis that those who reign with Christ are those who have been beheaded for their testimony to Jesus, and that these martyrs are those who have not worshipped the beast.[35] The NRSV renders it thus:

> Then I saw thrones, and those seated on them were given authority to judge. I also saw the souls of those who had been beheaded for their testimony to Jesus and for the word of God. They had not worshiped the beast or its image and had not received its mark on their foreheads or their hands. They came to life and reigned with Christ a thousand years. (Rev. 20.4)

It is important to note that there is an exegetical issue at stake here that is much discussed. The question is whether or not those who participate in the millennium are solely those who have been martyred,[36] or whether John also includes those who are '"Confessors" – in other words ... those whose confession of Jesus is genuine but does not issue in their martyrdom.'[37] One possible reading is that in his description of those who had not worshipped the beast, John was not merely describing those who had been martyred, but was rather adding a second category to those who reign in the millennium. Some would widen the scope even further, with Boring suggesting that 'we should not picture those seated on the thrones as any different from faithful Christians themselves'.[38] It is apparent from the many discussions that have taken place around this issue that it is not going to be decided on textual grounds; the text is simply ambiguous. Instead, the conclusion reached will be determined by the interpretation of the millennium that is being followed.

If the millennium is interpreted in anything other than a strictly metaphorical manner, this question becomes significant, because it becomes important *who* actually reigns for the thousand years. A perceived unfairness begins to creep in with questions such as: why should the martyrs be singled out for special treatment, while the person tortured to the point of death but who survived is denied this glory?[39] However, if the millennium is understood to be a metaphor that John is using to communicate the heavenly perspective on the earthly situation being faced by the recipients, this problem disappears. John is not advocating 'some kind of special reward for martyrs as a sub-class of saints'.[40] Rather, he is demonstrating theologically that those who overcome to the point of death – that very point where the beast seems to overcome them – are in actual fact those who truly overcome in an eschatological sense.[41]

The book of Revelation was not written for the dead to tell them what is happening to them, but was written for the living, for those who go through persecution and see others being martyred. This passage is therefore no description of the way the vindication of the martyrs and those who overcome will be worked out in history. Rather, it provides an alternative perspective on the life of suffering and death that awaits those who hold fast to their testimony to the word of God.

Why is Satan released again after the millennium?

The millennium functions in two ways within the narrative scheme of this section of the Apocalypse. First, it separates one aspect of the final judgement (20.4) from the main description itself (20.12–13), thereby allowing John's inclusion of his image for the vindication of the martyrs, with judgement being given in their favour and the beast's kingdom being transferred to them.[42] Second, the millennium delays the destruction of Satan so that it is not an immediate consequence of the parousia.

This second function needs to be understood with reference to John's overriding pastoral concern to provide his recipients with a new perspective on martyrdom. Bauckham suggests that the release of Satan, and his unsuccessful attempt to destroy the camp of the saints, serves to 'demonstrate that their triumph in Christ's kingdom is not one which evil can again reverse, that it is God's last word for good against evil.'[43]

In the same way that the millennium functions metaphorically, so does the release of Satan. Those to whom John was writing were not only those who feared they might themselves face martyrdom, but those who had survived seeing their sisters and brothers martyred. In spite of John's assurance that martyrdom was actually victory over the beast, their present experience was one where evil continued to be experienced as rampant in the land. It could appear to them that the victory of the martyrs was short-lived to say the least. By depicting Satan rampant in the land again, even after the vindication of the martyrs, and then showing his unsuccessful attempts to re-take the kingdom of the righteous, John was providing assurance to his recipients that martyrdom was not in vain. Satan is defeated even though he is still rampant in the land; his fate has been sealed by the victory of Christ and the evidence of the blood of the martyrs.[44]

Where does John locate his audience within the narrative?

The rhetorical strategy that John utilizes in Revelation is one that encourages readers of the Apocalypse to locate themselves within the text. Those reading the work are invited not only to identify themselves as various characters within the narrative,[45] but also to find their circumstances reflected in the imagery that John constructs. Thus John's first audience could equate their own experiences of suffering and martyrdom with those of Jesus the slain Lamb, while finding their hope of resurrection expressed through the continued existence of the Lamb on the throne. Some of John's audience may have found themselves suffering the betrayal of Maundy Thursday, or the fear of Good Friday morning, or they may have seen others join Jesus on the cross through a martyr's death. In its invitation to identify with Jesus, Revelation therefore encourages its audience to interpret their own lives according to the lived example of Jesus himself, with the events of the cross becoming real in their lives.

A helpful way to understand John's imagery of the millennium and the subsequent release of Satan is thus to read it in the light of the crucifixion story. The audience are thereby invited to locate themselves in the space of Easter Saturday, awaiting resurrection and restoration, confidently hopeful, but still living with the present pain of Friday's grief and horror. By this reading, the martyrs have departed the present life of suffering and gone to vindication (20.1–7), and Satan's hold on the world has been broken through the sacrificial deaths of both Jesus and the martyrs. However, in the present experience of John's audience, Satan is still loose in the world making war on the dwelling places of the saints. In this way, the Easter weekend can be seen as a paradigm for reading the story of the Church as presented in 20.1–10. The following table expresses these correspondences:

Crucifixion narrative	Revelation Ch. 20
Death of Jesus	Martyrdom of believers
Victory over Satan on the cross	Binding of Satan in the pit
Easter Saturday	Release of Satan 'for a little while'
Resurrection	Final judgement and new creation

What did the millennium mean for John?

The interpretation of the millennium offered above is based on an understanding of it as a metaphor. Few contemporary academic interpreters would claim to interpret the millennium literally so that it describes a period of exactly one thousand years, occurring as a consequence of the parousia, when those martyred will be raised to reign over the nations of the earth alongside Christ. However, many interpreters who hold the millennium as symbolic continue to interpret it as a symbol of the outworking of God in history in a temporal sense. Thus, the sequence of events in the passage is taken literally, with importance assigned to the precise order in which things occur. On the one hand, any expectation that the events described by John will really happen in history is rejected, yet on the other hand the text is treated as if John *thinks* he is describing events that will happen in history.[46]

Interpreting the millennium as a metaphor avoids these difficulties. Once it is accepted that John was consciously writing using metaphor, any compulsion to reconcile the temporal difficulties within the text is relieved, and the interpreter is freed to concentrate on the theological meaning of the passage. By this account John uses the metaphor of the millennium for a very specific function; to provide his audience with the perspective they need to understand the relationship between martyrdom and victory in Christ.

In this way, the questions to which many interpreters of the millennium devote many pages cease to be relevant. The reason these questions have proved so insoluble is because they are the wrong questions. As Bauckham notes:

John does not answer [them] because they are irrelevant to the function he gives ... [the millennium] in his symbolic universe ... [These interpreters] have to ask: whom do the saints rule? Do they rule from heaven or on earth? How is the eschatological life of resurrection compatible with an unrenewed earth? Who are the nations Satan deceives at the end of the millennium? And so on.[47]

Thus the millennium functions for John as a metaphor to provide a perspective on the very real human experience of martyrdom. However, it does not attempt to predict the manner of the vindication of the martyrs, and therefore should not be taken as such.

It is important to note that the preceding interpretation does not preclude there being a biblical basis for belief in the personal return of Christ since there are texts throughout the New Testament that provide Christian orthodoxy with its belief in the parousia.[48] What John achieves in the millennium passage is a reworking of the commonly held expectation of the return of Christ as a theological point about martyrdom. In this way, while he is not attempting to provide additional detail about *how* the parousia will occur, neither is he questioning that it *will* occur. John therefore reworks the Christian belief in the parousia for theological effect, in order to provide pastoral and prophetic advice to his audience on how they can live their lives before God in their current contexts.

Heaven's perspective on cities
Revelation 21.1—22.21

A tale of two cities: from New York to the new Jerusalem

Surely *the* defining moment of the opening years of the twenty-first century was the terrible terrorist atrocity perpetrated in New York City on

11 September 2001, when two aeroplanes were deliberately flown into the twin towers of the World Trade Centre.[49] The subsequent attacks on the Madrid train network on 11 March 2004, and the London public transport system on 7 July 2005, while not on a comparable scale in terms of their death-toll, have nonetheless acquired similar symbolic importance. These events have raised many questions, and provoked responses that span the globe.

It is interesting to note that the events of New York, Madrid and London have dominated the international arena in a way that other deaths on a similar scale have not. It seems that there is something symbolic about these attacks on internationally important cities that transcends the death-toll statistics, however horrifying those statistics may be. In the popular imagination, these cities have come to stand for more than the sum of their parts. In terms of New York, the 'Big Apple' is, for millions of people, more than just a city: it is a dream, a symbol of happiness and prosperity; it is the gateway to the promised land, to the New World.[50] Similarly, the World Trade Centre was more than an office block, it was a symbol of Western capitalist success.[51]

Tragic though the deaths in New York were, the attention that they attracted far exceeded that attached to similar levels of death and suffering around the globe that do not carry such symbolic power.[52] This symbolic function of cities, with their ability to represent more than the sum of their parts, is nothing new. Since the earliest days of civilization, cities have represented the best and the worst of humanity. They represent both humanity's greatest achievements and also the scene of its greatest evils.[53]

In Revelation, John recognizes this and uses the image of two cities to represent the best and the worst of humanity. To this end, he juxtaposes Babylon and Jerusalem. Of course, the real city of Babylon had been long destroyed by the time Revelation was written: the great and beautiful city of ancient times with its hanging gardens and its impressive architecture stood no more. No longer was it a place of cruelty and evil, where captives were killed for the pleasure of the citizens with countless hordes watching in fascination as innocent people were murdered in front of their eyes. But Babylon as an *image* still lived on in the Jewish imagination. It had come to represent all that was evil and corrupt; to stand for those aspects of human society that were opposed to God's ideal for humanity.

In Revelation, John uses this image of Babylon to signify the satanic tendency of humanity to construct idolatrous empires that challenge the dominion of the one on the throne in heaven. He uses it as a powerful reminder that no matter how great and beautiful human achievements may be, no matter how powerful and impressive the cities that are constructed, evil still remains a part of the human experience, raining death and destruction on innocent people through the imperial pretensions of those who deny the kingdom of heaven.

The image of Babylon in the book of Revelation tells its audience that there is nowhere they are completely safe from the threat of evil. Even in the great cities, places that inspire feelings of safety and security, people find no true protection from death and suffering. John's deconstruction of the mythology of the imperial city, through his identification of Rome as Babylon, demonstrates that no matter how hard humans may try to construct heaven on the earth, ultimately all that is achieved is idolatry and suffering.

It is against this bleak vision of humanity that John gives his audience another picture, another image, another city, in his description of the new Jerusalem.[54] Traditionally Jerusalem, the capital city of Israel, was regarded as the city of God, the place where the Jews had their focus of worship in the temple. In Jewish understanding, Jerusalem represented a city of hope, a city of peace, and was the place where God lived among his people. Jerusalem, too, was a city that had come to stand for more than the sum of its parts. In reality it was simply the capital city of Israel, beset by fighting and difficulty just like any other human community. But in the popular mindset, in people's imaginations, Jerusalem had come to stand for a lot more than this. It became a symbol of hope that one day God would right the world's wrongs, and that it would itself become a place where people would live at peace with their God. John picks up on this image and tells his audience of what he calls the new Jerusalem, which he depicts as the heavenly alternative to the city of Babylon. He holds before his first-century Roman audience an alternative reality; a vision of a city that subverts everything Babylon stands for.

To people facing despair at the evil of the world in which they live, to those who fear they are trapped in Babylon and will never find their way out, to those who look at the world and weep with anger and frustration and pain at the evil that seems so unavoidable, the vision of the new Jerusalem presents a hope that the world will not always be like this. For those in John's churches, struggling against the might of Babylon expressed as the Roman Empire, John's picture of the people of God as the new Jerusalem provides an alternative vision of humanity, where God is in his rightful place among his people. In this way, the vision of the new Jerusalem gives the heavenly perspective on the lived earthly reality: it is God's alternative city. Revelation presents the tantalizing vision of a world transformed, a world with different priorities. It encourages its audience to persevere and overcome when confronted with the true nature of Babylon.

John invites his audience to see themselves as citizens of the new Jerusalem, as citizens of the dawning kingdom of God. He invites them to become participants with Christ in bringing this new city into being.

Those in John's churches become the seeds of good news planted among the ashes of destruction, freedom fighters of peace in a world of fighting and unrest. To those who look at the world and see Babylon all around, John presents the option of saying that in Christ, this is not the way it should be. He offers two alternatives, inviting his audience to make a choice as to which city they will inhabit. They can either keep their citizenship in the attractive, cosmopolitan, seductive, exciting, frightening, and ultimately satanic city of Babylon, or they can align themselves with the small and subversive, with the hidden and the dangerous, and start living as citizens of the new Jerusalem.

The choice to move citizenship from Babylon to the new Jerusalem does not come without its cost. John's first-century audience faced both economic hardship and the possibility of persecution and even martyrdom for taking their stand against the might of the satanic empire. Martin Luther King, Jr. applies the concept of a battle against an empire fought without bombs, guns and terrorism, to the racial rights struggle of the mid-twentieth century. To those who were seeking to use violence against him, he said:

> [T]hrow us in jail and we will still love you. Threaten our children and bomb our homes and our churches and as difficult as it is, we will still love you. Send your hooded perpetrators of violence into our communities at the midnight hours and drag us out on some wayside road and beat us and leave us half-dead, and as difficult as that is, we will still love you. But be assured that we will wear you down by our capacity to suffer and one day we will win our freedom. We will not only win freedom for ourselves, we will so appeal to your heart and your conscience that we will win you in the process and our victory will be a double victory.[55]

Those who have sought, in any age, to establish their version of the kingdom of heaven on the earth by the use of force have inevitably ended up re-inventing Babylon in their own day and age. This is John's great insight into the human tendency to construct empire. Even those which begin with the best of intentions end up as idolatrous alternatives to the one on the throne in heaven, and are therefore fundamentally satanic. The battle against idolatry can, according to John, only be won by those who choose to place their citizenship with the new Jerusalem, and who work for its establishment on the earth.[56] Jesus compared the coming kingdom to yeast; small, invisible, hard to understand, and yet that which ultimately transforms the entire batch into bread (Matt. 13.33; Luke 13.20–1). This call of Jesus finds resonances in the theology of John, who encourages his audience to become those who participate in the coming of the kingdom of God to the earth.[57]

The new Jerusalem is described by John as descending from heaven to the earth (21.2, 10). It was argued above that through Chapters 1—4 John structured his work rhetorically to draw his first-century audience from the earth into his vision of heaven.[58] Here in Chapter 21 he returns them back to the earth again, as the heavenly manifestation of the Church descends to the earth. However, the way John describes this descent is interesting: following their journey with him through the heavenly realm, when they finally get back to the earth, John's audience find that everything is different. At the time of their initial ascent with John through the door opened in heaven (4.1), they were simply those attending the seven congregations of Asia Minor, living under the dominion of Rome, struggling in their faith and their worship. By the time they are returned to the earth at the end of the vision, they are seen to be the new Jerusalem, the eternal glorious Church. Their witnessing of the destruction of the satanic empire and the salvation of the nations of the earth has changed everything. John's vision has had its intended effect, transforming its hearers' imagination and the way in which they perceive and understand the world. The first heaven and the first earth have passed away, and John has taken his audience to a new understanding of creation where God and people live in harmony with each other, where the hold of death is broken, and where suffering has passed.

John's vision of the new heaven and the new earth draws on a similar vision from Isaiah (Isa. 65.17; 66.22). Boxall helpfully summarizes:

> [T]his is not to be understood in terms of destroying the old or the obsolete in order to replace it with something completely different (neither Isaiah nor John use the language of destruction). Rather, John sees a profound renewal of that which is already there ...[59]

However, there remains a question as to whether this renewal occurs entirely in the future, or if there is also a present fulfilment of this vision of transformation. There are many who seek to locate this vision in the distant future, as the goal towards which all of human history is heading.[60] However, against this it is important to recognize that, as with all of Revelation's imagery, John's vision of the new heaven and earth evokes not simply a future but also a present realization. The one seated on the throne declares in the present tense: ἰδοὺ καινὰ ποιῶ πάντα ('see, I am making all things new' 21.5).[61]

Tom Wright suggests that the New Testament language of heaven and earth coming to an end, followed by re-creation, functions as a metaphor for socio-political renewal:

> [T]here is virtually no evidence that Jews were expecting the end of the space-time universe. There is abundant evidence that they, like

Jeremiah and others before them, knew a good metaphor when they saw one, and used cosmic imagery to bring out the full theological significance of cataclysmic social events.[62]

John's audience are thus invited to realize that the existing world-order *has been* destroyed (cf. 16.17, 'it is done'), that Babylon *is* fallen (cf. 14.8; 18.2), and that all things *are being* made new (cf. 21.5). They come to a realization that when the earth is seen from heaven's perspective, everything is different. The future eschatological hope is therefore seen to be breaking into the present through the faithful, witnessing to the alternative heavenly reality of which they are a part.

In this way, the act of re-creation within John's scheme is presented as an ongoing, present-day activity, made manifest on the earth by the army of the Lamb, as creation moves towards its ultimate destination. Thus the Church becomes the fulfilment of the promise to Abraham that all nations would be blessed through him.[63] The spiritual heirs of Abraham, the faithful people of God, sing the 'new song', that only they can learn, of the victory won by Christ on the cross (14.3; cf. 5.8–10),[64] and so proclaim the good news to all nations that Babylon is fallen and the way to the new Jerusalem is open.

Through all this, the challenge that Revelation presents to its audience is for them take up their citizenship in the new Jerusalem, and become those who witness faithfully to the dawning heavenly kingdom. By John's understanding, everything depends on the faithful saints persevering with endurance through tribulation, as they demonstrate through their lives the testimony to the Lamb that was slain. It is only as the Church fulfils this calling, exercised through suffering and possible martyrdom, that the first fruits become the great harvest. This is John's bitter-sweet message, and it lies at the heart of his great visionary apocalypse.

Draw your own conclusions

- How is 'martyrdom' understood in contemporary culture?
- It is correct to describe suicide-bombers as 'martyrs'?
- Why does John address the issue of martyrdom?
- What message does John offer to those who survive while others are 'martyred'?
- How would you summarize John's presentation of the competing cities of Babylon and the new Jerusalem?
- What do you think John means when he speaks of 'a new heaven and a new earth' (21.1)?
- Do you think the *new heaven* and *new earth* are future possibilities or present realities?

Notes

1 For a discussion of the significance of the great multitude, see pp. 99–102.

2 As Boxall comments: 'The Lord's Prayer is never explicitly cited in the Apocalypse, yet its spirit permeates the whole.' Ian Boxall, 2006, *The Revelation of St John*, London: Continuum, p. 268.

3 See the discussion of the twenty-four elders on pp. 95–6, and the discussion of the four living creatures on pp. 128–9.

4 See the discussion of the rider on the white horse on pp. 76–8.

5 Within John's scheme, the scarlet beast functions as an image for Rome, with the false prophet as a symbol for Nero, see pp. 163–5, 171.

6 See the discussion on pp. 137–9, concerning those whose names are not written in the book of life, for a possible interpretation of their fiery fate.

7 See the discussion of the martyrs on pp. 107–9.

8 See the discussion on pp. 26–32 above for an introduction to the main approaches. R. Clouse provides a helpful discussion of four different interpretations of the millennium, each one proposed by a different interpreter. Cf. Robert G. Clouse (ed.), 1977, *The Meaning of the Millennium: Four Views*, Illinois: InterVarsity Press.

9 Beale points to the fact that John speaks of the 'thousand years' in the context of a vision, indicating that it should therefore be understood symbolically. Cf. G. K. Beale, 1999, *The Book of Revelation*, Carlisle: The Paternoster Press, pp. 973–4. See also pp. 1017–21 for his more detailed argument in favour of interpreting the millennium figuratively.

10 Court gives the following example of an extreme literal interpretation: 'It is calculated that about 40% of the United States population are "Born Again" Christians. Many may look for the end of the world in terms of a Rapture of the Saved "to meet the Lord in the air" (1 Thess. 5.17) and a Millennium (to reign with Christ for a thousand years). There will be "high management openings for can-do Christians". Jesus "needs saints who develop success patterns in this present real-life testing ground ... Many leaders will be needed to reign over cities, nations, territories and millennium projects".' John M. Court, 1994, *Revelation*, New Testament Guides, Sheffield: Sheffield Academic Press, p. 65.

11 See the discussion of first and second resurrections on pp. 108–9.

12 Midrash is the Jewish tradition of allegorical interpretation.

13 Robert W. Wall, 1991, *Revelation*, Carlisle: Paternoster Press p. 236.

14 For example, 1 Enoch says: 'Then after that there shall occur the second eighth week – the week of righteousness. A sword shall be given to it in order that judgement shall be executed in righteousness on the oppressors, and sinners shall be delivered into the hands of the righteous ... Then, after this matter ... there shall be the eternal judgement ... The first heaven shall depart and pass away; a new heaven shall appear; and all the powers of heaven shall shine forever'. 1 Enoch 91.12, 15. Translated by E. Isaac in James H. Charlesworth (ed.), 1983, *The Old Testament Pseudepigrapha Vol. 1*, New York: Doubleday, p. 73.

15 Leon Morris, 1987, *Revelation*, revised edn, The Tyndale New Testament Commentaries, Leicester: Inter-Varsity Press, pp. 227–8. Sweet suggests that this is the way in which to understand the millennium. Cf. John Sweet, 1979,

Revelation, London: SCM Press, pp. 68, 288. This time-frame can also be found in early Christian interpretations of the millennium. Cf. Hans Bietenhard, 1953, 'The Millennial Hope in the Early Church', *Scottish Journal of Theology*, vol. 6, no. 1: 12–30. The similarity with premillennial dispensationalism is also obvious. See above, pp. 29–30.

16 The *Dictionary of Biblical Imagery*, in its article on millennial expectation, comments that: 'Old Testament millennial visions are set in a temporal framework, as the prophets make it clear that the golden age they envision lies in the future. The millennium exists in the future sense.' Leland Ryken, James C. Wilhoit, and Tremper Longman III (eds), 1998, *Dictionary of Biblical Imagery*, Leicester: InterVarsity Press, p. 552. For more information on the concept of the millennium in the Pseudepigrapha and Rabbinic sources, see J. Massyngberde Ford, 1992, 'Millennium', in D. N. Freedman (ed.), *The Anchor Bible Dictionary*, New York: Doubleday, p. 832.

17 Aune makes much of the Jewish background in his suggested solution to the millennium question. He suggests that the millennium functions as a temporary messianic kingdom which is invented as a matter of necessity to reconcile 'the expectation of a messianic kingdom with the notion of the final realization of the eternal reign of God'. He says that John seeks to accommodate this provisional state of the kingdom by reduplication of the images in Revelation, resulting in what he calls a 'somewhat awkward' schema. He concludes that: 'A preliminary and temporary messianic kingdom solves the problem of how to conceive of the transition from the Messiah to the eternal reign of God. A messianic interregnum, therefore, functions as an anticipation of the perfect and eternal theocratic state that will exist when primordial conditions are reinstated for ever.' David E. Aune, 1998b, *Revelation 17–22*, Nashville: Thomas Nelson, p. 1108. The problem with Aune's suggestion is that it relegates the millennium to being an awkward compromise, with John including it as a matter of necessity in order to successfully redact the eschatological schemes he was inheriting. This fails to do justice to the text as a finished work, and seems at odds with the obvious literary skill with which the work has been composed.

18 Richard Bauckham, 1993, *The Climax of Prophecy: Studies on the Book of Revelation*, Edinburgh: T&T Clark, p. 106.

19 G. B. Caird, 1984, *The Revelation of St John the Divine*, London: A & C Black, p. 251.

20 This can be clearly seen in the following list of section headings: 'Allusions to Ezekiel 38—39 in 19.17-21 and 20.8-10'; 'The Connection between Recapitulation in Ezekiel 38—39 and in Revelation 19.17f.'; 'The Relation of the Structure of Daniel 7 to that of Revelation 19.11-20.6'. Beale, *Revelation*, pp. 976–82.

21 In other words, they take place between the first and second comings of Jesus.

22 Beale, *Revelation*, p. 985.

23 Beale, *Revelation*, p. 991.

24 Beale, *Revelation*, pp. 1005, 1012, 1015 respectively.

25 He says that in Revelation, 'John's Old Testament allusions are not merely decorative but carry precise meaning.' Bauckham, *Climax*, p. 248. It should be noted that N. Cohn looks not simply to the Jewish background for Revelation,

but also posits the possibility that John was drawing on Zoroastrianism in his prophecy of a future transformation and a coming kingdom. See Norman Cohn, 1993, *Cosmos, Chaos and the World to Come*, London: Yale University Press, p. 219.

26 Bauckham, *Climax*, pp. 106–7. J. J. Collins interprets this Daniel passage against the background of Canaanite myth, with an enthronement scene being acted out to emphasize the superiority of God as the son approaches the father. John J. Collins, 1977, *The Apocalyptic Vision of the Book of Daniel*, Missoula, Montana: Scholars Press, pp. 99–101.

27 Mealy draws an additional parallel between Rev. 20.4a and Dan. 7.22, on the basis of which he concludes that 'it is clear that giving judgement to someone can mean passing judgement in their favour, and not just delegating judicial authority to them'. J. Webb Mealy, 1992, *After the Thousand Years*, Sheffield: JSOT Press, pp. 108–9. He goes on to conclude that it is unlikely that those seated on the thrones are actually the martyrs themselves. Rather, he suggests that the thrones represent the judgement which is given to vindicate the martyrs.

28 Beale suggests that 'the book of Daniel may be more determinative on the overall theology and structure of the Apocalypse than any other traditional O.T. source.' G. K. Beale, 1984, *The Use of Daniel in Jewish Apocalyptic Literature and in the Revelation of St. John*, New York: University Press of America, p. 271.

29 Bauckham, *Climax*, p. 107.

30 Resseguie makes a similar point: 'Reigning with Christ for a thousand years vindicates the martyrs.' James L. Resseguie, 1998, *Revelation Unsealed, a Narrative Critical Approach to John's Apocalypse*, Biblical Interpretation, Leiden: E. J. Brill, p. 190.

31 See pp. 15–16 for a discussion on how the dating of Revelation relates to the experience of martyrdom in the context of John's recipients.

32 Smalley notes that biblical symbols provide a 'picture ... which is used to evoke or represent a spiritual reality'. Stephen S. Smalley, 1994, *Thunder and Love: John's Revelation and John's Community*, Milton Keynes: Nelson Word, p. 160.

33 Bauckham, *Climax*, p. 107.

34 'The temporal disparity between the beast's reign and the reign of the saints is an encouragement to the reader, for, although the period of the beast's kingdom seems interminable (3, 5 years), it is brief compared to the thousand-year reign of the saints.' Resseguie, *Revelation Unsealed*, pp. 46–7.

35 See the discussion of John's characterization of 'the martyrs' on pp. 107–8.

36 This is the position taken by, for example, Aune and Mounce. See Aune, *Revelation 17–22*, p. 1085; Robert H. Mounce, 1977, *The Book of Revelation*, revised edn, Grand Rapids: William B. Eerdmans, p. 360.

37 Mealy, *After the Thousand Years*, p. 110.

38 M. Eugene Boring, 1989, *Revelation*, Louisville: John Knox Press, p. 203.

39 It is worth noting that in the early Church this question caused much debate. Imaginative suggestions were proposed, such as that described by Stuart Hall: 'A martyr, μάρτυς, is simply a 'witness'. So living martyrs are quite

possible. They have given their testimony, μαρτυρία. If they ratify it, confirming their testimony by dying, it becomes stronger ... But essentially it is no different from 'confession', ὁμολογια, which can be 'unto death'. Confessors and martyrs are one and the same.' Stuart G. Hall, 1993, 'Women among the Early Martyrs', in Diana Wood (ed.), *Martyrs and Martyrologies*, Oxford: Blackwell, p. 2.

40 Mealy, *After the Thousand Years*, p. 114.

41 As Resseguie comments: 'The millennium is the heavenly or eschatological point of view, the antithesis to an earthly point of view. Although it appears in this age that the beast has triumphed, that it has conquered the saints and that it reigns at will over the earth, this point of view is merely a fiction.' Resseguie, *Revelation Unsealed*, p. 62.

42 Bauckham, *Climax*, p. 107.

43 Bauckham, *Climax*, p. 107.

44 In his description of the release of Satan and the attempt to retake the camp of the saints, John makes reference to the vision in Ezekiel 38—9, where Israel is seen as being attacked by the heathen nations who are led by a leader named Gog. In this way, John is picking up on a theme already present in Israelite teaching, and reinterpreting it with reference to Satan's continued attack on the believers. Cf. D. S. Russell, 1994, *Prophecy and the Apocalyptic Dream*, Peabody, Massachusetts: Hendrickson Publishers, pp. 74, 80–1.

45 See pp. 91–3 for an examination of the various images which John employs for the people of God.

46 Boettner exemplifies this approach. He argues cogently and forcefully for understanding the millennium as a symbolic figure, but does not go on to say what it is symbolic of in any theological sense. Rather, he says that, 'the "thousand years" is to be understood "symbolically" as relating to an indefinitely long period of time'. Loraine Boettner, 1957, *The Millennium*, Philadelphia: The Presbyterian and Reformed Publishing Company, p. 66.

47 Bauckham, *Climax*, p. 108.

48 For an examination of the parousia in 1 Thessalonians, Mark 13, and Matthew 24—5, see C. Freeman Sleeper, 1999, 'Christ's Coming and Christian Living', *Interpretation*, vol. 53, no. 2: 131–42.

49 The total death toll of the 11 September 2001 terrorist attacks on the World Trade Centre, the Pentagon, and United Airlines Flight 93 is listed as 2996. http://www.september11victims.com/. Accessed 7.11.07

50 Columbus believed he had discovered the new Jerusalem, writing in October 1500: 'Of the New Heaven and Earth which our Lord made, as St John writes in the Apocalypse ... He made me the messenger thereof and showed me where to go ... I undertook a new voyage to the New Heaven and World which hitherto had been hidden.' Quoted in William Joseph Federer, 1996, *America's God and Country*, St Louis: Amerisearch, p. 127. Howard-Brook and Gwyther comment: 'In the minds of the first religious interpreters of the New World, America was often interpreted in imagery that combined the Garden of Eden, the Promised Land, and the Endtime City-on-a-Hill. Seventeenth-century New England preachers such as Cotton Mather and eighteenth-century successors such as Jonathan Edwards frequently gave eschatological meaning to the colonial adventure.' Wes Howard-Brook and Anthony Gwyther, 2001, *Unveiling Empire: Reading Revelation Then and Now*, New York: Orbis Books, p. 7.

51 The symbolic function of significant buildings is well known. From the iconic Empire State Building in New York, to the domineering Communist Palace of Science and Culture in Warsaw, from the Dome of the Rock in Jerusalem to St Paul's Cathedral in London, such buildings represent far more than the sum of their bricks, stone, steel and concrete. Within the world of the New Testament, the Jerusalem temple and its destruction in AD 70 provide the background to John's imagery of the new Jerusalem in Chapters 21 and 22. Cf. the chapter on 'Symbol and Controversy' in N. T. Wright, 1996, *Jesus and the Victory of God*, Christian Origins and the Question of God, vol. 2, London: SPCK, pp. 369–442.

52 For example, in 2001, the total number of road fatalities in the UK was 3,450. http://www.dft.gov.uk/pgr/statistics/datatablespublications/accidents/casualtiesgbar/roadcasualtiesgreatbritain2001. Accessed 7.11.07.

53 The story of the tower of Babel represents an exploration of human imperial aspiration expressed through the building and destruction of a city and a tall tower (Gen. 11.1–9).

54 See the discussion of the new Jerusalem as an image for the people of God on pp. 110–13.

55 Martin Luther King, Jr. speaking to Western Michigan University on 18 December 1963. http://www.wmich.edu/library/archives/mlk/transcription.html. Accessed 7.11.07.

56 Cf. Ian Smith, 2002, 'A Rational Choice Model of the Book of Revelation', *Journal for the Study of the New Testament*, vol. 85: 97–116.

57 John's image of the church as the 'first-fruits' to the greater harvest is in view here. See p. 99.

58 See the discussion of heaven's perspective on the church on pp. 181–5.

59 Boxall, *Revelation*, p. 293.

60 See the discussion of dispensationalism on pp. 29–30.

61 Cf. Isa. 43.19.

62 N. T. Wright, 1992, *The New Testament and the People of God*, London: SPCK, p. 333. Italics his. It should be noted that Adams has recently argued that Wright is incorrect in this assertion, claiming that 'in all of the catastrophe passages [in the New Testament] the reference is to an expected "real" calamity on a universal scale, as the accompaniment of the parousia or the form of the coming judgement.' Edward Adams, 2007, *The Stars Will Fall from Heaven: Cosmic Catastrophe in the New Testament and its World*, London: T&T Clark, p. 17. In this way Adams asserts that in the book of Revelation: 'We do not have here a miraculous transformation of the existing created order. Rather, the first creation is taken back to its pre-created, chaotic state and a new creative act takes place. The picture is indeed that of the renewal of creation, but the renewal is accomplished precisely by destruction and re-creation.' (p. 238).

63 Cf. Gen. 18.18; 22.18; 26.4.

64 See the discussion of the 'new song' on p. 97.

Select Bibliography

Introductions to Revelation

Barr, David L. (ed.), 2003, *Reading the Book of Revelation: A Resource for Students*, SBL Resources for Biblical Study, vol. 44, Atlanta: Society of Biblical Literature

Bauckham, Richard, 1993, *The Theology of the Book of Revelation*, New Testament Theology, Cambridge: Cambridge University Press

Boxall, Ian, 2002, *Revelation: Vision and Insight: An Introduction to the Apocalypse*, London: SPCK

Cory, Catherine A., 2006, *The Book of Revelation*, New Collegeville Bible Commentary, Collegeville, Minnesota: Liturgical Press

Court, John M., 1994, *Revelation*, New Testament Guides, Sheffield: Sheffield Academic Press

Desrosiers, Gilbert, 2000, *An Introduction to Revelation*, T&T Clark Approaches to Biblical Studies, London: Continuum

Howard-Brook, Wes, and Anthony Gwyther, 2001, *Unveiling Empire: Reading Revelation Then and Now*, The Bible and Liberation Series, New York: Orbis Books

Koester, Craig R, 2001, *Revelation and the End of All Things*, Grand Rapids: Wm. B. Eerdmans Publishing Company

Metzger, Bruce M, 1993, *Breaking the Code: Understanding the Book of Revelation*, Nashville: Abingdon Press

Michaels, J. Ramsey, 1992, *Interpreting the Book of Revelation*, Guides to New Testament Exegesis, vol. 7, Grand Rapids: Baker Books

Moyise, Steve (ed.), 2001, *Studies in the Book of Revelation*, Edinburgh: T&T Clark

Paul, Ian, 2003, *How to Read the Book of Revelation*, Cambridge: Grove Books

Paul, Ian, 2005, *The Ethics of the Book of Revelation*, Cambridge: Grove Books

Peterson, Eugene H., 1988, *Reversed Thunder: The Revelation of John and the Praying Imagination*, San Francisco: Harper Collins

Smalley, Stephen S., 1994, *Thunder and Love: John's Revelation and John's Community*, Milton Keynes: Nelson Word

Spilsbury, Paul, 2002, *The Throne, the Lamb & the Dragon: A Reader's Guide to the Book of Revelation*, Illinois: InterVarsity Press

Wainwright, Arthur W., 1993, *Mysterious Apocalypse: Interpreting the Book of Revelation*, Nashville: Abingdon Press

Wilson, Mark, 2007, *Charts on the Book of Revelation: Literary, Historical, and Theological Perspectives*, Kregel Charts of the Bible and Theology, Grand Rapids: Kregel Publications

Commentaries

Aune, David E., 1997, *Revelation 1—5*, Word Biblical Commentary, vol. 52A, Dallas: Word Books

Aune, David E., 1998a, *Revelation 6—16*, Word Biblical Commentary, vol. 52B, Nashville: Thomas Nelson

Aune, David E., 1998b, *Revelation 17—22*, Word Biblical Commentary, vol. 52C, Nashville: Thomas Nelson

Barker, Margaret, 2000, *The Revelation of Jesus Christ*, Edinburgh: T&T Clark Ltd

Beale, G. K., 1999, *The Book of Revelation*, The New International Greek Testament Commentary, Carlisle: The Paternoster Press

Beasley-Murray, G. R., 1974, *The Book of Revelation*, New Century Bible, London: Oliphants

Boring, M. Eugene, 1989, *Revelation*, Interpretation, Louisville: John Knox Press

Boxall, Ian, 2006, *The Revelation of St John*, Black's New Testament Commentaries, London: Continuum

Caird, G. B., 1984, *The Revelation of St. John the Divine*, 2nd edn, London: A & C Black

Charles, R. H., 1920, *A Critical and Exegetical Commentary on the Revelation of St John*, 2 vols., Edinburgh: T&T Clark

González, Catherine Gunsalus, ánd Justo L. González, 1997, *Revelation*, Westminster Bible Companion, Louisville, Kentucky: Westminster John Knox Press

Harrington, Wilfrid J, 1993, *Revelation*, Sacra Pagina, vol. 16, Collegeville, Minnesota: The Liturgical Press

Keener, Craig S., 2000, *Revelation*, The NIV Application Commentary Series, Grand Rapids: Zondervan

Kiddle, Martin, 1940, *The Revelation of St John*, The Moffatt New Testament Commentary, London: Hodder & Stoughton

Knight, Jonathan, 1999, *Revelation*, Sheffield: Sheffield Academic Press

Kovacs, Judith L., and Christopher Rowland, 2004, *Revelation*, Blackwell Bible Commentaries, Oxford: Blackwell

Lupieri, Edmondo F., 2006, *A Commentary on the Apocalypse of John*, trans. Maria Poggi Johnson and Adam Kamesar, Italian Texts and Studies on Religion and Society, Cambridge: Wm. B. Eerdmans Publishing Company

Morris, Leon, 1987, *Revelation*, revised edn, The Tyndale New Testament Commentaries, Leicester: InterVarsity Press

Mounce, Robert H., 1997, *The Book of Revelation*, revised edn, The New International Commentary on the New Testament, Grand Rapids: Wm. B. Eerdmans Publishing Company

Osborne, Grant R., 2002, *Revelation*, Baker Exegetical Commentary on the New Testament, Grand Rapids, Michigan: Baker Academic

Richard, Pablo, 1995, *Apocalypse: A People's Commentary on the Book of Revelation*, trans. Phillip Berryman, The Bible & Liberation, New York: Orbis Books

Rowland, Christopher, 1993, *Revelation*, Epworth Commentaries, London: Epworth

Schüssler Fiorenza, Elisabeth, 1991, *Revelation: Vision of a Just World*, Proclamation Commentaries, Minneapolis: Fortress Press

Smalley, Stephen S., 2005, *The Revelation to John: A Commentary on the Greek Text of the Apocalypse*, London: SPCK

Sweet, John, 1979, *Revelation*, London: SCM Press

Thompson, Leonard L., 1998, *Revelation*, Abingdon New Testament Commentaries, Nashville: Abingdon Press

Wall, Robert W., 1991, *Revelation*, New International Biblical Commentary, Carlisle: Paternoster Press

Witherington III, Ben, 2003, *Revelation*, New Cambridge Bible Commentary, Cambridge: Cambridge University Press

Monographs and Other Works

Bauckham, Richard, 1993, *The Climax of Prophecy: Studies on the Book of Revelation*, Edinburgh: T&T Clark

Bredin, Mark, 2003, *Jesus, Revolutionary of Peace: A Nonviolent Christology in the Book of Revelation*, Paternoster Biblical Monographs, Milton Keynes: Paternoster

Charles, R. H., 1913, *Studies in the Apocalypse*, Edinburgh: T&T Clark

Charlesworth, James H. (ed.), 1983, *The Old Testament Pseudepigrapha Volume 1*, The Anchor Bible Reference Library, New York: Doubleday

Charlesworth, James H. (ed.), 1985, *The Old Testament Pseudepigrapha Volume 2*, The Anchor Bible Reference Library, New York: Doubleday

Court, John M., 1979, *Myth and History in the Book of Revelation*, London: SPCK

Garrow, A. J. P., 1997, *Revelation*, New Testament Readings, London: Routledge

Grenz, Stanley J., 1992, *The Millennial Maze: Sorting out Evangelical Options*, Illinois: InterVarsity Press

Johns, Loren L. (ed.), 2000, *Apocalypticism and Millennialism: Shaping a Believers Church Eschatology for the Twenty-First Century*, Studies in the Believers Church Tradition, Kitchener, Ontario: Pandora Press

Keller, Catherine, 1996, *Apocalypse Now and Then: A Feminist Guide to the End of the World*, Boston: Beacon Press

Kraybill, J. Nelson, 1996, *Imperial Cult and Commerce in John's Apocalypse*, Journal for the Study of the New Testament Supplement Series, vol. 132, Sheffield: Sheffield Academic Press

Kyle, Richard, 1998, *Awaiting the Millennium*, Leicester: InterVarsity Press

Ladd, George Eldon, 1956, *The Blessed Hope: A Biblical Study of the Second Advent and the Rapture*, Grand Rapids: Wm. B. Eerdmans Publishing Company

Lyons, William John, and Jorunn Økland (eds), 2008, *The Way the World Ends? The Apocalypse of John in Culture and Ideology*, Sheffield: Sheffield Phoenix Press

McKelvey, R. J., 1999, *The Millennium and the Book of Revelation*, Cambridge: The Lutterworth Press

Mealy, J. Webb, 1992, *After the Thousand Years, Journal for the Study of the New Testament* Supplement Series, Sheffield: JSOT Press

Newport, Kenneth G. C., and Crawford Gribben (eds), 2006, *Expecting the End: Millennialism in Social and Historical Context*, Waco, Texas: Baylor University Press

Pippin, Tina, 1999, *Apocalyptic Bodies: The Biblical End of the World in Text and Image*, London: Routledge

Polkinghorne, John, and Michael Welker (eds), 2000, *The End of the World and the Ends of God: Science and Theology on Eschatology*, Harrisburg, PA: Trinity Press International

Resseguie, James L., 1998, *Revelation Unsealed, a Narrative Critical Approach to John's Apocalypse*, Biblical Interpretation, Leiden, The Netherlands: Brill

Rowland, Christopher, 1982, *The Open Heaven: A Study of Apocalyptic in Judaism and Early Christianity*, New York: Crossroad

Schüssler Fiorenza, Elisabeth, 1998, *The Book of Revelation: Justice and Judgment*, 2nd edn, Minneapolis: Fortress Press

Swinburne, Richard, 1992, *Revelation, from Metaphor to Analogy*, Oxford: Clarendon Press

Thompson, Leonard L., 1990, *The Book of Revelation: Apocalypse and Empire*, Oxford: Oxford University Press

Waddell, Robby, 2006, *The Spirit of the Book of Revelation*, Journal of Pentecostal Theology Supplement Series, vol. 30, Blandford Forum: Deo Publishing

Index of References to Revelation

Index of Subjects

1,000 years *see* 'Millennium'
1,260 years 28, 117 n.49
1260 days 103, 106, 117 n.49, 131
144,000 47, 50–1, 74, 96–100, 105,
  124, 133–5, 144 n.28, 153, 191,
  205–6, 208
3½ years 103
42 months 49, 103, 105, 131,
  164
666 *see* 'Number of the beast'

Abaddon, Apollyon *see* 'Angel of the
  bottomless pit'
Abraham x, 29, 72, 105–5, 113–4,
  127, 132–3, 134, 139, 142, 201,
  206, 236
Allegory 25, 38 n.11, 237 n.12
Alpha and Omega 65, 67, 79
America 5, 24, 29, 35, 39 n.27, 117
  n.46, 214, 215, 217 n.27, 240 n.50
Amillennialism 21, 26, 27–28, 29,
  30, 32, 38 n.15
Angel from the rising sun 124–5, 134
Angel from the sun 126–7, 129, 153
Angel of Jesus Christ 44, 49, 120,
  121–2
Angel of the bottomless pit 48, 134–
  5, 154, 174 n.30–31, 196, 210
Angel of the waters 51, 126
Angel with a golden censer 125, 127,
  129
Angel with the key to the bottomless
  pit 128, 148, 149, 174 n.32
Angel, interpreting 95, 121, 167
Angelic multitude 123, 162
Angels of the churches 69, 94–5
Angels of the presence 90 n.104,
  120, 143 n.8
Angels, bowl 51, 52, 53, 120–1, 122,
  126, 159
Angels, four bound at the

Euphrates 129, 141, 155–6, 193,
  196
Angels, four restraining the four
  winds 123–4, 135, 153, 173 n.25
Angels, six 127
Angels, trumpet 48, 51, 120, 121,
  122
Antichrist 23, 37 n.5, 60, 62, 180
Antiochus IV Epiphanes 103, 175
  n.40, 176 n.62
Apocalypse, apocalyptic ix, 8–16, 17
  n.9–11, 18 n.14, 18 n.23, 35, 37
  n.1, 40 n.34–5, 44–5, 47, 58 n.13,
  63, 68, 82, 86 n.43, 89 n.94, 119,
  143 n.4, 153, 162, 174 n.40, 194,
  199 n.22, 202, 210, 220 n.58
Archangels 85 n.28, 119–123, 143
  n.7
Ark of the covenant 201, 216 n.2
Armageddon *see* 'Harmagedon'
Army of angels 125–6, 144 n.28
Army of locusts 174 n.30
Army of the beast from the sea 165,
  171
Army of the faithful 53, 74, 78, 96–
  8, 99, 107, 127, 139–40, 144 n.28,
  148, 150, 161, 165, 204, 212, 236
Ascension 49, 64, 72, 79, 81, 106,
  122
Augustine 27–31, 38 n.15–6, 38
  n.18
Augustus Caesar 159, 166, 172 n.3
Author of the seven letters 69–70, 82
Authorship 10, 33, 44–5

Baal 131, 192
Babylon 16, 20 n.57, 23, 33, 35–6,
  43, 50, 51–3, 55, 65, 79, 101, 110–
  4, 121–2, 126–7, 134, 139–40,
  151, 156–72, 175 n.39–40, 176
  n.62, 176 n.67, 177 n.69, 187–90,